The Gaseous Phase

The Gaseous Phase

W. H. Thorning
Second Master and Head of Science,
Merchant Taylors' School

John Murray Albemarle Street London

Physics Topics Series

Already published

Motion and Forces
Vibrations and Waves
The Gaseous Phase

In preparation

Electromagnetic Radiation
The Electric Field
The Condensed Phase

Text set in 10/11 pt IBM Press Roman, printed by photolithography, and bound in Great Britain at The Pitman Press, Bath

0 7195 2954 9

Contents

Preface

This book provides a survey of the basic properties of matter in its gaseous form, and aims at showing the extent to which these properties may be predicted and explained on the basis of a simple kinetic theory. This of necessity includes an account of the phenomena associated with the transition between the liquid and gaseous phases, and I therefore considered it appropriate to include an account of the processes used for the liquefaction of gases. The first law of thermodynamics occupies a central position in much of this work and I felt it desirable to introduce the second law, although only in the most brief and simple manner. I have not attempted a detailed consideration of temperature measurement; on the other hand, it seemed essential to make a brief reference to this subject in the early chapters.

The major part of the book should be well within the understanding of a pupil pursuing a sixth-form Physics course, but there are a few parts where the treatment goes beyond the basic requirements at this stage. Wherever possible, experiments which the pupil may himself carry out or observe in the school laboratory are included, although full practical details are not given. In some parts of the study, particularly Chapter 6, I felt it more appropriate to adopt a historical approach to the subject. The questions at the end of each chapter are intended to provide a test of the understanding which has been achieved, and are not in any way typical examination questions.

I was most fortunate throughout the preparation of the text to be able to take advantage of the advice and helpful criticism of L. R. Middleton. The book has certainly gained greatly by the removal of the errors he pointed out and the comments which caused me to think again – and, I hope, to better effect. My colleague Ray Slade read the text and made many helpful comments. I am also aware that I have gained much from discussions with him, John Aylmer and other colleagues in the past, to say nothing of the provoking and stimulating questions raised by pupils over many years.

The laborious task of typing the manuscript was shared by Hilda Sealy and Caroline Hinderwell, and I am indeed grateful to both of them and to Tony Mould for the clarity of his diagrams.

Finally I wish to thank the editorial staff of John Murray for their patient forbearance and helpful consideration at all times.

Kingsbridge, 1974

1 An Introduction to the Behaviour of Gases

The idea that matter consists of small particles called atoms which are in continuous motion was first propounded by Democritus in the fourth century B.C., but it was not until the eighteenth century that Bernoulli attempted to explain the fact that gases obeyed Boyle's law in terms of the continuous movement of small corpuscles. In the nineteenth century Dalton expounded his atomic theory to explain the combination of atoms into molecules of compounds and the basic laws governing chemical combination. From that time onward there was a steady development of the ideas of particles in motion in order to explain the properties of matter in its different states; this concept is usually referred to as the *kinetic theory of matter.*

1 KINETIC THEORY OF MATTER

The kinetic theory of matter envisages an assembly of atoms or molecules which are in motion and thus possess energy. Matter in bulk, or on the *macroscopic* scale, exhibits different properties according to the manner in which these constituent particles are arranged. In elementary science it is common to refer to the three common ways in which the molecules are arranged as leading to the solid, liquid, and gaseous *states.* However, it is preferable to refer to each of these forms as a *phase*; the term *state* can then be used to represent specified conditions of pressure, volume and temperature.

Our division of matter into these three phases comes from our recognition of the differences in their macroscopic or large-scale properties.

Solids appear to have a definite volume and, in the case of small enough samples, a definite shape; it would be more precise to say that very large forces are needed to bring about changes in either volume or shape. For example, a steel wire can be stretched or an iron bar compressed by sufficiently large forces, and a cylinder of metal such as copper may have its shape changed by correctly applied forces.

Liquids offer no resistance to a change of shape although very large forces are needed to bring about changes in volume. They show the property of *fluidity* as opposed to the *rigidity* of solids. However, in a liquid there is a measure of limited resistance to the *maintenance* of relative motion between its different parts. The property responsible for this resistance is known as *viscosity*; treacle is an obvious example of a particularly viscous liquid.

Gases offer relatively little resistance to a change in volume, and their viscosity is also very much less than that of liquids. A gas such as bromine can readily be seen to spread very rapidly through an evacuated tube, and this indicates the relative freedom of the molecules; we shall see later it is only the large number of collisions which occur between molecules which prevents this *diffusion* taking place even more rapidly. Similarly two gases readily diffuse through one another until each is uniformly distributed throughout the space available to it.

We shall see later that all molecules at normal room temperature and atmospheric pressure travel on the average a distance of the order of only 10^{-5} cm between collisions; this mean distance is known as the *mean free path* (λ) and is a most important and useful concept in the kinetic theory description of gases.

These facts, together with the very much smaller densities normally associated with the gaseous phase, suggest that the molecules of a gas are on the average relatively remote from one another with, at any instant, large regions of empty space between them. The phenomenon of diffusion also clearly indicates that the gas molecules must be in motion.

When the gas has condensed to a solid or liquid the molecules are very much closer together, and in the case of a solid are held in definite positions by forces which act between them. This regular array of molecules or atoms is referred to as *long range order.* From a point inside a solid we would see rows and rows of atoms stretching away into the infinite distance. There is order in each row and the rows themselves are arranged in a definite manner; we refer to such an arrangement as a *lattice.* The molecules are at such a separation that there is equilibrium between the forces of attraction and repulsion which they exert on each other. An increase of this separation results in a larger mutual attraction than repulsion, whilst if the separation is decreased, the repulsion grows more rapidly than the attraction and so predominates.

In a liquid the inter-atomic distances are very little different, being of the order of 3×10^{-10} m; the atoms possess very considerable kinetic energy as they travel about, but for very short time-intervals of the order of 10^{-13} s occupy fixed positions, so that they and their nearest neighbours form a fleeting geometrical structure; for this reason we speak of *short range order* in a liquid. The mean free path of an individual atom is only slightly larger than the diameter of the atoms themselves, and at any instant a particular atom or molecule is touching at least three others; the ordered arrangement only extends over a few molecular diameters, and beyond this distance the arrangement in one part of the liquid has little effect on that elsewhere.

When a liquid is heated the identity and number of the immediate neighbours of a particular atom are both likely to change, so that a liquid may be considered to correspond to a continuous series of crystal phases, each with a short-range lattice arrangement, which is only stable at one particular temperature. In general we may think of a liquid as a disordered crystal with a number of equally likely structures: furthermore it is always changing from one of these structures to another.

2 BROWNIAN MOTION

The first direct evidence of molecular movement was obtained by Brown in 1827, when he observed through a microscope very small pollen grains in an aqueous suspension. The grains, which were seen as specks of light, moved in short random jerks. A similar effect can be readily seen if smoke particles in a small glass cell are observed as in Fig. 1.1, where the illumination is provided from the side.

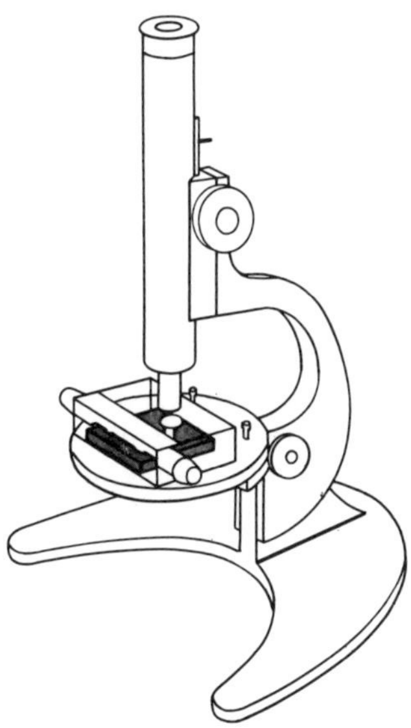

Fig. 1.1

The particles showing this Brownian motion are of course much larger and more massive than molecules, but are nevertheless small enough for there to be a considerable likelihood that more molecules hit them on one side, or in one direction, than the other, and consequently they are set in motion. Slightly later they will similarly receive an impulse in a different direction and consequently move in a jerky and apparently random manner. The smaller the particles under observation, the greater the chance of this lack of balance in the bombardment they receive; at the same time the larger the effect on them of these impulses from collisions, and thus the more violent their motion. It can also be shown that for particular particles the higher the temperature of the fluid, the greater the observed motion.

Although examples of Brownian motion are found in many parts of physics, two typical difficulties arising from it may now be mentioned. When particularly delicate suspensions are constructed for very sensitive balances or galvanometers, the random bombardment of the very fine thread by the air molecules may well produce sufficient Brownian motion for the zero position to show a random and continual oscillation. Also, in Millikan's well-known experiment to determine the electronic charge, the bombardment of the air molecules on the very small oil drops used may well lead to a random motion which hampers the observation of their steady motion under either gravity or an electric field.

3 MOLECULAR MOTION AND PRESSURE

While Brownian motion shows that molecules in both the liquid and gaseous phases are continually in motion, a liquid is characterized by the possession of *surface tension* which can only be explained in terms of forces of attraction between molecules; similar forces are needed to explain the definite volume of a liquid. Both of these effects are absent in the gaseous phase, and this entitles us to believe that the molecules of a gas are relatively free of the constraints imposed by such forces. A gas is therefore pictured as made up of a large number of molecules in continuous motion. These molecules continually collide with each other and with the walls of the containing vessel, and they only experience forces during these collisions.

They rebound from a solid surface because a force has been exerted on them which changes their velocity and momentum. By the third law of motion the walls experience an equal and opposite reaction, which is the *pressure* of the gas. If there is no container to confine the gas, their motion enables them to carry on into the space open to them, thereby *diffusing.*

We would expect that heating the gas increases the kinetic energy of the molecules and they thereby travel faster. Thus, they hit the walls more often and have a greater momentum when they do collide. On these two counts the pressure of the gas should therefore increase. If the gas is in a container which is able to withstand this increased pressure, we simply observe an increase in pressure. If, on the other hand, the container responds to this pressure increase by expanding, the pressure falls again. In the ideal case where the gas is confined in a cylinder with the equivalent of a frictionless piston, the volume of the gas increases until the pressure returns to its original value.

These two possibilities, *expansion at constant pressure* and *increase in pressure at constant volume*, represent two of the ways in which a gas may behave when heated. Each will now be considered in detail from an experimental point of view. It should, however, be appreciated that in general the pressure and volume of a gas will both alter when it is heated, unless special steps are taken to keep one of them constant.

4 EXPANSION AT CONSTANT PRESSURE

The apparatus shown in Fig. 1.2 can be used to investigate the expansion at constant pressure of a gas such as air. The air is confined in the central bulb B, above either a light oil or concentrated sulphuric acid. Both are preferable to mercury, being less dense and therefore able to indicate a much smaller difference in pressure. The sulphuric acid has the advantage of ensuring the dryness of the gas but it does require greater care than oil in its use.

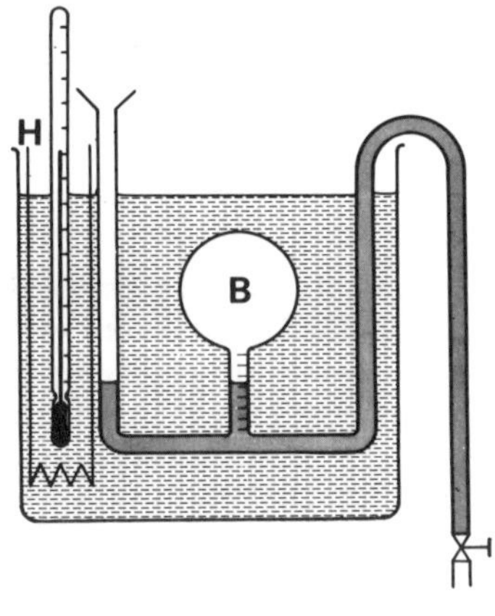

Fig. 1.2

The gas is heated by an electric heater H in the water bath surrounding the apparatus, but great care is necessary to ensure that the water temperature read on the thermometer is equal to that of the enclosed gas. Before attempting to take a reading, the heat supply should be cut off and the water stirred thoroughly so that the whole apparatus reaches a true thermal equilibrium; in order to ensure this, the process should be repeated to see if the reading of gas volume remains constant at a particular thermometer reading. Prior to taking the final reading the manometer levels must be made equal. But little error is likely to arise in judging equality by eye, since a level difference of half a centimetre, which is readily avoidable, is equivalent to only about half a millimetre of mercury, or approximately 1/10 per cent of the normal atmospheric pressure; the volume change resulting from this would be quite undetectable on the scale of the central tube.

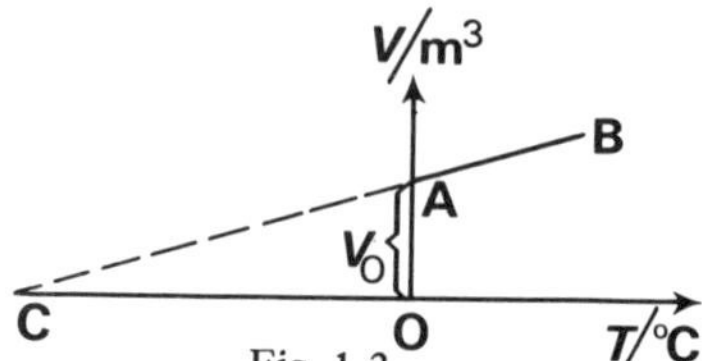

Fig. 1.3

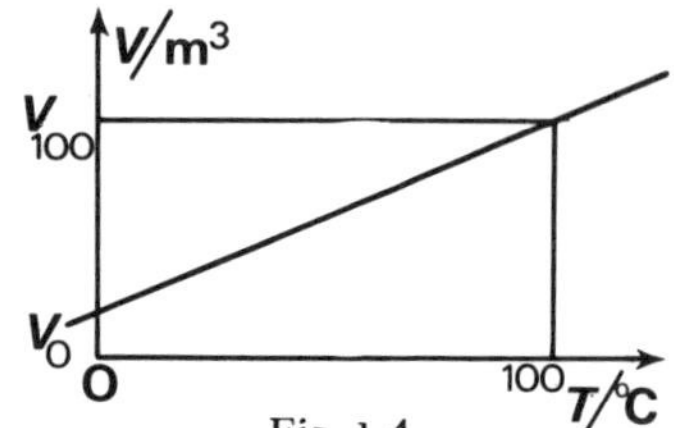

Fig. 1.4

When a graph of volume against temperature is plotted, a straight line is obtained, as in Fig. 1.3; the negative intercept on the temperature axis is approximately −273. By consideration of the triangle ACO, we see that the change in volume for each Celsius degree rise in temperature is 1/273 of the volume at 0 °C. This graph is, however, a somewhat unsatisfactory method of portraying the results, since the experimental points occupy only a very small region between A and B, and considerable extrapolation with large possibility of error is involved. It is more satisfactory to plot the graph on a larger scale as in Fig. 1.4, and to read from the graph the volumes at 0 °C and 100 °C. The coefficient of volume expansion (α) is then calculated from

$$\alpha = \frac{V_{100} - V_0}{100\, V_0}. \tag{1.1}$$

In more elaborate experiments such as those originally carried out by Regnault, separate baths were used for the bulb and the manometer, but this introduces a complication since the gas above the liquid in the manometer is not at the same temperature as the gas in the bulb, and a correction needs to be applied. It also becomes necessary to allow for the expansion of the container, although this will normally be less than one per cent of that of the gas.

Simple experiments may also be carried out with graduated glass syringes of the type shown in Fig. 1.5: pressure constancy is obtained by ensuring a near frictionless contact between the walls of the syringe and the piston. The surfaces in contact should be smeared with a mixture of a light vacuum oil and vaseline, and the piston moved up and down a number of times. The syringe is then placed vertically in a gas jar of water so that almost the whole of the barrel is immersed in the water. An electric immersion heater in the liquid is then used to raise the temperature of the water.

The relatively thick glass wall of the syringe makes it particularly important to take steps to ensure a true thermal equilibrium if reliable results are to be obtained. The gas syringe is particularly convenient for carrying out experiments with various gases. The syringe is thoroughly flushed out several times with the particular gas under test in order to remove any air before the final filling with gas.

Fig. 1.5

Any gases which are remote from their point of liquefaction give values of α approximately equal to 1/273, but the more easily liquefiable gases such as carbon dioxide and sulphur dioxide do have rather larger values of the volume coefficient.

5 INCREASE OF PRESSURE AT CONSTANT VOLUME

The increase of pressure with temperature whilst the volume is kept constant can be investigated using the apparatus of Fig. 1.6. The right-hand limb containing mercury is raised or lowered in order to keep the mercury level in the left-hand tube exactly at the tip of the glass pointer G; pro-

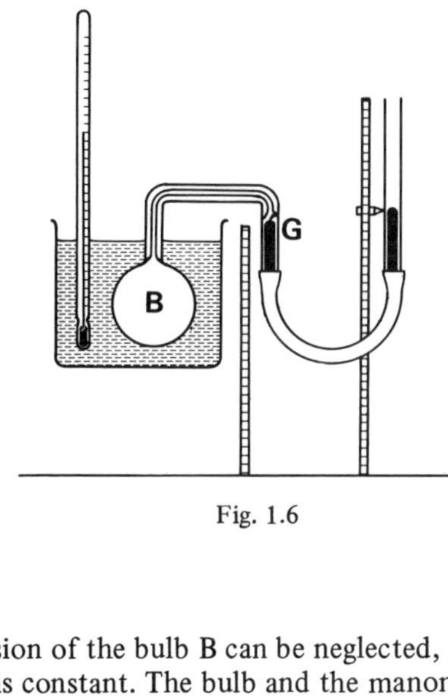

Fig. 1.6

vided the expansion of the bulb B can be neglected, the volume of the gas therefore remains constant. The bulb and the manometer are connected by a capillary tube so that the volume of the gas not at the temperature of the bath surrounding the bulb is reduced as much as possible. However, this 'dead space' is a factor which must be allowed for in very accurate investigations. Once again it is important to take steps to ensure that the gas in the bulb is at the temperature which is read by the thermometer in the bath, and a procedure similar to that outlined in the last section should be adopted.

The manometer gives the difference between the pressure of the enclosed gas and atmospheric pressure, and in order to obtain the absolute gas pressure the barometer in the laboratory must be read in the course of the experiment to check that no change occurs. In more accurate forms of the apparatus it is necessary to correct for the change in temperature and hence density of the mercury in the manometer, and also for the expansion of the bulb B.

A graph of pressure against temperature is plotted and the coefficient of increase of pressure (β) deduced in a manner similar to that used for the volume coefficient, from the relation

$$\beta = \frac{P_{100} - P_0}{100 P_0}. \tag{1.2}$$

The table below shows typical results for some common gases, and the equality of the values of the two coefficients α and β for gases remote from their liquefaction points is clearly evident.

Gas	$1/\alpha$	$1/\beta$
Helium	273.4	273.2
Hydrogen	273.3	273.1
Nitrogen	273.2	273.1
Carbon dioxide	267.3	268.4
Sulphur dioxide	256.6	260.8

It is clear from the results that a gas such as sulphur dioxide shows a behaviour significantly different from those gases like air which are so much more difficult to liquefy.

6 BOYLE'S LAW

The two previous sections have been concerned with experiments on gases in which the pressure and volume respectively were maintained constant. A third investigation may be carried out using, in a simple case, the apparatus shown in Fig. 1.7, where the temperature is maintained constant and the pressure and volume of a fixed mass of gas are varied. The volume is obtained from the length of air column in the tube A, and the difference from atmospheric pressure by measuring the difference in the mercury levels at B and C. The experiment can be carried out at any required temperature by suitably modifying the apparatus, and the graph of pressure against 1/volume is a straight line through the origin, showing the constancy of the product PV at a constant temperature.

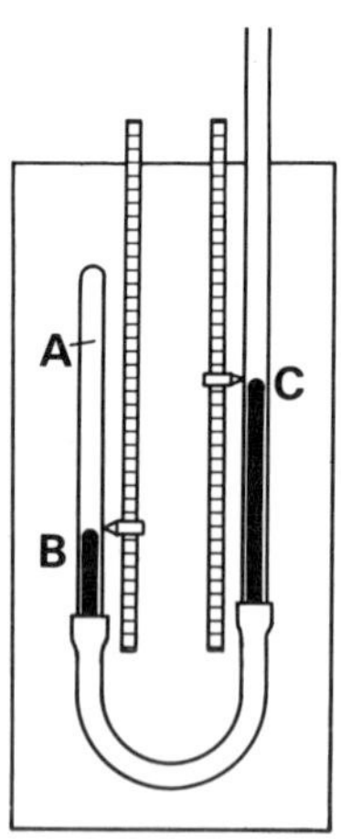

Fig. 1.7

The apparatus of Fig. 1.7 is somewhat inconvenient for an investigation involving various gases; for this purpose it is more satisfactory to use a gas syringe. Whatever the gas, the syringe is first thoroughly flushed out with the gas under test in order to remove any air from the apparatus, and of course the piston is well lubricated as described in Section 4. The syringe is then clamped vertically as indicated in Fig. 1.8 and a large pan affixed to the top of the piston. Various weights calibrated in newtons are then added to the pan to produce pressures greater than atmospheric, and the corresponding gas volume is recorded in each case. When a series of readings with increasing pressures have been taken, the loads are reduced in the same sequence. In this manner an averaging of the volume readings obtained for a particular pressure will reduce any effects arising from friction. In order to determine the pressure for any particular load it is necessary to make a measurement of the diameter of the piston of the syringe; this is easily carried out with vernier callipers.

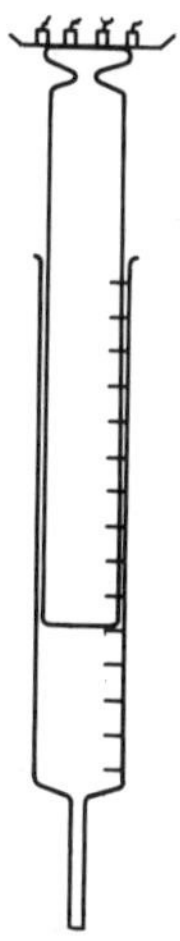

Fig. 1.8

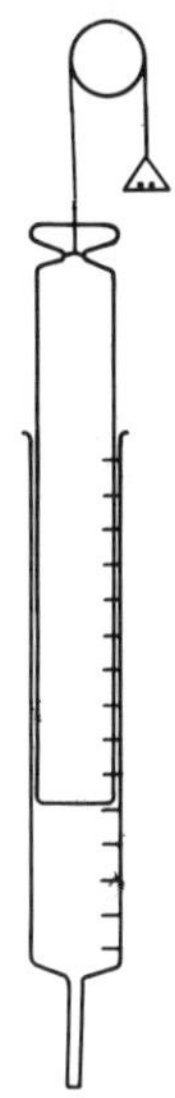

Fig. 1.9

The use of a pulley as shown in Fig. 1.9 enables readings to be obtained for pressures less than that corresponding to normal atmospheric pressure. The gas syringe can conveniently be adapted for use over a wide range of pressures, and by placing the syringe in a container of water maintained at any desired temperature by an immersion heater, the investigation can be further extended.

A more rigorous investigation of the type considered in detail in Sections 4 and 5 of Chapter 6, shows that the further a gas is away from its liquefying point, the more accurately does it obey Boyle's law. So those gases whose volume and pressure coefficients are most nearly equal are the gases whose behaviour is most in accord with Boyle's law.

7 THE IDEAL GAS

The results of experiments on a fixed mass of gas which occupies a volume V_0 under a pressure P_0 at 0 °C, may be expressed by the two relations

$$V_t = V_0 (1 + \alpha t) \quad (1.3)$$

$$P_t = P_0 (1 + \beta t) \quad (1.4)$$

where V_t is the volume at t °C after a change at constant pressure, and P_t is the pressure reached at the same temperature after heating at constant volume. The values of α and β for any particular gas are found to be more nearly equal the lower the initial pressure of the gas under investigation. A lower pressure implies fewer molecules in any specified volume and consequently that the gas is further from liquefying into the condensed phase.

These results lead to the concept of an *ideal* or *perfect* gas, which accurately obeys equations (1.3) and (1.4) under all conditions. Furthermore, the coefficients α and β are equal for an ideal gas. We see that under normal atmospheric pressures, gases such as hydrogen, nitrogen etc. are good approximations to the ideal, whilst sulphur dioxide under normal laboratory conditions is certainly not such a good approximation. In general, for any particular gas the lower its pressure, the better approximation to the ideal it will prove.

For an ideal gas, we have

$$\alpha = \beta$$

and thus under these circumstances, eqn. (1.3) and (1.4) can be combined to give

$$P_t V_t = P_0 V_0 (1 + \alpha t). \quad (1.5)$$

In eqn. (1.5), if either P or V is kept constant, it is seen that the equation reduces to either (1.3) or (1.4), showing that it combines in one relation the results of the two separate equations. It should, however, be appreciated that these are *not* simultaneous equations, since the separate relations cannot possibly be true at the same time, involving – as they do – mutually exclusive conditions.

Eqn. (1.5) is an *equation of state* for an ideal gas, showing the relation between possible values of P, V and t for any particular mass of gas. If we apply the restriction of constancy of temperature it reduces to

$$PV = \text{constant} \quad (1.6)$$

which is, of course, Boyle's law.

We have seen that the extent to which any particular real gas may be considered as ideal depends on how remote it is from liquefaction. In order to realize the factors which are responsible for liquefaction, it must be appreciated that a liquid *coheres*; its molecules exert attracting forces on one another which hold it together. These are the forces which give rise to the surface tension of the liquid and the phenomena associated with its meniscus, and it is clear that the forces decrease rapidly with increasing distance between the molecules. Consequently molecules which are close enough together and travelling sufficiently slowly can be caught by the forces and held together in the condensed phase. Remoteness from liquefaction therefore implies that the forces between molecules are relatively unimportant; in an ideal gas there are no attractions between the molecules and it would, of course, never liquefy. In the case of any real gas the lower the density (and hence the greater the mean distance between the molecules) the nearer it approaches the ideal.

8 ABSOLUTE TEMPERATURE AND THE IDEAL GAS EQUATION

Eqn. (1.5) shows that at a temperature $(-1/\alpha)$, which is approximately $-273\ ^\circ\mathrm{C}$, the product PV for an ideal gas would become zero. This could only happen if the molecules ceased moving and also occupied no space, so we must envisage the molecules of an ideal gas to be particles which occupy no volume. It is necessary for both these conditions to apply since the equations indicate that each of P and V can become zero separately. Since we cannot imagine a gas either exerting a negative pressure or occupying a negative volume, this temperature at which PV is zero must represent the lowest possible temperature, and it is known as *absolute zero.*

More accurate determinations than those we have considered indicate that absolute zero is $-273.15\ ^\circ\mathrm{C}$, and temperatures measured from this zero are known as *absolute* temperatures. Originally the scale was defined by stating that there were 100 degrees between the ice and steam points, so that the degrees were identical in size with the Celsius degree. Thus, the melting point of ice on this scale was 273.15 K, where K represented the *kelvin*, the unit of temperature. The definition of a scale of temperature is considered further in Section 10.

If T represents temperature measured from this zero,

$$T = t + 1/\alpha. \tag{1.7}$$

Since eqn. (1.5) can be written

$$P_t V_t = P_0 V_0\ \alpha\left(\frac{1}{\alpha} + t\right)$$

we can now write

$$\frac{P_t V_t}{T} = \frac{P_0 V_0}{1/\alpha}. \tag{1.8}$$

The right-hand side of this equation is independent of temperature; it depends only on the mass of gas considered since $1/\alpha$ is a fundamental constant. Thus the equation can be written

$$PV = (\text{constant})T. \tag{1.9}$$

It is evident that the constant in the above relation will be proportional to the mass of gas under consideration, and if r is the value for unit mass we can write

$$PV = mrT \tag{1.10}$$

for a mass m of gas.

Eqn. (1.10) shows that the units of r, the gas constant for unit mass, are

$$\frac{\text{N m}^{-2} \times \text{m}^3}{\text{kg} \times \text{degrees}} = \text{N m kg}^{-1}\ \text{K}^{-1} = \text{J kg}^{-1}\ \text{K}^{-1}.$$

Example 1. The density of hydrogen at normal atmospheric pressure (10^5 N m^{-2}) and 273 K, is approximately 0.090 g l^{-1}. Use these values to calculate the gas constant for unit mass of hydrogen

Expressed in correct SI units, the density = 9.0×10^{-2} kg m^{-3}. Thus

$$r = 10^5 \times \frac{1}{9 \times 10^{-2}} \times \frac{1}{273}$$
$$= 4.1 \times 10^3\ \text{J kg}^{-1}\ \text{K}^{-1}.$$

The gas equation is particularly useful in the solution of problems where different parts of a mass of gas are at different temperatures; this is illustrated in the worked example which follows.

Example 2. Two containers whose volumes are in the ratio 2:1 contain gas at 10 °C and 760 mm mercury pressure, and are connected by a narrow capillary tube of negligible volume. Calculate the pressure in the apparatus when the temperature of the larger container is increased to 100 °C, while the other is maintained at 10 °C, ignoring the expansion of the containers.

When the temperature is raised some gas passes from the larger container to the smaller one, but the total mass of gas in the two vessels remains constant.

If r' is gas constant in (mm of Hg) (m^3) per kg per deg.,

$$\text{initial mass of gas} = \frac{760 \times 3V}{283r'}$$

where V is the volume of the smaller container.

If P is the pressure in the apparatus after heating,

$$\text{mass of gas in larger container} = \frac{2PV}{373r'},$$

$$\text{mass of gas in smaller container} = \frac{PV}{283r'}.$$

Since total mass of gas in constant,

$$\frac{PV}{r'}\left\{\frac{2}{373}+\frac{1}{283}\right\}=\frac{2280V}{283r'}.$$

Dividing by V/r', we obtain an expression which expresses the constancy of PV/T, before and after the change occurs, i.e.

$$P\,\frac{566+373}{373\times 283}=\frac{2280}{283}$$

or

$$P=\frac{2280\times 373}{939}$$

$$=906 \text{ mmHg}.$$

9 THE MOLE

The *mole* is defined as the amount of substance containing as many elementary units as there are carbon atoms in 0.012 kg of carbon-12.

This number is known as the *Avogadro constant*, and has the value $6.022\ 52\times 10^{23}$; it is normally represented by either L or N_A.

Thus a mole of the normal isotope of carbon corresponds to a mass of 0.012 or 12×10^{-3} kg. It follows from our knowledge of the relative masses of atoms and molecules, that the Avogadro number of helium atoms has a mass of 4×10^{-3} kg. Similarly, a mole of hydrogen molecules has a mass of 2×10^{-3} kg. In general, if the relative molecular mass is M a mole of these molecules have a mass $M\times 10^{-3}$ kg.

The density of any gas may be obtained by a direct weighing of a flask containing gas, when the flask has previously been weighed empty. A gas syringe is a convenient apparatus for carrying out such a direct determination.

In this way the densities of various gases may be obtained at s.t.p., i.e. 0 °C and 760 mm of mercury pressure. Examination of such results shows that a mole of any gas which approximates to the ideal occupies the same volume, approximately 22.4 litres or 0.0224 m^3. This result is equivalent to the statement known as *Avogadro's hypothesis*, which asserts that equal volumes of gases at the same temperature and pressure contain equal numbers of molecules, since by definition a mole of any gas is the same number (L) of molecules.

The constancy of the volume occupied by a mole of any ideal gas at a particular pressure and temperature, in conjunction with eqn. (1.9) shows that the gas constant has a constant value for a mole of any such gas.

This particular value of the constant is represented by R, and thus for a mole of gas, eqn. (1.9) becomes

$$PV=RT \tag{1.11}$$

where $$R = \frac{10^5 \times 0.0224}{273} = 8.32 \text{ J mol}^{-1} \text{ K}^{-1}.$$

Although this is the correct value as expressed in SI units, there are occasions when it is convenient to use the molar gas constant R in

litre x atmosphere per degree

and thus $$R = \frac{1 \times 22.4}{273} = 0.082\ 1 \text{ at mol}^{-1} \text{ K}^{-1}.$$

An example of the use in these units is provided by the following worked examples.

Example 3. 8.0 g of a particular gas occupies a volume of 2.8 l at 273 °C and a pressure of four atmospheres. What is the molecular weight of the gas?

Gas constant for this amount of gas

$$= \frac{4 \times 2.8}{546} \text{ l at K}^{-1}.$$

Thus number of moles $$= \frac{4 \times 2.8}{546 \times 0.082} = 0.25.$$

Thus 8.0 g is 0.25 mol and consequently a mole of this gas has a mass 32.0 g. Therefore molecular weight is 32.0.

The gas constant is also of great use in solving problems involving the dissociation of a gas, as is shown in the following example.

Example 4. 2.3 g of solid nitrogen tetroxide is heated and the gaseous products are found to occupy a volume of 1.04 l at 60 °C and a pressure of 1 atmosphere. What proportion of the original N_2O_4 molecules have dissociated into NO_2 molecules at this temperature?

Since the molecular weight of $N_2O_4 = 28 + 64 = 92$, there are originally $2.3/92 = 1/40$ moles of N_2O_4 present.

If α is the fraction of molecules dissociating, $\alpha/40$ moles have dissociated to form $2\alpha/40$ moles of NO_2.

There are also $(1 - \alpha)/40$ moles of N_2O_4.

Thus total number of moles

$$= \frac{2\alpha + 1 - \alpha}{40} = \frac{\alpha + 1}{40}.$$

These occupy a volume of 1.04 l at atmospheric pressure and 333 K; so substituting in $PV = nRT$,

$$1 \times 1.04 = \frac{(1 + \alpha) \times 0.082 \times 333}{40}$$

$$\therefore\ 1 + \alpha = \frac{1 \times 1.04 \times 40}{0.082 \times 333}$$

$$= 1.52$$

Thus $\alpha = 0.52.$

10 TEMPERATURE AND THERMOMETERS

We have already considered several experiments in which the variation of certain properties with temperature has been investigated. In order to measure *temperatures* we need a *thermometer.* It is therefore necessary at this stage to consider both how temperature is defined and how it is measured by a thermometer.

There are many properties – of which volume is an obvious example – which increase as the substance in question becomes hotter; any such property can be used to measure temperature. The familiar mercury thermometer employs the volume expansion of mercury relative to glass, but other liquids could well be used, although cohesion and good thermal conductivity make mercury particularly useful, apart from the considerable range of conditions over which it is liquid.

A simple mercury thermometer is calibrated by marking the liquid level when the thermometer is in melting ice, repeating the procedure when it is in the steam from water boiling under standard atmospheric conditions and dividing the range between these two *fixed points* into 100 equal *Celsius degrees.* In this way temperature is defined so that it is linearly related to the volume of mercury measured by a glass container; such a temperature scale is entirely arbitrary and depends on the particular materials chosen – in this case mercury and glass.

Any other temperature scale, similarly defined using some other property or other materials, would of necessity agree with the mercury scale at the two fixed points, but there is no reason why it should agree with it at any other point.

There is a scale of temperature which does not depend on a particular property of any individual substance. This scale, known as the *thermodynamic scale* (which is briefly considered in Chapter 4, Section 9), can be shown to be identical with a scale based on the properties of an ideal gas. Thus a *gas thermometer* using an ideal gas can be considered as a means of measuring temperatures on this thermodynamic scale.

The thermodynamic scale could be defined using two fixed points as earlier suggested for the mercury thermometer, and for many years this was the method adopted. However, the accepted procedure now is to use *one* fixed point and also fix the *size of the degree.*

The *triple point of water* – the temperature at which water, ice and water vapour can exist in equilibrium with each other (Chapter 5,

Section 6) – is found to be much more accurately reproducible than the ice point, and is used as the fixed point.

The degree size is defined by defining the triple point of water as 273.16 K, where K represents the kelvin, the degree of temperature so defined.

Definition of the scale in this way may be considered as using two fixed points; the second fixed point is the *absolute zero* of temperature which is made O K. Thus the size of the kelvin is defined by having 273.16 temperature intervals each 1 K, between absolute zero and the triple point.

Since the ice point is found to be 0.01 K lower than the triple point, the the ice point zero of the Celsius (or common) scale is 273.15 K.

It has already been mentioned that it can be shown that an *ideal gas scale* is identical with the thermodynamic scale; the ideal gas thermometer utilises the variation in the product PV for an ideal gas. It can thus be used to define thermodynamic temperature (T), according to the relation

$$\frac{PV}{(PV)_{\mathrm{tr.pt.}}} = \frac{T}{273.16}. \tag{1.12}$$

In the next chapter – Section 5, eqn. (2.7) – we establish on the basis of the simple kinetic theory that PV is proportional to the translational kinetic energy of the molecules; it is therefore the translational kinetic energy of the gas molecules which is, in effect, being used to define the temperature scale.

11 THE GAS THERMOMETER

No ideal gas exists and it is therefore necessary to use real gas thermometers in the first instance; the ideal gas scale is then obtained by applying corrections for the known deviations from ideal behaviour of the gas in question. At temperatures above room temperature it is convenient and satisfactory to use nitrogen, but for lower temperatures hydrogen and helium are more suitable.

Since we are concerned with the variations in the product PV, the precise conditions under which the gas is confined are not important, but in practice it is convenient to use a gas which is maintained at a *constant volume.* Generally speaking, changes of pressure can be more easily measured than volume changes. The apparatus of Fig. 1.6 is the basic form of constant volume gas thermometer, but it is desirable to incorporate a barometer so that the total gas pressure is measured; Fig. 1.10 shows a simple form of such apparatus.

With suitable choice of gas, the gas thermometer can be used over a very wide range of temperatures. At the lower temperatures the deviations from the ideal become more serious, although they may be reduced by using gas

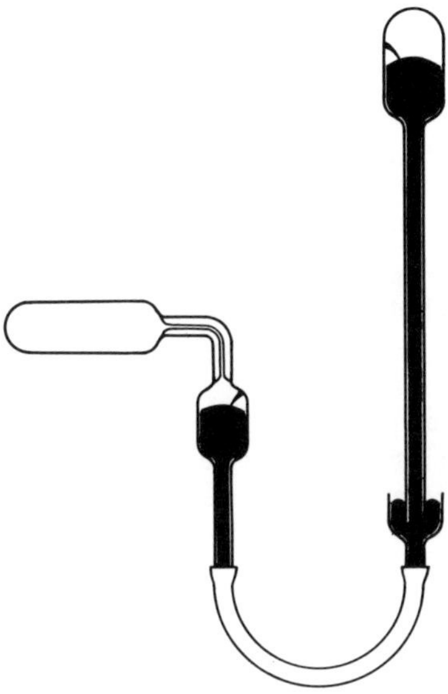

Fig. 1.10

at a lower pressure. At high temperatures problems arise from the porosity of the bulb, even when it is constructed of platinum; the relative chemical inertness of nitrogen prevents further difficulties. It should also be appreciated that amongst the corrections to be applied is one for the expansion of the bulb itself.

The size and large heat capacity of the gas thermometer make it most inconvenient for use. A large bath is needed to accommodate it and a very considerable time must be allowed for all parts of the gas to reach the temperature to be measured. For this reason it is much more convenient to use other types of thermometer which are calibrated to read temperatures on the gas scale.

12 INTERNATIONAL PRACTICAL TEMPERATURE SCALE AND OTHER THERMOMETERS

In order to facilitate the calibration of various other thermometers on the gas scale, it is desirable to have a number of subsidiary fixed points whose values have been determined by an ideal gas thermometer. These fixed points may be considered to define the International Practical Temperature Scale; this scale normally uses the Celsius degree, whose size is identical with the kelvin.

The fixed points chosen are:

Boiling point of oxygen	−182.97 °C
Boiling point of water	100.0 °C
Boiling point of sulphur	444.6 °C
Freezing point of silver	960.8 °C
Freezing point of gold	1063.0 °C

Details of the establishment of this scale can be found in text books on heat together with details of the mode of operation of the particular thermometers used in the various ranges of temperature, but the following outline can be of interest.

Between the oxygen point and the freezing point of antimony, which is 630 °C, the platinum resistance thermometer can be calibrated to read temperatures on the international scale. For temperatures above 0 °C, the relation between resistance R and temperature t is of the form

$$R = R_0(1 + At + Bt^2) \qquad (1.13)$$

where A and B are constants determined from the values of the resistance at the two fixed points in the range.

For the lower temperatures a more complicated equation involving a further constant and higher powers of t is required.

In the region between the antimony point and the freezing point of gold, temperatures can be determined with a *thermocouple* consisting of one junction of platinum and the other of an alloy of platinum and rhodium. The relation between e.m.f., E and temperature is of the form

$$E = a + bt + ct^2. \qquad (1.14)$$

Above the gold point the scale is realized by the use of a *radiation pyrometer* which relates the temperature to the energy of a particular wavelength, which is emitted by a hot body.

QUESTIONS

1. If nitrogen is found to have a mass of 1.25 gram per litre at a temperature of 0 °C and a pressure of 10^5 N m^{-2}, calculate the gas constant for a mole of nitrogen.

2. What volume of liquid oxygen (density 1.14 g cm^{-3}) may be produced by the complete liquefaction of the contents of a cylinder of volume 100 l which contains oxygen at a pressure of 20 atmospheres and a temperature of 20 °C? Assume that the oxygen in its initial state may be considered an ideal gas, that atmospheric pressure = 10^5 N m^{-2}, and that the gas constant = 8.32 J mol^{-1} K^{-1}.

3. A cylinder contains 5.8 kg of oxygen at a pressure of five atmospheres. If an exactly similar cylinder contains 3.8 kg of nitrogen at the same temperature, what is the pressure of the nitrogen?
(M.W. of oxygen = 32; M.W. of nitrogen = 28).

4. Two glass vessels of volume 4 litre and 1 litre are connected by a glass capillary of negligible volume. The apparatus is sealed and contains an ideal gas at a pressure of 760 mm of mercury and a temperature 300 K. Calculate the pressure in the apparatus if the temperature of the larger vessel is raised to 400 K, whilst the smaller one is maintained at 300 K.

5. Outline the experiments which lead to the concept of an ideal gas obeying the relation $PV = mrT$, for a mass m of gas, showing how this result follows from the experimental results.

What is the further experimental evidence that the constant in this equation can be replaced by a universal constant R for a mole of any gas which approximates to the ideal?

6. A sealed glass bulb contains 29 cm³ of mercury and 1.00 cm³ of air at 0 °C and 760 mm mercury pressure. If the vapour pressure of mercury is ignored, calculate the pressure of the air when the temperature is raised to 50 °C.

Coefficient of linear expansion of glass = 8×10^{-6} °C^{-1}; coefficient of cubical expansion of mercury = 8×10^{-5} °C^{-1}.

7. Two vessels A and B with volumes 1 and 3 litres respectively are connected by a tube of negligible volume containing a tap which is initially closed. The air in A is at a temperature of 20 °C and a pressure of 65 cm mercury, whilst that in B is at 50 °C and a pressure of 90 cm mercury. Calculate the pressure in the apparatus if the tap is opened and the temperature of the whole apparatus is maintained at 30 °C.

8. A simple type of constant volume apparatus consists of a glass bulb of volume 100.0 cm³ and a small dead space volume of 2.0 cm³. With the bulb in melting ice, the pressure is 80.0 cmHg and the dead space is estimated to be at 7° C. What will be the pressure when the bulb is in steam if the estimated temperature of the dead space is then 27 °C?

9. Two containers whose volumes are in the ratio 2:1 contain an ideal gas at a temperature of 15 °C and atmospheric pressure. The temperature of the smaller container is kept constant whilst that of the other is increased; the pressure in the apparatus becomes 1.20 atmospheres. What is the temperature of the larger container?

10. A gas thermometer has a bulb of volume 60 cm³ connected by a tube of negligible volume to a pressure measuring device which has a volume of 6.0 cm³. With the bulb immersed in melting ice the pressure of the gas is 720 mm mercury. What will be the pressure when the bulb is in a bath at 50 °C, if the pressure gauge is assumed to be at a room temperature of 17 °C for both measurements?

11. Air is contained in two glass bulbs of volume 100 cm³ and 10 cm³, which are joined by a tube of negligible volume. The pressure is 100 cmHg when the large bulb is at −23 °C and small bulb at +27 °C. What is the pressure when both are heated to 57 °C?

12. A certain mass of a diatomic gas exerts a pressure of 10^5 N m^{-2} at 0°C, but when it has been heated to 500 °C the pressure has risen to 3.5×10^5 N m^{-2}. What can be deduced from this data?

13. Helium is stored in a cylinder at 200 atmospheres pressure. The volume of the cylinder is 30 litres and its temperature 15 °C. How many atoms are there in the cylinder, and what is the mass of gas stored? (Gas constant = 8.4 J mol^{-1} K^{-1}. Avogadro's number = 6.02×10^{23} per mole. Atomic weight of helium = 4. Atmospheric pressure = 10^5 N m^{-2}.)

14. Two identical vessels filled with hydrogen are connected by a tube which contains a small thread of mercury. The hydrogen in one vessel is at 0 °C, and that in the other is at 20 °C. Will the mercury move if both vessels are heated through 10 °C and, if so, in which direction?

The Kinetic Theory of an Ideal Gas

2

The previous chapter established some of the basic properties of gases and developed the concept of an ideal gas; at the same time we introduced the idea of the kinetic theory based on the proposition that a gas consists of a large number of particles in rapid and random motion. We now proceed to build on this basic idea in greater detail in order to construct a quantitative model of a gas in terms of such particles; we shall then investigate the properties we should expect of such a gas and compare them with those found experimentally.

1 BASIC ASSUMPTIONS

The molecules are considered to act as if they are particles; thus their size is negligible compared with the space which they occupy. It will also be assumed that they exert no forces on each other except when they collide. The collisions which do occur will be assumed to be perfectly elastic. If the molecules are effectively points this is a reasonable assumption as far as collisions between any pair of gas molecules are concerned, since the only energy they can be imagined to possess is translational kinetic energy. If a collision was not perfectly elastic it might be suggested that some kinetic energy was converted into heat as is the case with macroscopic bodies. But the kinetic theory pictures heat as the kinetic energy of the molecules and it would therefore seem impossible for collisions between such particles to be other than perfectly elastic. However, we will return to a consideration of this particular point later. If the collisions between molecules and the walls of the container were not perfectly elastic there would be a steady transfer of energy from the gas to its container, even when they are both originally at the same temperature, and this is certainly not reasonable. In any case, it should be appreciated that such collisions are also between molecules, and there is no reason why they should be any different in nature from those between gas molecules.

We would expect that the addition of heat to a gas (thereby raising its temperature) makes the molecules travel more rapidly, so increasing their kinetic energy. This is a vague picture of temperature, but at this stage we have no precise concept of temperature as far as the kinetic theory is concerned.

The absence of any forces between molecules except when they collide, implies that the collisions take place in a negligible time and also means that in the interval between collisions the molecules travel in straight lines.

The motion of the molecules is completely random in so far as direction is concerned; if at a particular instant a certain number are travelling in a specified direction, an equal number are travelling in exactly the opposite direction. There are no preferred directions and all directions are equally likely. The random nature of the motion also means that we cannot predict the motion of a particular molecule, but may only make assertions concerning the likelihood of it moving in a certain direction.

2 COLLISIONS AND ROOT MEAN SQUARE SPEEDS

The molecules of a gas are frequently colliding with each other; the Brownian motion described in the previous chapter suggests that this should be so, and we have already mentioned that the mean free path of air molecules at room temperature is of the order of 10^{-5} cm. We will establish later that the speeds of most of the molecules are such that distances of this order are travelled in a very short time indeed. Thus an individual molecule suffers very many collisions in any short time or in travelling any short distance. It also follows that there will be a very large number of collisions occurring in any small region of the gas, and although an individual molecule is continually suffering changes of direction as a result of collisions, there are so many molecules in any small region, that whenever a particular molecule is diverted so that it is no longer travelling in a certain direction with a particular speed, there is another collision occurring nearby so that some other molecule emerges from it travelling in exactly the same direction and with the same speed as the original one.

This is a statistical argument and can be applied because in any small space the number of molecules travelling in a certain direction with a particular speed remains constant. So as far as the large-scale effect of the molecular motions is concerned we are able to ignore the inter-molecular collisions and carry out our calculations as if a particular molecule travelled with constant speed in a particular direction. It is important to realize that this argument could not be applied if the pressure was so low that the concentration of molecules was very small.

Provided the temperature does not alter, the total kinetic energy possessed by the gas molecules remains unchanged but we do not assume that all molecules are travelling with the same speed; we consider that they have speeds distributed over a range but the number with any particular speed does not vary.

If there are n_1 molecules with a speed c_1, n_2 with a speed c_2, n_r with a speed c_r and so on, until we have included all the molecules, their total kinetic energy is

$$\tfrac{1}{2}n_1mc_1^2 + \tfrac{1}{2}n_2mc_2^2 \,\ldots\ldots + \tfrac{1}{2}n_rmc_r^2 + \ldots$$
$$= \tfrac{1}{2}m\Sigma\,(n_rc_r^2)$$

for molecules of mass m.

This is the energy possessed by an equal number of molecules, each with a speed $\sqrt{\overline{c^2}}$ or $\left(\overline{c^2}\right)^{\frac{1}{2}}$, where

$$\overline{c^2} = \frac{\Sigma\left(n_r c_r^2\right)}{n} \tag{2.1}$$

and
$$n = n_1 + n_2 \ldots\ldots n_r \ldots\ldots$$

The speed $\left(\overline{c^2}\right)^{\frac{1}{2}}$ defined by eqn. (2.1) is known as the *root mean square speed*, and is often written c_{rms}.

An imaginary molecule moving with the r.m.s. speed is typical of the molecules at that particular temperature, and it is such a molecule which we frequently consider in the kinetic theory of gases. If all molecules travelled with a speed c_{rms}, we would have a gas with the same total kinetic energy.

It should be realized that although the energy of a particular molecule is continually changing as a result of collisions, the number of molecules with any particular energy remains unaltered, provided the temperature does not change; since we are unable to distinguish one molecule from another it follows that on the macroscopic scale these collisions are of little concern.

3 CALCULATION OF GAS PRESSURE

We now consider a mass of gas contained in a sphere of radius r, as shown in Fig. 2.1. If a particular molecule of mass m travelling with a speed c_1 strikes the sphere at A, at an angle θ to the radius at A, its velocity along

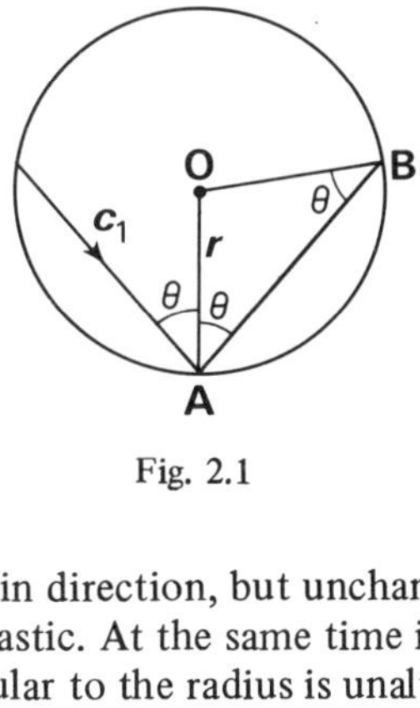

Fig. 2.1

the radius will be reversed in direction, but unchanged in magnitude since the collision is perfectly elastic. At the same time its velocity component in the direction perpendicular to the radius is unaltered. Thus it travels away from the surface along AB, which also makes an angle θ with AO.

Since AOB is an isosceles triangle the molecule travels a distance $2r \cos\theta$

before it again hits the wall at B. Thus if a molecule is travelling at an angle θ to the radius where it first hits the wall, the perfectly elastic nature of the collisions ensures that it always hits the wall at this same angle to the radius. It follows that it always takes the time $2r \cos\theta/c_1$ to travel the constant distance between impacts with the wall. We are, of course, assuming that since no forces act on the molecule between collisions with the wall, it travels in a straight line.

This molecule thus collides with the wall $c_1/2r \cos\theta$ times per second and at each of these collisions it suffers a momentum change $2mc_1 \cos\theta$ normal to the surface of the sphere.

Thus in one second the magnitude of the total momentum change normal to the surface of the sphere

$$= 2mc_1 \cos\theta \times \frac{c_1}{2r\cos\theta}$$

$$= \frac{mc_1^2}{r}.$$

If there are n_1 molecules per unit volume with this speed, the corresponding momentum change per second has magnitude,

$$\frac{4}{3}\pi r^3 n_1 \times \frac{mc_1^2}{r}$$

$$= \frac{4}{3}\pi mn_1 c_1^2 r^2.$$

These impacts must be equally distributed over the surface of the sphere so that the rate of change of momentum brought about per unit area is

$$\frac{4}{3}\pi mn_1 c_1^2 r^2 \Big/ 4\pi r^2 = \frac{1}{3} m n_1 c_1^2.$$

By Newton's second law of motion this is the force per unit area exerted by the walls on these molecules. Since pressure is force per unit area, the equal and opposite reaction is the pressure exerted by these molecules on the wall.

We can now add the contributions to the total pressure exerted by molecules of various speeds, thus

$$P = \frac{1}{3} m (n_1 c_1^2 + n_2 c_2^2 + \ldots\ldots)$$

which by eqn. (2.1) becomes

$$P = \frac{1}{3} mn\overline{c^2}. \tag{2.2}$$

Although this result for the pressure has been derived for the particular case of molecules in a spherical container, it applies equally whatever the shape of the vessel.

Fig. 2.2 shows a cube of side l; a particular molecule with speed c_1 will have velocity components $(u_1 v_1 w_1)$ parallel to the three edges of the cube. Provided we ignore the effect of collisions between molecules in accordance with the statistical argument given previously, a particular molecule has to

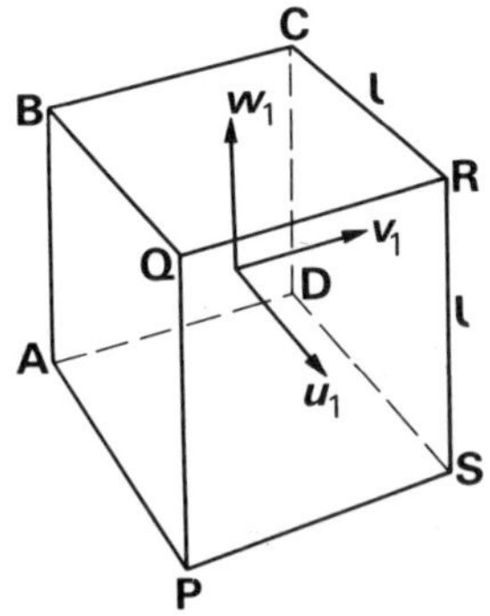

Fig. 2.2

travel a distance $2l$ in a direction parallel to AP between successive collisions with the wall PQRS; the molecule referred to above travels this distance in a time $2l/u_1$, and thus makes $u_1/2l$ collisions per second with this wall. At each of these perfectly elastic collisions its momentum perpendicular to PQRS changes by $2mu_1$.

Thus the rate of change of momentum parallel to PA for this molecule

$$= (u_1/2l)(2mu_1) = mu_1^2/l.$$

Adding such changes for all the molecules in the cube, we obtain

$$\frac{m}{l}(n_1 u_2^2 + n_2 u_2^2 + \ldots\ldots)$$

$$\frac{m}{l} nl^3\, \overline{u^2} = mnl^2\, \overline{u^2}$$

since there are nl^3 molecules in the cube, if there are n per unit volume.

This is the force exerted on the face of area l^2, and thus the pressure P_x on this face is given by

$$P_x = mn\,\overline{u^2}.$$

A similar argument in respect of the other two faces CDSR and CBQR leads to

$$P_y = mn\overline{v^2};\ P_z = mn\overline{w^2}.$$

Since there is no mass movement of the gas in any particular direction we would expect that $P_x = P_y = P_z$; this is also in accord with the experimental fact that the pressure is equal in all directions.

Thus
$$P = P_x = P_y = P_z$$
$$= \frac{1}{3}(P_x + P_y + P_z)$$
$$= \frac{1}{3} mn \left(\overline{u^2} + \overline{v^2} + \overline{w^2}\right)$$
$$= \frac{1}{3} mn \overline{c^2}$$

as before.

4 MOLECULAR VELOCITIES

Since m is the mass of a single molecule and n is the number of molecules per unit volume

$$\rho = mn$$

where ρ is the density of the gas.

Thus eqn. (2.2) can be written

$$P = \frac{1}{3} \rho \overline{c^2} \tag{2.3}$$

which can be re-arranged to

$$\left(\overline{c^2}\right)^{\frac{1}{2}} = \sqrt{\frac{3P}{\rho}}. \tag{2.4}$$

The density of hydrogen at 0 °C and standard atmospheric pressure of approximately 10^5 N m^{-2} is approximately 9×10^{-2} kg m^{-3}; so, substituting these values in eqn. (2.4), we obtain

$$\left(\overline{c^2}\right)^{\frac{1}{2}} = \sqrt{\frac{3 \times 10^5}{9 \times 10^{-2}}} = \sqrt{(3.33 \times 10^6)}$$
$$= 1.86 \times 10^3 \text{ m s}^{-1}.$$

In the case of nitrogen the density under the same conditions of pressure and temperature is greater by a factor of 14: thus we obtain

$$\left(\overline{c^2}\right)^{\frac{1}{2}} = 1.86 \times 10^3/\sqrt{14}$$
$$= 497 \text{ m s}^{-1}.$$

An important test of the validity of the ideas so far developed is provided by direct measurement of the speeds of the molecules of a gas. Such measurements were first carried out by Maxwell in the last century, but two rather more modern methods will now be outlined, although the particular experiments described refer to atoms of bismuth and potassium, respectively.

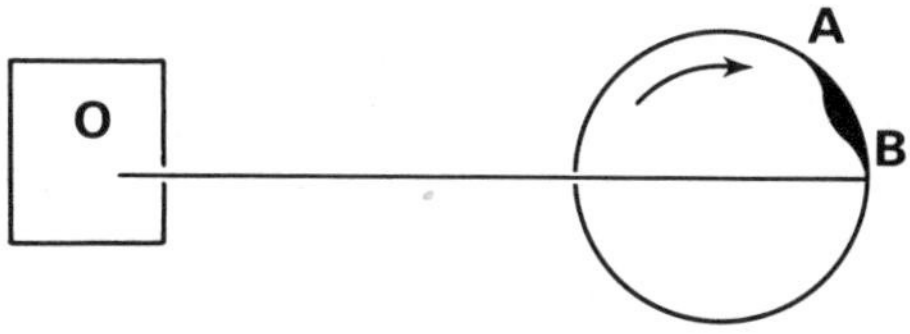

Fig. 2.3

In 1930 Zartmann and others used the apparatus indicated schematically in Fig. 2.3 where a high degree of vacuum was maintained in all parts of the apparatus outside the oven O. Bismuth molecules in the gaseous state were first produced in the oven O and then allowed to escape as a molecular beam which is well defined by a pair of slits. The beam then passed through a further slit in a rotating cylinder, and the molecules entering travelled across the cylinder and condensed on its opposite surface, so forming a deposit. The more slowly-moving molecules were deposited at A, and the faster ones at points such as B. Knowing the diameter and speed of rotation of the cylinder, the distribution of velocities in the molecular beam could be calculated from the relative density of the deposit at various points. This result was then used to calculate the velocity distribution of the molecules in the oven; this is rather different from the velocity distribution of those emerging, since there is a greater chance of faster-moving molecules escaping in any time-interval.

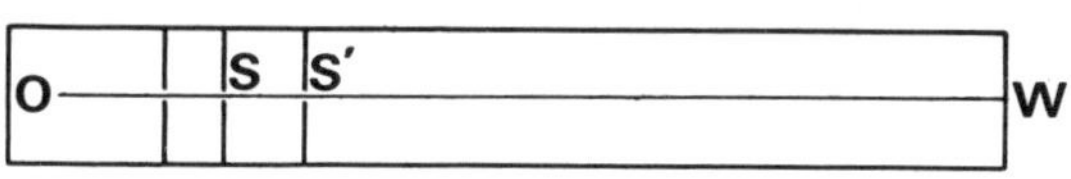

Fig. 2.4

An alternative arrangement is shown in Fig. 2.4: potassium atoms are vaporized in an oven O at about 270 °C from a special lump of potassium which has previously been kept under paraffin in order to avoid any problems arising from impurity atoms. The oven was previously highly evacuated, and the potassium atoms emerge from the oven through two very fine slits S and S′ as a narrow beam, and enter a tube which is about 2 m in length. Special pumps are used to reduce the pressure in the tube to 3×10^{-6} torr (mm of mercury) and under these conditions the emerging atoms are unlikely to be involved in collisions as they travel along the tube. The two narrow slits are positioned so that only molecules travelling exactly horizontally emerge into the tube. However, in their transit of the tube they acquire a vertical component of velocity from the gravitational field and are a depth h below the level of the slits when they reach the detector at the end of the tube. If they have taken a time t for this journey

$$h = \frac{1}{2} gt^2.$$

Thus any value of h corresponds to a particular value of t, and hence of original horizontal velocity on emergence into the tube.

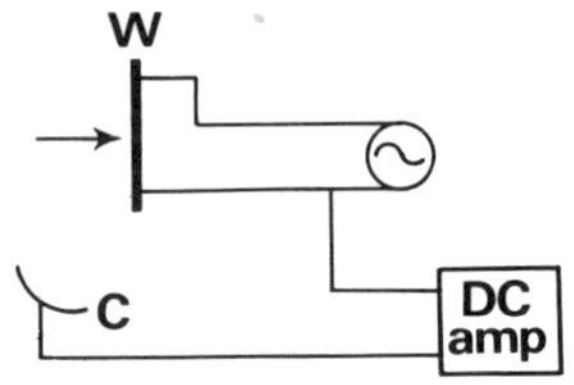

Fig. 2.5

The detector is shown in plan view in Fig. 2.5 and consists of a very fine horizontal wire W through which a current passes; when atoms hit the wire, positive ions are accelerated away from the wire towards the collecting electrode C. The very small current so produced passes through a d.c. amplifier, and the output is read on a microammeter. The wire is moved vertically by a micrometer, and in a typical experiment currents which were of the order of 10^{-11} A were measured over a range of positions of W covering approximately $\frac{1}{2}$ mm. The maximum current corresponding to the most probable velocity occurred for a drop of about 0.1 mm.

If $h = 10^{-4}$ m, $t^2 = 2h/g = 2 \times 10^{-5}$ and t is approximately 4.5×10^{-3} s. For a tube of length 2 m this represents atoms with a velocity of $2/(4.5 \times 10^{-3})$ or about 450 ms^{-1}.

Experiments of this nature establish that the velocity distribution among the molecules is of the form shown below, where $N(c)$ the number with a given speed c is plotted against c.

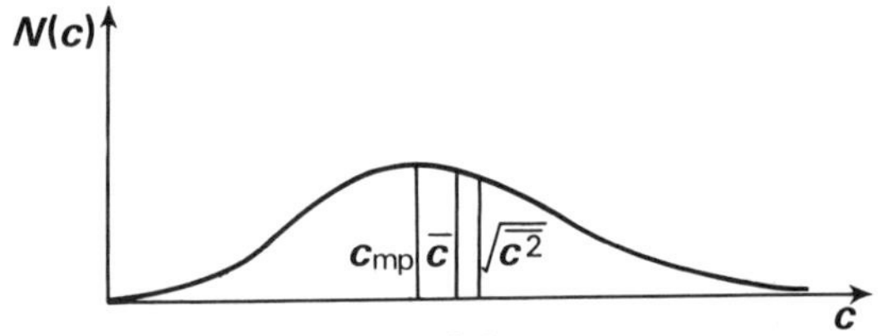

Fig. 2.6

A distribution of this form had already been predicted theoretically by Maxwell. The *most probable* speed c_{mp} corresponds to the maximum of the distribution curve; since the curve is not symmetrical about this value the *mean* speed $\bar{c}$ is somewhat greater than the most probable velocity as is shown in Fig. 2.6.

In calculating the r.m.s. speed greater weight is given to the higher speeds and consequently c_{rms} is rather larger than $\bar{c}$. The values of c_{rms}

deduced from the distribution curve are found to be in agreement with those calculated from eqn. (2.4). It should be emphasized that c_{rms} is only one particular average speed obtained by a particular method of averaging; it is that speed which, if possessed by each molecule, would give the same total translational kinetic energy as does the spread of speeds in the Maxwell distribution.

The detailed expression for the distribution function is given later but some indication of the way in which speeds are distributed is shown by the following table showing the fraction of molecules in various ranges of speed, for nitrogen at room temperature.

Speeds between	Fraction of molecules
0 and 100 m s^{-1}	0.01
100 and 300 m s^{-1}	0.25
300 and 500 m s^{-1}	0.42
500 and 700 m s^{-1}	0.24
700 and 900 m s^{-1}	0.07
above 900 m s^{-1}	0.01

The corresponding values of the most probable, the mean and the root mean square speeds are

$$c_{mp} = 412 \text{ m s}^{-1}$$

$$\bar{c} = 466 \text{ m s}^{-1}$$

$$\sqrt{\overline{c^2}} = 503 \text{ m s}^{-1}.$$

An increase of temperature moves the maximum of the distribution curve towards higher speeds and at the same time spreads the molecular speeds over a larger range as is indicated in Fig. 2.7.

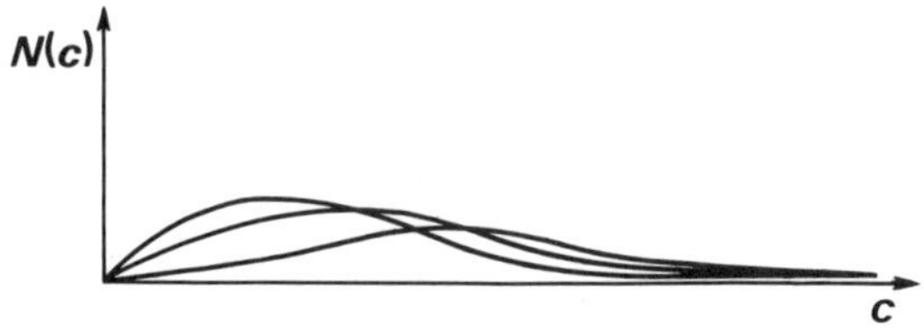

Fig. 2.7

5 KINETIC THEORY INTERPRETATION OF TEMPERATURE

Heating a gas involves an increase in the velocity and kinetic energy of the molecules. If the temperature of a gas does not change we should expect that the velocity of its molecules remains unaltered; thus by eqn. (2.3), P/ρ should be constant under these conditions. This is equivalent to Boyle's law which states that the product of pressure and volume of a fixed mass of gas is constant if the temperature remains constant.

At this stage it is necessary to introduce into the kinetic theory of gases a more precise concept of temperature; our intuitive test of temperature equality of two bodies, asserts that no heat passes from one to the other of such bodies when they are in contact. In fact, we do not observe heat passage directly, but infer it from a change in the temperature of a body. Thus two gases are at the same temperature if, when we allow them to mix, there is no net interchange of energy between the two sets of molecules.

If we imagine a container of molecules of gas A, and then add a large number of molecules of another type B, the two types of molecules collide with each other, and normally one would expect there to be a transfer of energy either from type A to type B or in the reverse direction. It can be shown by considering the mechanics of a large number of identical particles that the absence of any net transfer of energy between two types of molecules can only result when the *mean translational kinetic energies* of the two types are equal. It is important to include the word 'translational' in this statement since we are here concerned with the kinetic energy the molecules possess by virtue of their motion as point masses – this being the only type of energy we have so far envisaged the molecules possessing – and it is this energy which they can freely exchange in collisions.

Thus for two gases, whose respective molecules are represented by the suffices 1 and 2, we have, for equality of temperature,

$$\frac{1}{2} m_1 \overline{c_1^2} = \tfrac{1}{2} m_2 \overline{c_2^2}. \tag{2.5}$$

It is important to stress that it is the mean kinetic energies and not the speeds of the two sets of gas molecules which are equal. Since the mass of the oxygen molecules is sixteen times that of the hydrogen molecule, it follows from eqn. (2.5) that the root mean square speed of oxygen molecules will, at any temperature, be one-quarter that of hydrogen molecules at the same temperature.

Considering eqns. (2.2) and (2.5), we see that if two gases are exerting equal pressures at the same temperature,

$$\frac{1}{3} m_1 n_1 \overline{c_1^2} = \frac{1}{3} m_2 n_2 \overline{c_2^2}$$

and

$$\frac{1}{2} m_1 \overline{c_1^2} = \frac{1}{2} m_2 \overline{c_2^2}$$

and thus

$$n_1 = n_2.$$

If the number of molecules per unit volume is the same for the two gases it follows that

equal volumes contain equal numbers of molecules,

–which is the statement previously referred to as *Avogadro's hypothesis.* Thus on the basis of the simple model of a gas which we have derived from the basic assumptions of the kinetic theory, we can predict that Avagadro's hypothesis will be obeyed.

We have already seen that temperature is directly related to the kinetic energy and we can now make the following definition:

> *absolute temperature is directly proportional to the mean translational kinetic energy of the molecules.*

This can be expressed in the form of an equation,

$$\frac{1}{2}m\,\overline{c^2} = \frac{3}{2}kT \tag{2.6}$$

where k is an absolute constant, independent of the particular gas under consideration; k is known as *Boltzmann's constant.*

We could equally well have replaced $3k/2$ in eqn. (2.6) by a single symbol, but the reason for this particular numerical factor will appear shortly.

If N molecules of a gas occupy a volume V, eqn. (2.2) can be written,

$$P\,V = \frac{1}{3}\,mN\,\overline{c^2}. \tag{2.7}$$

Combining eqn. (2.7) with (2.6), we obtain

$$P\,V = NkT. \tag{2.8}$$

We now see that eqn. (2.8) is identical with the ideal gas equation (1.10) provided Nk is equal to the gas constant for the particular amount of gas under consideration.

If we consider a mole of gas, N in this particular case becomes L, Avogadro's number, and thus

$$Lk = R. \tag{2.9}$$

We can consider eqn. (2.9) as defining Boltzmann's constant, and it shows that k can be looked upon as the *gas constant per molecule.*

Rewriting eqn. (2.6) as

$$m\overline{c^2} = 3\,kT$$

and substituting in eqn. (2.7), we obtain

$$PV = LkT$$

which in view of eqn. (2.9) becomes

$$PV = RT,$$

the ideal gas equation for a mole. Thus a definition of temperature by eqn. (2.6) is identical with definition in terms of the behaviour of an ideal gas.

The temperature of a gas has been defined to be directly proportional to the mean kinetic energy of translation of the molecules. If the molecules are particles, one cannot conceive of any other form of energy they could possess, provided they are not in a field of force. Thus the total *internal energy* of the gas is the sum of all the individual translational kinetic energies; representing this internal energy by U, we have

$$U = \frac{1}{2} mN \overline{c^2}$$

for N molecules.

Comparing this eqn. with eqn. (2.7), we can write

$$U = \frac{3PV}{2} \tag{2.10}$$

for any quantity of gas. In the particular case where we consider a mole,

$$U = \frac{3RT}{2}. \tag{2.11}$$

A mole of air at s.t.p. occupies 22.4 litre or 0.0224 m^3, and the gas constant for this quantity of gas has already been shown to be 8.3 J. Thus from eqn. (2.11) the total translational kinetic energy of the molecules in this volume under these conditions is

$$\frac{3}{2} \times 8.3 \times 273$$

$$= 3400 \text{ J.}$$

Some indication of the magnitude of this quantity of energy is obtained by realizing that it is the energy given out by a one-unit electric fire in just under $3\frac{1}{2}$ seconds. Alternatively, it is the kinetic energy of a mass of 2 kg moving with a speed of approximately 58 m s^{-1}, which is of the order of 130 miles per hour.

If the energy of a gas is entirely of this translational nature, raising its temperature by 1 K, would require $3R/2$ joule per mole. Thus the specific heat capacity would be $3r/2$ J kg^{-1} K^{-1}, where r is the gas constant for unit mass of gas, i.e. 1 kg. This value should be constant so that the specific heat capacity would seem to be independent of temperature. A more detailed consideration of the specific heat capacities of gases will be found in the next chapter.

6 DIFFUSION AND EFFUSION

We have already mentioned the ability of a gas to spread out and fill any space which is available to it, and we now consider this phenomenon in greater detail.

Diffusion is the intermingling of two gases so that eventually there is a uniform distribution of each gas throughout the space. If a closed container of gas is opened in a room, the gas eventually diffuses through the air to all parts of the room, and at the same time air diffuses into the container.

Effusion is a one-way motion involving the efflux or flowing of a gas through holes, which are normally of a small size. It is a rather simpler phenomenon to analyse than diffusion and it is correspondingly easier to measure the rate of effusion. The term *transpiration* is frequently used to describe the effect when there are a large number of small orifices through which the gas can flow. The flow through the holes in a porous pot or plug is of this nature.

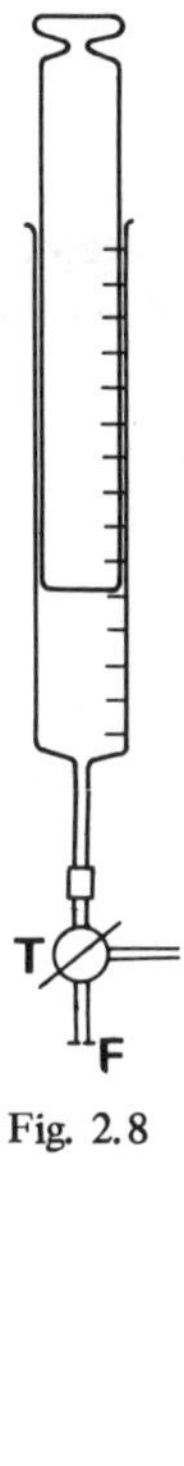

Fig. 2.8

The effusion of gases can be investigated by the use of the gas syringe shown in Fig. 2.8. A tap T is fixed to the end of the syringe and the vertical tube from the tap is closed by a piece of metal foil F with a tiny hole pierced in it. The size of hole is chosen so that with the gas syringe containing air under the pressure provided by the weight of the piston, all the air effuses from the barrel of the syringe in a few minutes.

The syringe is fixed vertically and the time for the bottom end of the piston to fall a distance representing a measured volume is recorded. This is therefore the time for a particular volume of gas to effuse through the hole.

The syringe is then thoroughly flushed out with another gas, using the horizontal tube, and the experiment is repeated. If the investigation is extended to a number of gases, it can be established that the rate of effusion is inversely proportional to the molecular weight.

In the case of a mole of gas the transitional kinetic energy is $\frac{1}{2}M\overline{c^2}$ where M is the total mass of the molecules in a mole. Thus using eqn. (2.11)

$$\frac{1}{2}M\overline{c^2} = \frac{3RT}{2}$$

and

$$\left(\overline{c^2}\right)^{\frac{1}{2}} = \sqrt{\frac{3RT}{M}}. \qquad (2.12)$$

When substituting particular values in eqn. (2.12) it is most important to realize that M, the mass of a mole, must be expressed in the SI unit of mass, i.e. kilograms. In the case of oxygen, $M = 32 \times 10^{-3}$ kg, and thus for molecules at 17 °C

$$\left(\overline{c^2}\right)^{\frac{1}{2}} = \frac{3 \times 8.3 \times 290}{1 \times 32 \times 10^{-3}}$$

$$= 475 \text{ m s}^{-1}.$$

If a small hole is made in the wall of a vessel containing gas, any molecule which would hit the area corresponding to the hole will pass out of the container. If the pressures inside and outside the vessel are equal, a similar flow of molecules will take place through the hole in the opposite direction and there will be no net effect. If, however, we imagine the space outside to be evacuated we can calculate the rate at which molecules escape from the vessel.

The number of molecules escaping will be proportional to $\bar{c}$ and also to the number per unit volume. At a given pressure and temperature this latter quantity is constant for all gases. Since $\bar{c}$ is proportional to $\left(\overline{c^2}\right)^{\frac{1}{2}}$ (see Section 9), eqn. (2.12) shows that the rate of efflux should be inversely proportional to $\sqrt{M}$ for any fixed temperature.

We can also consider eqn. (2.4) instead of eqn. (2.12) and thus for a given pressure, the number escaping should be proportional to $1/\sqrt{\rho}$.

Under many circumstances the passage of gases through the interstices of a porous pot or plug takes place so that the flow of each gas can be considered quite independently of the other. Flow of this type is found to obey Graham's law of Diffusion, which states that

the rate of diffusion is inversely proportional to the square root of the density.

It should, however, be emphasized that the rate of flow must be considered in terms of *number of molecules.* In accordance with Avogadro's hypothesis, volume flow under identical conditions of temperature and pressure will obey the same relation. However, since the mass of the molecules is proportional to the gas density under these circumstances, the rate of *mass* flow will be *directly proportional* to $\sqrt{\text{density}}$.

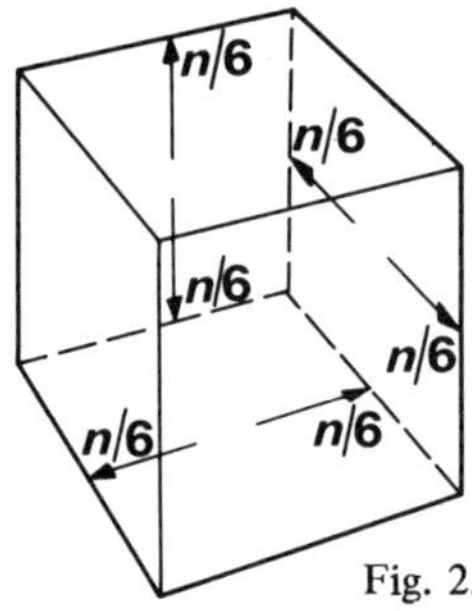

Fig. 2.9

In view of the random distribution of the molecular velocities in space, Joule found it useful to envisage these movements in all directions replaced by six equal streams, one flowing each way in each of three perpendicular directions. Thus in Fig. 2.9 we show a unit cube with n molecules, and at any instant, $n/6$ are travelling towards each of the faces of the cube.

From this picture we can calculate the rate of which molecules should reach any area. Those molecules which, at the beginning of a second, are within a distance c of the area A in Fig. 2.10 and which are travelling towards A, should reach it in the second. These molecules are contained within the volume shown; the total number in this volume is ncA, and one-sixth are moving towards A.

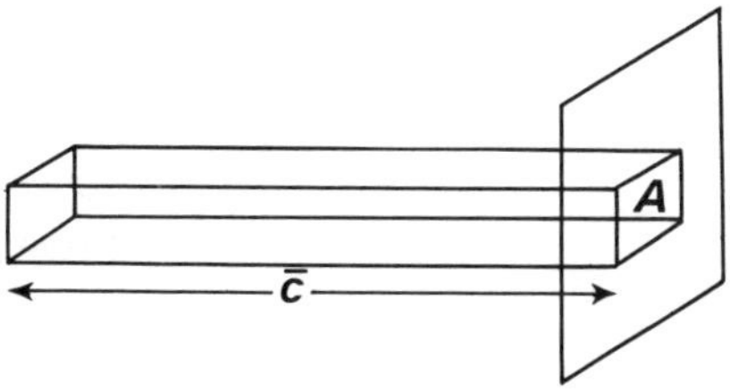

Fig. 2.10

Thus $ncA/6$ hit the area per second.

Considering all speeds follows that the total number hitting unit area per second

$$= n\bar{c}/6. \qquad (2.13)$$

It will be seen later (in Section 10 of this chapter) that the result of eqn. (2.13) is not accurate; however, it is of the correct order of magnitude, and is often of considerable use in elementary calculations.

We can use this simplified picture of the motion of molecules per unit volume towards any surface to calculate the pressure. If there are n_1 molecules with a velocity c_1, $n_1c_1/6$ of them hit unit area per second: each of these molecules suffers a momentum change $2mc_1$ when its velocity perpendicular to the area is reversed as a result of the collision. Thus the change in momentum per second is

$$\frac{n_1 c_1}{6} \times 2mc_1 = \frac{1}{3} n_1 m\, c_1^2.$$

If there are also n_2 with a velocity c_2, n_3 with a velocity c_3 and so on, the total rate of change of momentum occurring on unit area

$$= \frac{1}{3} m\, (n_1 c_1^2 + n_2 c_2^2 \ldots\ldots\ldots)$$

$$= \frac{1}{3} m \Sigma (n\, c^2).$$

$$= \frac{1}{3} mn\, \overline{c^2}.$$

which is the result already obtained in eqn. (2.2) for the pressure exerted by a gas.

7 LAW OF PARTIAL PRESSURES

Fig. 2.11 shows three identical containers; the upper two each contain a gas, and they produce pressures P_1 and P_2 as a consequence of the impact

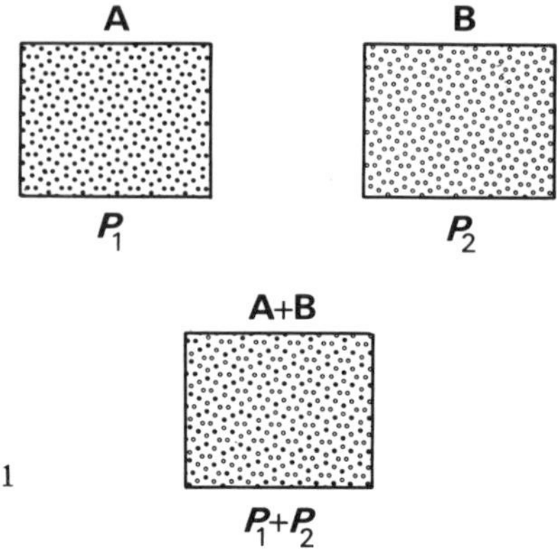

Fig. 2.11

of their molecules on the walls of the vessels: with the usual meaning for the symbols,

$$P_1 = \frac{1}{3} n_1 \, m_1 \, \overline{c_1^2}$$

$$P_2 = \frac{1}{3} n_2 \, m_2 \, \overline{c_2^2}.$$

Although they are not producing equal pressures, the gases are at the same temperature; thus, their mean translational kinetic energies are equal. If the molecules from both vessels are now placed in a third identical container so that they are free to mingle and collide, there will be no net transfer of energy from molecules of one type to the other.

The law of partial pressures – first propounded by Dalton – states that each gas continues to exert the same pressure as it did previously; thus the

total pressure (P) in the third container is the sum of the pressures in the two separate containers.

or

$$P = P_1 + P_2$$

$$= \frac{1}{3} n_1 \, m_1 \, \overline{c_1^2} + \frac{1}{3} n_2 \, m_2 \, \overline{c_2^2}. \qquad (2.14)$$

This can only be so if the frequency of collisions of one sort of molecule with the wall is unaffected by the presence of the molecules of the other type. It was seen earlier in calculating the pressure exerted by a gas that the overall effect of collisions could be neglected, since there were so many molecules in any small region that if a collision prevented a particular molecule from hitting the wall at some instant there would be another collision which causes another molecule, which otherwise would *not* have hit the wall in that instant, now to do so. The same situation applies here and the frequency of collisions is unaltered.

It should be realized that the situation would certainly be modified if the actual space taken up by the molecules themselves represented an appreciable fraction of the total volume of vessel available to them. Since the molecules would be unable to occupy that part of the space occupied by the molecules of the other gas, they would be effectively moving in a smaller space and would make more collisions in any time.

Thus we see that, provided no chemical action or heat exchange occurs,

each gas exerts the pressure it would exert if it occupied the space to the exclusion of the other, and the total pressure is the sum of these partial pressures.

Dalton's law of partial pressures is seen to be a consequence of the basic ideas of the kinetic theory of an ideal gas. A number of example of its application will be encountered in Chapter 5.

8 MOLECULAR COLLISIONS AND MEAN FREE PATH

We have already referred to the small size of the mean distance travelled by molecules between collisions; it is important, however, to appreciate that at each collision a molecule changes its direction of motion; its path is therefore of the form indicated in Fig. 2.12 where, of course, only a very small number of changes of direction are shown. The actual directions are chosen entirely at random, but each distance between a pair of collisions is

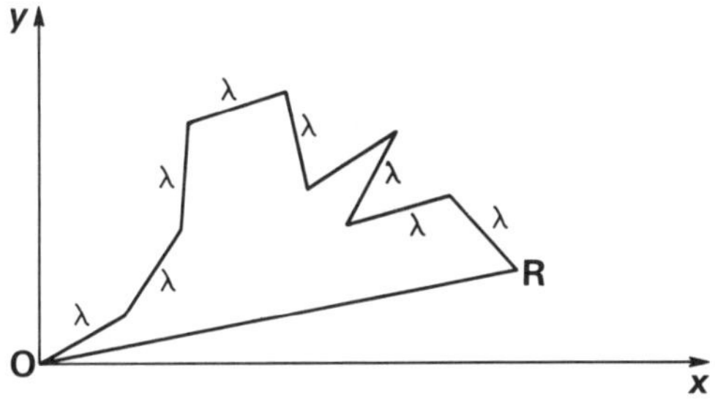

Fig. 2.12

equal to the mean free path λ. As a result of these paths, each of this length, the molecule travels from O to R.

We now draw two perpendicular axes through O; each path length can now be resolved into two component displacements $(x_1y_1)(x_2y_2)$ etc., and thus the total displacement along the X axis is $(x_1 + x_2 + x_3 + \ldots\ldots)$ and the corresponding displacement along the Y axis is $(y_1 + y_2 + y_3 + \ldots)$

$$\therefore \mathrm{OR}^2 = (x_1 + x_2 + x_3 + \ldots\ldots)^2 + (y_1 + y_2 + y_3 + \ldots\ldots)^2$$

$$= \Sigma(x_r)^2 + \Sigma(y_r)^2 + 2\Sigma(x_rx_s) + 2\Sigma(y_ry_s)..$$

Since these molecular paths are randomly distributed in space, positive and negative values of x and y occur with equal frequency, provided we consider a large enough number of paths. Thus the sum of products such as $x_r x_s$ will be zero; similarly $\Sigma\,(y_r y_s) = 0$.

$$\therefore \mathrm{OR}^2 = \Sigma\,(x_r^2 + y_r^2)$$
$$= r\lambda^2$$

since the original displacement was made up of r individual free paths. Thus, OR

$$\mathrm{OR} = (\sqrt{r})\lambda. \tag{2.15}$$

Although this result has been derived for the particular case of motion in two dimensions it can be extended to the case of three-dimensional motion.

We have already referred to the very rapid effusion of a gas such as bromine into an evacuated space (Chapter 1, Section 1); if, however, the bromine diffuses into a space in which there are many air molecules, the observed spread of the colour is very much slower. This is a consequence of the large number of collisions which any bromine molecule makes with air molecules, which thus act as a 'barrier'. In spite of the bromine molecules having a mean speed of the order of 200 m s^{-1} at room temperature, experiment shows that bromine takes a time of the order of 500 seconds to spread some 10 cm through the air.

This can be explained with the aid of eqn. (2.15); we make the simplifying assumption that the average distance travelled by a bromine molecule between collisions with an *air* molecule is λ, the mean free path for the air molecules. Thus if the bromine diffuses a distance q as a result of N collisions and mean free paths, eqn. (2.15) gives

$$q = (\sqrt{N})\,\lambda$$

and thus,

$$N = q^2/\lambda^2.$$

If the molecules travel with a velocity c, they make ct/λ collisions in time t, and therefore

$$ct/\lambda = q^2/\lambda^2$$

or

$$\lambda = q^2/ct.$$

Substituting, $q = 0.1$ m, $c = 200$ m s^{-1}, and $t = 500$ s,

$$\lambda = \frac{10^{-2}}{200 \times 500} = 10^{-7}\ \mathrm{m}.$$

This value of 10^{-7} m for the free path is of the correct order of magnitude and agrees with the result deduced by other methods.

It is instructive to work out the number of collisions that would be made by a bromine molecule in these circumstances.

Since $N = 10^{-2}/10^{-14} = 10^{12}$, the number of collisions per second is $10^{12}/500 = 2 \times 10^{9}$.

If the molecules of a gas were true particles they would move about indefinitely without colliding with one another; however, it is obvious that the assumption of negligible size can only be an approximation, and that they should more correctly be considered as spheres with a diameter d. Although the path of a particular molecule contains many changes of direction we can imagine it to be straightened out as in Fig. 2.13.

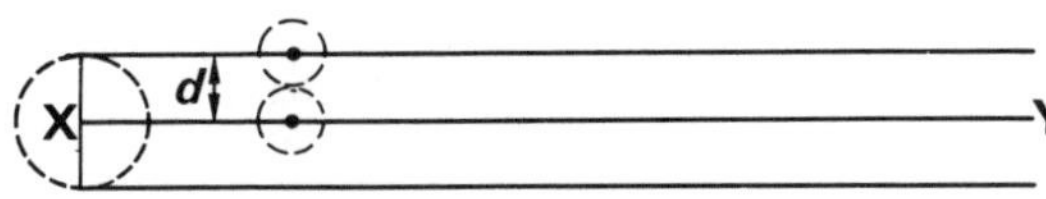

Fig. 2.13

A particular molecule travelling along this straightened-out path XY will just touch any other molecule whose centre lies within the cylinder shown; this is of radius equal to the molecular diameter d. Thus, in describing a path of length L it collides with any molecules whose centres lie in a volume $\pi d^2 L$; if there are n molecules per unit volume, it thus makes $\pi n d^2 L$ collisions. Since these occur in a path of length L, the mean free path λ is given by

$$\lambda = \frac{L}{\pi n d^2 L} = \frac{1}{\pi n d^2}. \qquad (2.16)$$

If the gas may be considered as obeying Boyle's law, n (the number of molecules per unit volume) is inversely proportional to the pressure, and it follows from eqn. (2.16) that provided the molecular diameter is independent of pressure, the mean free path is *inversely proportional to the pressure.*

The result of eqn. (2.16) was arrived at by assuming a particular molecule to be moving through a mass of stationary molecules; a more rigorous treatment taking into account the fact that all molecules are in motion leads to the result

$$\lambda = \frac{1}{\sqrt{2}\,\pi n d^2}\,. \qquad (2.17)$$

The mean free path of air at near atmospheric pressure is of the order of 10^{-7} m; the inverse proportionality between λ and pressure indicates that at a pressure of 10^{-1} N m^{-2} (less than 0.001 mm of mercury) the mean free path would be of the order of 0.1 m. At room pressure a molecule encounters many others on its journey across even a small vessel; however, at low pressures – of the order referred to above – it might well travel from one side of the vessel to the other without hitting another molecule. Thus collisions with the containing wall may become much more significant than encounters with other molecules, and this fact has considerable effect on the properties of gases at these very low pressure; phenomena at low pressures are considered in detail in Section 4 of Chapter 9.

It will be seen in Section 2 and 3 of Chapter 9 that the mean free path is of great importance in considering such gaseous properties as thermal conductivity and viscosity, and that eqn. (2.17) combined with other results not only provides important evidence for the validity of the ideas of the kinetic theory of gases, but also enables estimates to be made of molecular diameters.

9 THE MAXWELL-BOLTZMANN DISTRIBUTION LAW

Fig. 2.6 showed the nature of the curve obtained when the number of molecules, n_c, travelling at a particular speed c, is plotted against the speed. The equation corresponding to this curve, which is known as the *Maxwell-Boltzmann* distribution, is as follows:

$$n_c = A\, c^2 \exp(-mc^2/2kT) \tag{2.18}$$

where m is the mass of a molecule and A is a constant given by

$$A = 4\pi\,(m/2\pi kT)^{3/2}. \tag{2.19}$$

Eqn. (2.18) can be used to evaluate

$$\int n_c\, c^2\, \mathrm{d}c$$

and thus to deduce the value of c_{rms}.

This gives

$$c_{rms} = \sqrt{\frac{3kT}{m}} \tag{2.20}$$

which is the value previously obtained and stated in eqn. (2.12). In a similar manner both the mean speed, $\bar{c}$, and the most probable speed, c_{mp}, may be calculated from integrations over all speeds of molecules; the values obtained are

$$\bar{c} = \sqrt{\frac{8kT}{\pi m}} \tag{2.21}$$

$$c_{mp} = \sqrt{\frac{2kT}{m}}. \tag{2.22}$$

From these results it may be calculated that

$$c_{\mathrm{rms}}/\bar{c} = 1.08 \tag{2.23}$$

$$c_{\mathrm{rms}}/c_{\mathrm{mp}} = 1.22. \tag{2.24}$$

These results were shown in Fig. 2.6 in Section 4, where some particular values of these speeds were given for the case of nitrogen at room temperature.

10 RATE OF MOLECULAR EFFLUX

In order to calculate the rate at which molecules escape through a hole, we must consider molecules reaching the aperture of area A in Fig. 2.14 from all directions. Those approaching at an angle θ to the normal to the area, with velocity c will, if they are at a particular instant in the volume UVYX, reach the area in the next second if XU = c.

Thus if n_θ is the number of molecules per unit volume with velocities in this particular direction, the number of such molecules reaching the area A at XY per second, is

$$(Ac\cos\theta)\,n_\theta. \tag{2.25}$$

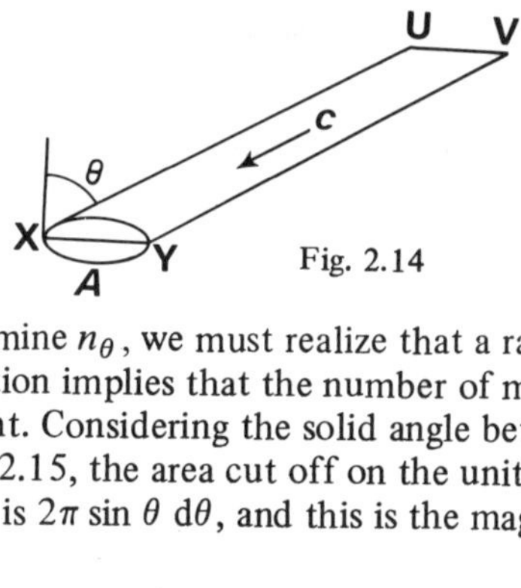

Fig. 2.14

In order to determine n_θ, we must realize that a random distribution with regard to direction implies that the number of molecules per unit solid angle is constant. Considering the solid angle between the directions θ and $\theta + \mathrm{d}\theta$ in Fig. 2.15, the area cut off on the unit sphere between these two directions is $2\pi \sin\theta\, \mathrm{d}\theta$, and this is the magnitude of the solid angle.

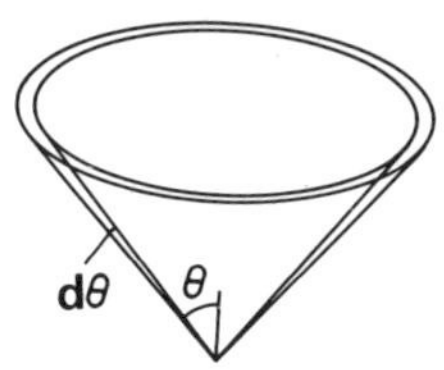

Fig. 2.15

This angle represents a fraction $2\pi \sin\theta\,\mathrm{d}\theta/4\pi = (\sin\theta\,\mathrm{d}\theta)/2$ of the total solid angle, which in turn represents the proportion of the molecules which have velocities in this direction. Therefore if there are n molecules per unit volume,

$$n_\theta = (n \sin\theta \, d\theta)/2. \tag{2.26}$$

Combining eqns. (2.25) and (2.26) the number of molecules travelling in the θ direction, reaching area A per second

$$= \frac{1}{2}(n \sin\theta)(Ac \cos\theta)\, d\theta.$$

Thus the total number reaching A per second from all directions

$$= \frac{nAc}{2}\int_0^{\pi/2} \sin\theta \cos\theta \, d\theta$$

$$= \frac{nAc}{2}\left[\frac{\sin^2\theta}{2}\right]_0^{\pi/2}$$

$$= nAc/4.$$

In deriving this result we have assumed all the molecules to be travelling with the same speed; if we consider molecules with different velocities, c is simply replaced by $\bar{c}$, the mean speed of the molecules. It follows that the number hitting unit area per second is

$$n\bar{c}/4. \tag{2.27}$$

This would therefore appear to be the correct expression rather than that ($n\bar{c}/6$) which was obtained by a more elementary analysis in Section 5.

QUESTIONS

1. Calculate the root mean square speed of oxygen molecules at 27 °C, given that the root mean square speed of hydrogen molecules at 0 °C is 1.84×10^3 m s^{-1}. Assume that both gases are ideal and that the molecular weights of oxygen and hydrogen are 32 and 2 respectively.

2. Calculate the root mean square speed of nitrogen molecules at 17 °C, using the facts that a mole of the gas occupies 22.4 litres at s.t.p., the molecular weight of nitrogen is 28, and that a standard atmosphere is 10^5 N m^{-2}.

3. Calculate the percentage change in the root mean square speed of the molecules of air when the temperature increases from 15 °C to 20 °C.

4. Estimate the total translational kinetic energy of the molecules of air in a room with a floor area 7 m by 4 m, and a height of 2.5 m, on a day when the temperature is 17 °C. Take the mean molecular weight of the air to be 29.

5. Molecules escape from a small hole of area 1 cm^2 in the surface of a sphere of radius 2 m. Assuming the space outside is evacuated, and that the air in the sphere is at a temperature of 300 K and an initial pressure of 10 N m^{-2}, how long would it take for the pressure in the sphere to fall to one-quarter of its original value. Assume no molecules remain in the space outside the sphere, but are rapidly removed by a pump?

6. The total translational kinetic energy of the helium molecules in a vessel is 0.2 J, when the temperature of a helium is 20 °C. If another vessel contains twice the mass of helium, and the total translational kinetic energy of the molecules is 0.8 J, what is the temperature in the second vessel?

7. A box contains gas at a very low pressure so that the molecules very rarely collide with each other, and normally pass from one end of the box to the other without a collision. In the middle of the box is a partition with a small hole; if there are n_1 molecules per unit volume with mean speed $\bar{c}_1$ in one half of the box, and n_2 per unit volume with mean speed $\bar{c}_2$ in the other half, show that a steady state is reached when

$$n_1 \bar{c}_1 = n_2 \bar{c}_2 .$$

Hence show that if the two halves are at different temperatures T_1 and T_2, the pressures in the two halves at equilibrium are not equal and determine the ratio of these pressures.

Discuss why the situation is different when the pressures are of the order of atmospheric pressure.

8. How does the pressure exerted by the molecules of a gas on a surface change if the surface moves towards the gas at a speed of $c/10^3$, where c is the r.m.s. speed of the molecules? Make clear any assumptions you have made in the calculation.

9. A closed vessel contains mercury vapour which has a molecular weight of 200, at a pressure of 50 N m^{-2} and a temperature of 327 °C. Assuming that each mercury atom striking a small area of cooled surface remains on the wall, estimate the mass of mercury so deposited per unit area per second, provided the pressure is maintained constant.

10. A mixture of 10.5 g of nitrogen and 16 g of oxygen is maintained at a pressure of 1 atmosphere. Calculate the partial pressures exerted by each gas.

11. A high pressure cylinder of argon, which has a volume of 15 litre increases in mass by 3.1 kg when it is filled with the gas to a pressure of 120 atmospheres at 15 °C. Calculate a value for the gas constant for 1 kg of argon.

Heat Capacities of Gases

3

If a gas is envisaged as consisting of a collection of particles, the only kinetic energy it can possess is translational kinetic energy. In the case of a mole of gas, it is seen from eqn. (2.11) that the translational kinetic energy of the mass points constituting the gas is $3RT/2$, at an absolute temperature T.

At 17 °C a mole of such a gas would possess

$$\frac{3}{2} \times 8.3 \times 290 = 3600 \text{ J}.$$

In order to raise the temperature of such a gas this kinetic energy must be increased and a simple calculation shows that for an increase of 1 K, approximately 12 J of energy are required.

It is convenient in the case of gases to consider the heat required to raise the temperature of 1 mole of gas by 1 K, rather than the corresponding quantity for unit mass, since the great similarity in the behaviour of different gases is then more readily evident. Therefore, in this chapter we will frequently consider *molar heat capacities* instead of *specific heat capacities.*

If the gas is confined in a box which is sufficiently strong to withstand the extra pressure resulting from the rise of temperature, without itself expanding, the heat capacity measured is that at *constant volume* (c_v).

Under these conditions the energy supplied goes entirely into increasing the internal energy (U) of the gas. Thus in the case of a mass m of gas, whose temperature rises ΔT, we have,

$$\Delta U = mc_v \, \Delta T \qquad (3.1)$$

where c_v represents the specific heat capacity at constant volume.

In many cases, however, the extra pressure leads to an increase in the volume of the container. We consider the ideal extreme case where the gas is in a cylinder fitted with a frictionless piston, moving horizontally so that no work is done against gravity. Thus the slightest pressure difference brings about expansion, and the change occurs at constant pressure.

The energy supplied to bring about unit rise in temperature under these conditions is the heat capacity at *constant pressure*; in the case of unit mass, we have the specific heat capacity at constant pressure (c_p).

The two quantities c_p and c_v are known as the *principal specific heat capacities* of the gas. The corresponding heat capacities for a mole are usually written C_p and C_v.

1 DIFFERENCE IN PRINCIPAL HEAT CAPACITIES

In the case where the gas is heated at constant pressure, work has to be done in moving the piston against the external pressure and the energy to perform this work must come from the heat energy originally supplied. We can imagine that the molecules lose some of their increased kinetic energy as they rebound from the moving piston.

In order to calculate this work done, we consider a mole of gas originally occupying a volume V at absolute temperature T, which is in a cylinder fitted with a frictionless piston. As shown in Fig. 3.1 it expands horizontally so that no work is done against gravity. Since the piston moves even under an infinitesimal pressure difference, no finite acceleration occurs and the piston moves infinitely slowly. At no time is there a finite difference in pressure between the two sides of the piston, and therefore we can represent both the external pressure and that of the gas by the constant value P.

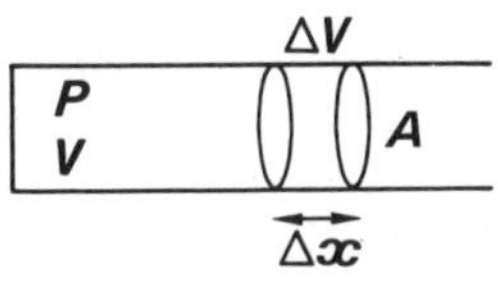

Fig. 3.1

The expansion takes place against a force PA, where A is the area of the piston; if the piston moves a distance Δx, the work done is consequently $PA\,\Delta x$.

Since $A\Delta x$ is ΔV, the increase in volume taking place, we can write

$$\text{work done} = P\,\Delta V. \tag{3.2}$$

If we supply sufficient energy to raise the temperature of the gas by an amount ΔT and at the same time allow it to expand in this manner so that its pressure remains constant, the heat supplied is $C_p\,\Delta T$, where C_p is the *molar heat capacity* of the gas at *constant pressure.*

This is greater than the corresponding *molar heat capacity* at *constant volume*, C_v, by the amount of work done in the expansion, since the change in energy of the molecules, which depends only on the temperature change, is the same in both cases. There are no attractions between the molecules of an ideal gas (Chapter 2, Section 1). No work can therefore be done against internal forces in an expansion, and the internal potential energy of the gas does not vary with changes in volume. Thus,

$$C_p\,\Delta T = C_v\,\Delta T + P\,\Delta V.$$

For an ideal gas,

$$PV = RT$$

where R is the gas content for a mole.

If the pressure remains constant,

$$P\,\Delta V = R\,\Delta T. \tag{3.3}$$

Substituting from this in eqn. (3.2) and dividing by ΔT, we obtain

$$C_p = C_v + R. \tag{3.4}$$

It is important to appreciate that in this relation all three of the quantities are expressed in J K^{-1} mol^{-1}.

Eqn. (3.4) shows that the difference between the molar heat capacities of any gases which may be considered as ideal should be constant and equal to the universal gas constant, i.e. 8.36 J K^{-1} mol^{-1}. This prediction can be tested by direct measurement of heat capacities at constant volume and constant pressure.

Although the result has been derived for a mole, it will sometimes be stated in terms of specific heat capacities and then eqn. (3.4) becomes

$$c_p - c_v = r \tag{3.5}$$

where r is the gas constant appropriate to unit mass of the particular gas.

2 HEAT CAPACITY AT CONSTANT VOLUME

A major difficulty in this determination arises from the relatively small value of the mass of gas and its consequent small heat capacity; this is to some extent overcome by using gas under considerable pressure as in the Joly differential steam calorimeter shown in Fig. 3.2.

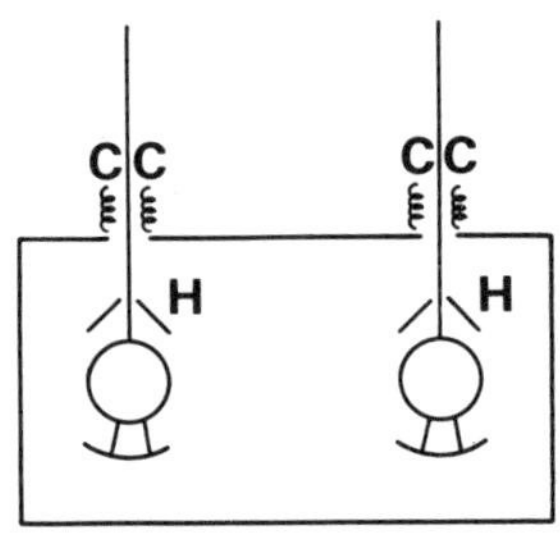

Fig. 3.2

The accuracy of the result is increased by a differential method involving two identical metal spheres suspended from the arms of an accurate balance. In the original form of the apparatus the spheres were about 7 cm in diameter and were in a chamber which could be filled with steam; one sphere contained gas under a pressure of the order of 20 atmospheres while the other was evacuated. The mass (m) of gas was first determined by weighing with the chamber at a temperature t_1 °C, and then the steam was admitted. The larger heat capacity of the sphere containing the gas causes a greater mass of steam to condense on it and give up its latent heat in order to raise the temperature. This continues until the whole apparatus is at the temperature of the steam t_2 °C. If it is then found that an extra mass M of steam has condensed on the sphere containing the gas,

$$mc_v(t_2 - t_1) = ML \tag{3.6}$$

where L is the specific latent heat of vaporization of the steam; thus the specific heat capacity at constant volume, c_v, may be calculated.

A number of points require special attention if an accurate result is to be obtained. Special hoods H are fitted above both spheres to prevent water condensed on the walls of the chamber from falling onto the pans. Condensation near the small holes by which the supporting wires enter the chamber can affect the free swinging of the balance; this is prevented by lining the holes with plaster of Paris which absorbs such water, and small heating coils C evaporate any water which is not so absorbed.

It is not possible to produce a pair of identical spheres, and error on this account is avoided by repeating the experiment with the gas in the other sphere. The small expansion of the spheres prevents the conditions being accurately those of constant volume so that it is also necessary to apply a small correction for the work done in this expansion.

3 SPECIFIC HEAT CAPACITY AT CONSTANT PRESSURE

The specific heat capacity of a gas is usually measured by a continuous flow method. In that of Swan, illustrated schematically in Fig. 3.3, the gas flows freely over a heating coil C, and each layer of gas serves as a piston confining the gas behind it at constant pressure.

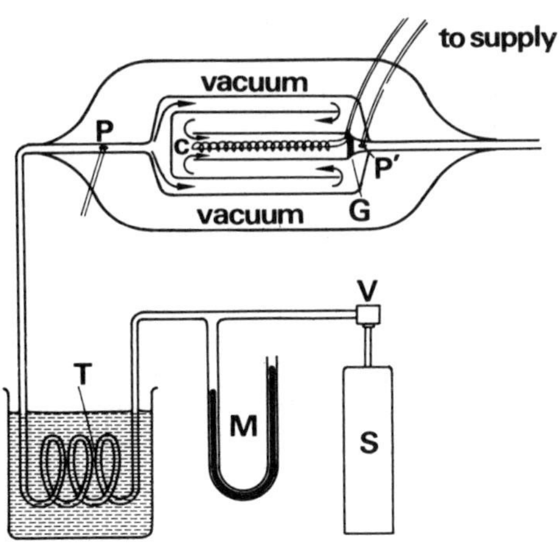

Fig. 3.3

The gas emerges from the storage cylinder S through a valve V so that the pressure can be maintained at a value slightly greater than atmospheric, and this pressure is indicated by the manometer M. The gas next passes through a coiled tube T in a water bath B in order to ensure a constant inlet temperature (t); this is read on the platinum resistance thermometer P.

The flow tube, which is surrounded by a vacuum jacket, is in the form of three concentric cylinders so that any heat escaping outwards from the heated gas is absorbed by gas which has yet to pass over the heating coil C. In this way the possible loss of heat is very greatly reduced. The flow of gas is indicated in the diagram by arrows, and after the heating coil it passes through a plug of copper gauze G in order to help mixing and ensure a uniform temperature; this temperature is then recorded by the platinum resistance thermometer P′.

The current (I) through the coil and the potential difference (V) across it are measured by potentiometer circuits. Thus if the final temperature of the gas is t', and the mass of gas flowing per second is m, the specific heat capacity at constant pressure c_p, is given by

$$IV = m\, c_p(t' - t). \tag{3.7}$$

It remains to determine the rate of mass flow of the gas through the apparatus; this can be done by determining the volume flow by a flow meter (e.g. of the rotameter type) and using the appropriate value of the density obtained from tables. Alternatively, the mass flowing out of the cylinder in a measured time can be deduced from the change in the pressure recorded on a pressure-gauge attached to the cylinder. A knowledge of the temperature and these pressure readings enables the mass of gas at the beginning and end of the time-interval to be calculated using the gas equation.

Eqn. (3.7) ignores the heat lost from the apparatus to its surroundings. If the apparatus is suitably designed this loss will be small but it can be eliminated by repeating the experiment with a different rate of flow of gas, and adjusting the supply of electrical energy to the heating coil in order to produce the same initial and final temperatures. Under these conditions the rate of loss of heat to the surroundings remains unchanged and it can thus be eliminated from the two simultaneous equations.

4 MOLAR HEAT CAPACITIES OF GASES

The results in the table opposite show the molar heat capacities for a number of gases. It is evident that the first six gases, all of which under normal conditions are remote from their liquefying points and may therefore be considered as likely to approximate in behaviour to ideal gases, have most remarkably constant values of $C_p - C_v$; this value is also in good agreement with the gas constant R, as is to be expected in view of eqn. (3.4). A number of other gases show larger values for the difference of the heat capacities. Since this difference represents the work done in an expan-

Gas	C_v/ J mol^{-1} K^{-1}	C_p	$C_p - C_v$	C_p/C_v
Hydrogen	20.1	28.4	8.3	1.41
Helium	12.6	21.0	8.3	1.66
Argon	12.4	20.8	8.4	1.67
Neon	12.7	21.3	8.3	1.64
Nitrogen	20.7	29.1	8.4	1.40
Oxygen	20.8	29.1	8.3	1.40
Mercury vapour	12.5	20.9	8.4	1.67
Hydrogen chloride	21.1	29.6	8.6	1.41
Chlorine	25.1	34.1	9.0	1.36
Carbon dioxide	28.2	36.5	8.3	1.25
Sulphur dioxide	31.4	40.6	9.2	1.29
Ether	129	139	10	1.08
Carbon monoxide	20.7	29.1	8.4	1.41
Nitric oxide	21.0	29.4	8.4	1.40
Ammonia	28.4	37.2	8.8	1.31

sion, the larger values suggest that in these cases additional work is done against inter-molecular attractions. The table indicates that these are gases rather nearer to their point of liquefaction, so that attractions between their molecules would be expected to be rather more significant.

If the only energy possessed by a gas is the translational kinetic energy of its molecules, we have for U', the energy of each molecule,

$$U' = \frac{3}{2} kT$$

by eqn. (2.6) on page 31.

Since by eqn. (2.9)

$$L\,k = R$$

we obtain for U the corresponding energy of a mole of such molecules,

$$U = \frac{3}{2} RT. \tag{3.8}$$

It follows that the molar heat capacity at constant volume C_v is given by

$$C_v = \frac{dU}{dT} = \frac{3}{2} R. \tag{3.9}$$

This equation would lead to results of the order of 12.6 J mol^{-1} K^{-1}, and the results in the table above show good agreement for the monatomic gases listed. It therefore seems reasonable to assert that the internal energy of a *monatomic ideal gas* is entirely due to the *translational kinetic energy of its molecules.*

The larger molar heat capacities of gases such as oxygen, nitrogen and hydrogen, which are good approximations to the ideal, suggest that these gases must possess some form of internal energy other than the translational energy possessed by the monatomic gases. The same point appears from a consideration of the last column which shows the values of γ, the ratio of the molar heat capacities (this will also be the ratio of the specific heat capacities).

In the case of monatomic gases which are good approximations to the ideal

$$C_v = 3R/2$$

and thus

$$C_p = 5R/2.$$

Consequently the value of γ should be $5/3$, and this agrees with the experimental results for helium, argon, neon and mercury vapour.

The other gases in the table have more complex molecules. The table shows them to have larger molar heat capacities; since in most cases the difference in the two principal heat capacities is very nearly the same, the values of γ are smaller.

The cases where $C_p - C_v$ is greater than approximately 8.3 J mol^{-1} K^{-1} (the value to be expected for an ideal gas) can be explained in terms of the extra energy needed to do work against attractive forces between the molecules. With these gases some of the energy supplied increases the mutual potential energy of the molecules.

The above discussion suggests that the larger values of C_v for gases such as oxygen indicates that they possess molecular energy other than translational kinetic energy, which depends on the temperature of the gas; so this energy increases when the temperature is raised. The energy must be internal to the molecule and could arise, either from a rotation of the molecule, or from a vibration of its constituent atoms, and these points are considered in detail in the next section.

It is important to appreciate that it is the translational kinetic energy which controls the temperature. We saw earlier that in a mole of monatomic gas at 17 °C, the translational kinetic energy of the molecules was approximately 3 600 J; the translational kinetic energy of a mole of oxygen molecules at the same temperature will also be 3 600 J. and the same is true for any polyatomic gas which is a good approximation to the ideal. However, in all these cases the molecules also possess in addition energy in other forms.

Equality of temperature implies that on mixing, there will be no net transfer of energy between the two bodies. In the case of two gases, one with monatomic molecules and the other with more complex molecules, it is clear that the extra energy possessed by the latter molecules cannot be transferred in the collisions which occur between the two types of molecules when the gases are allowed to mix. There may be individual collisions in which a transfer does occur, but on balance this extra energy is conserved in its original form throughout any collisions which take place. This is to be expected since we have seen that the pressure exerted by diatomic gases does obey the relation, $P = \frac{1}{3}mnc^2$. If the extra form of energy possessed by these molecules was not conserved we might expect the law obeyed by diatomic gases to be different from that for monatomic gases, and this is not the case.

This conservation of energy in a particular form gives a meaning to perfect elasticity applied to molecular collisions; if, for instance, we consider the case where the molecule has spin energy, there is no net transfer from the spin form into translational kinetic energy or vice versa. Thus, at the molecular level perfect elasticity implies that on balance the total translational energy remains constant, and so also does any spin energy or energy associated with vibration within the molecules.

5 EQUIPARTITION OF ENERGY

The total energy of a mechanical system may be expressed as a number of terms, each of which corresponds to one aspect of its motion. The motion of a point particle moving freely in space is completely described by its three velocity components, u, v and w; any change in the motion of the particle can be specified by alterations in one or more of these components. A particle moving under these conditions in a field-free space is said to possess *three degrees of freedom.*

If it has a mass m its total energy, entirely translational kinetic, is $\frac{1}{2}mu^2 + \frac{1}{2}mv^2 + mw^2$; this energy is made up of *three* terms added together. The number of terms so contributing to the total energy gives the number of *degrees of freedom.* The presence of a field of force in the region in which the particle moves, and the consequent potential energy term needed for a complete description, would therefore increase the number of degrees of freedom.

All directions are equally likely for the velocity of any molecule and it is therefore to be expected that the mean values of the three energy terms will be equal. Thus the mean translational kinetic energy of the gas molecules, $3kT/2$, is equally divided between the three translational degrees of freedom.

Thus each degree of freedom has $\frac{1}{2}kT$ *of energy.*

This is a particular case of Boltzmann's *Principle of Equipartition of Energy*, which states that if there are a number of degrees of freedom which can contribute to the total energy of the system *each will contribute equally.*

The principle of equipartition of energy is exemplified by the thermal equilibrium of two gases. No matter what their original temperatures, thermal equilibrium is established when the mean translational kinetic energies of the two types of gas molecule are both equal to $3kT/2$, where T is the final absolute temperature.

The same considerations can be applied to the case of a smoke particle which is subjected to bombardment by gas molecules as occurs in the

Brownian movement. The smoke particle of mass – say, 5×10^{-16} kg, or about 10^{10} the mass of the oxygen molecule – will eventually reach thermal equilibrium with the molecules so that it possesses translational kinetic energy $3kT/2$. Thus at a temperature 20 °C, its root mean square speed, v, is given by

$$\frac{1}{2}(5 \times 10^{-16})v^2 = \frac{3}{2} \times 1.38 \times 10^{-23} \times 293$$

or

$$v = 5 \times 10^{-3} \text{ m s}^{-1} \text{ (approx).}$$

6 ENERGY OF POLYATOMIC MOLECULES

We now consider the possible degrees of freedom of more complex molecules. In the first case we consider a diatomic molecule which can be represented approximately by two mass points A and B a fixed distance apart as in Fig. 3.4, and investigate the likelihood of its possessing rotational energy. It was seen in the case of the monatomic molecule that no

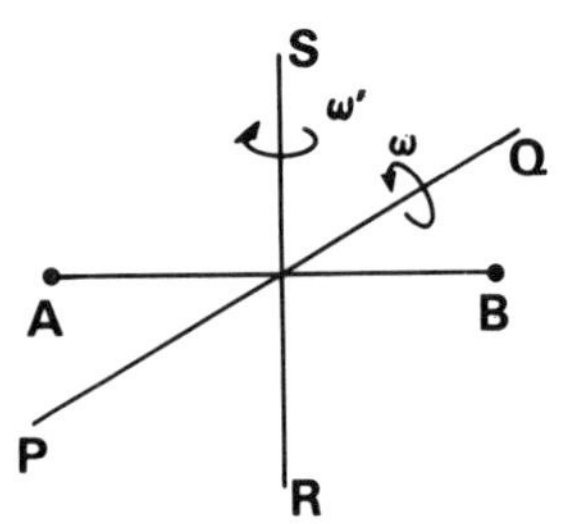

Fig. 3.4

energy contribution arose from spin of the molecule, and it would therefore seem reasonable that in this diatomic molecule there would be no energy contribution from rotation about the axis AB. If the molecule is rotating about the axes PQ and RS it will possess rotational energy which by the equipartition principle will be dependent on the temperature, thus increasing the heat capacity.

If I and I' are the moments of inertia about these axes, by the principle of equipartition of energy, the respective angular velocities ω and ω' must be such that

$$\frac{1}{2}I\omega^2 = \frac{1}{2}I'\omega'^2 = \frac{1}{2}kT. \tag{3.10}$$

These two extra degrees of freedom therefore contribute an amount kT to the energy of the molecule, and so, for each molecule,

$$U' = \frac{5}{2}kT.$$

and for a mole, $$U = \frac{5}{2} L\,kT = \frac{5}{2} RT$$

so that $$C_v = \frac{5}{2} R \tag{3.11}$$

and therefore $$C_p = C_v + R$$

$$= \frac{7}{2} R \tag{3.12}$$

$$\therefore\ \gamma = \frac{7}{5} = 1.4.$$

Reference to the table on page 49 shows this to be the value found experimentally for oxygen, nitrogen, hydrogen and hydrogen chloride at temperatures of the order of room temperature; this is also true for a number of other diatomic molecules.

It is of interest to calculate the angular velocity of rotation for the oxygen molecule at room temperature. We can picture it as consisting of two point masses, each 2.65×10^{-26} a distance apart equal to the accepted diameter of the oxygen atom, about 2.8×10^{-11} m. Since the masses are almost entirely concentrated in the nuclei, which have diameters of the order of 10^{-14} m, this assumption that they be treated as point masses is clearly justified.

The moment of inertia about either of the axes through the centre of mass, perpendicular to the line joining the nuclei is

$$2 \times 2.65 \times 10^{-26} \times (1.4 \times 10^{-11})^2$$

$$= 1.04 \times 10^{-47}\ \text{kg m}^2\text{, approximately.}$$

Thus at 300 K, the angular velocity ω is given by

$$\frac{1}{2} \times 1.04 \times 10^{-47}\ \omega^2 = \frac{1}{2} kT = \frac{1}{2}(1.38 \times 10^{-23} \times 300)$$

or $$\omega = 2.0 \times 10^{13}\ \text{s}^{-1}.$$

Since the atoms of a molecule are bound to each other by forces, any displacement of an atom along the line joining their centres leads to a vibration in exactly the same way as occurs with two masses joined by a spring. The energy of a vibration consists of two terms, one representing the potential energy in any position, and the other the corresponding kinetic energy. It would seem therefore that a vibration involves two degrees of freedom.

A diatomic molecule which possessed such a vibration in addition to the rotation previously considered, would have a total of seven degrees of freedom, which would lead to a value of $7R/2$ for C_v.

$$\therefore C_p = C_v + R = \frac{9R}{2}.$$

Thus for such a molecule $\gamma = 9/7 = 1.29$. This value is rarely found with diatomic gases at normal temperatures, but both air and hydrogen at temperatures of the order of 5 000 K do have values close to this.

A triatomic molecule, or any molecule with more than three atoms in its molecule would be expected to have three rotational degrees of freedom, since it should have significant moments of inertia about all three possible axes of rotation. Thus even if there were no internal vibration, such a molecule should have a value of $\gamma = 4/3$; a value of this order is found for carbon dioxide and sulphur dioxide.

If a molecule possesses a total of p degrees of freedom, each of which has the equipartition energy,

$$C_v = p\frac{R}{2}$$

and

$$\therefore C_p = C_v + R$$

$$= (p+2)\frac{R}{2}$$

and

$$\gamma = \frac{p+2}{p}$$

$$= 1 + \frac{2}{p}. \tag{3.13}$$

In general γ for gases with complex molecules is found to lie between 1.2 and 1.3 at room temperatures, a value which suggests that the molecules possess some vibrational energy. At 15 °C the value for ammonia is 1.31 whilst for ethane, which has a molecule containing two carbon atoms and six hydrogen atoms, γ is 1.22.

In practice γ varies considerably with temperature; in the case of hydrogen it is approximately 1.7 at 88 K and remains nearly constant over a considerable temperature range, but changes to 1.4 just below room temperature and subsequently falls to 1.3 at about 2 000 K.

The ratio of the principal specific (or molar) heat capacities is an important characteristic quantity for any gas, and it is often convenient to bring it into problems concerning ideal gases.

Since

$$c_p = c_v + r$$

we can write

$$\gamma c_v = c_v + r$$

or

$$c_v = \frac{r}{\gamma - 1}. \tag{3.14}$$

Similarly

$$C_v = \frac{R}{\gamma - 1}. \tag{3.15}$$

These two relations are often of use.

7 ENERGY DISTRIBUTION AND EQUIPARTITION

The discussion in the preceding section suggests that the specific heat capacities of gases should be constant, independent of temperature, unless there is a change in the number of degrees of freedom of the molecule. A further unsatisfactory feature of the argument is the assertion that single atoms are unlikely to possess spin energy and likewise that the 'dumb-bell' shaped molecule does not rotate about the line joining the nuclei of the atoms. Although the moments of inertia involved in either of these rotations would certainly be very small, there is no apparent reason why the associated angular velocities could not be correspondingly large.

The reason for these difficulties lies in our considering the energy of the average molecule rather than the detailed distribution of energy amongst the molecules. It is necessary to consider how many are in any particular energy state; this distribution is not easy to deduce in a formal manner, but we are able to obtain information concerning the form of the distribution by considering a somewhat different – but nevertheless similar – example.

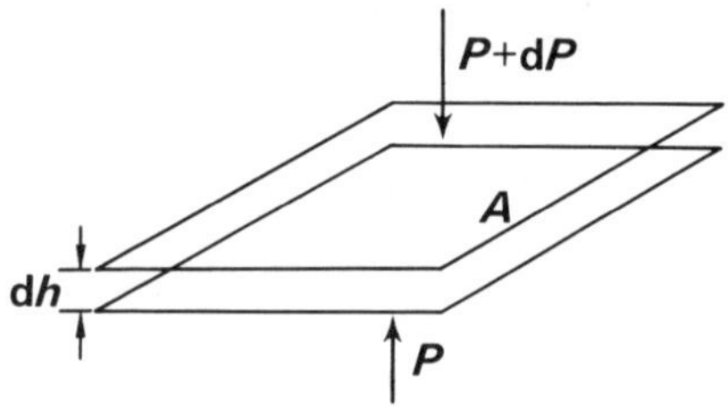

Fig. 3.5

Fig. 3.5 shows a layer of air of thickness dh at a height h above the ground in an atmosphere which is assumed to be of uniform absolute temperature T.

The upward pressure on the lower face of the layer is P, while the downward pressure on the upper face is P + dP, where dP is negative. If we consider a layer of area A, the mass of air in this layer is ρ (A dh) where ρ is the density of the air at this height. This air is in equilibrium under the combined action of the two pressures and its weight.

$$\therefore\ PA = (P + \mathrm{d}P)A + Ag\rho \mathrm{d}h$$

or

$$\mathrm{d}P = -g\rho\ \mathrm{d}h. \qquad (3.16)$$

If the molecular weight of the air is M, from the ideal gas equation

$$P\frac{M}{\rho} = RT. \qquad (3.17)$$

Combining equations (3.16) and (3.17),

$$\frac{\mathrm{d}P}{P} = -\frac{Mg\ \mathrm{d}h}{RT}.$$

Since we began by considering an atmosphere in which T is constant, this can be integrated to give,

$$\log_e (P/P_0) = -Mgh/RT \tag{3.18}$$

where P_0 is the pressure at ground level, i.e. $h = 0$.

Eqn. (3.18) shows the variation of pressure with height in an atmosphere at a constant temperature; it is more conveniently written

$$P = P_0 \exp\left(\frac{-Mgh}{RT}\right). \tag{3.19}$$

For a particular gas under isothermal conditions the pressure is directly proportional to the number of molecules per unit volume; if this quantity is n, we have

$$n = n_0 \exp\left(\frac{-Mgh}{RT}\right) \tag{3.20}$$

where n_0 is the number per unit volume at ground level. This variation of n with h is of the form shown in Fig. 3.6.

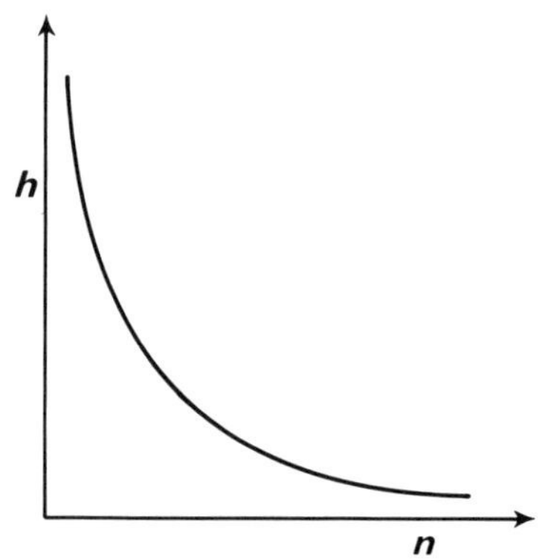

Fig. 3.6

If the mass of a molecule is m,

$$M = L\,m$$

$$= \frac{Rm}{k}$$

where L is Avogadro's number and k is Boltzmann's constant.

Substituting in eqn. (3.20), we obtain

$$n = n_0 \exp\left(\frac{-mgh}{kT}\right). \tag{3.21}$$

The gravitational potential energy of a molecule at a height h is mgh, if measured from a zero value of potential energy at $h = 0$; so expressing eqn. (3.21) in terms of this energy E,

$$n = n_0 \exp\left(\frac{-E}{kT}\right). \tag{3.22}$$

This relation gives the number of molecules with a particular energy E. The exponential factor $\exp(-E/kT)$ is proportional to the probability of a molecule having a particular energy E, if we consider all the molecules making up the atmosphere.

In order to calculate the precise number with a specified energy we have to use the fact that the molecules must all be in one of the possible energy states; thus the total probability over all the possible energy states must add up to unity.

The result in eqn. (3.22) is a general relation which can be applied in all cases of energy distributions, although it has here been obtained for the particular case of the potential energies of molecules in an isothermal atmosphere.

If this result is applied to molecules moving in space with a velocity v the probability of a molecule having this particular velocity is proportional to

$$\exp\left(\frac{-mv^2}{2kT}\right) \tag{3.23}$$

if the temperature of the gas is T.

This result can be used to calculate the average energy of the molecules as a result of motion with a velocity component v_x along the x axis, by summation over all the possible values of v_x. In this way the result $\frac{1}{2}kT$ is obtained, exactly as indicated by the idea of equipartition of energy already discussed. Extending this to three dimensions leads of course to the result $3kT/2$ already obtained for the translational kinetic energy of a molecule.

Before applying this result to the possible rotational energies of a diatomic molecule it is necessary to appreciate that where such small particles are concerned there are certain rules embodied in the *quantum theory* which must be applied; these ideas in their simplest form will now be considered.

8 QUANTUM THEORY AND ITS APPLICATION

The basic principle of the quantum theory is that a system may only have certain definite energies; these permissible energy states are so close together that in the macroscopic world we are not normally aware of the forbidden energies between them. These discrete possible energies gain paramount importance, however, when we are concerned with systems on the atomic scale.

Energy associated with a vibration of frequency ν can only arise in *quanta* of energy $h\nu$, where h is *Planck's constant* which has the value 6.6×10^{-34} J s.

It is the extremely small value of h which accounts for our not being aware of the existence of these quanta of energy in the large-scale world with which we are familiar. Although energy is essentially discontinuous in nature, the minute magnitude of the corpuscles of energy, even for very large frequencies indeed, ensures that we are under the impression that energies of all possible values are permissible, i.e. that energy is continuous.

The application of the quantum hypothesis to rotating bodies leads to the postulate that their angular momentum can only have one of a series of values; these can be represented by

$$nh/2\pi$$

where n is a positive integer.

The lowest rotational state arises from $n = 1$, and if I is the moment of inertia, the angular velocity ω must be such that

$$\omega = h/2\pi I.$$

Thus the rotational kinetic energy in this state, E, is given by

$$E = \frac{1}{2}I\omega^2 = h^2/8\pi^2 I. \tag{3.24}$$

Eqn. (3.24) shows that with a small moment of inertia, as is the case for a monatomic molecule, this lowest energy will be relatively large. The same applies to a diatomic molecule rotating about the line joining the centres of its constituent atoms. Since I for this axis may well be 10^{10} times smaller than that for one of the perpendicular axes, the energy corresponding to this lowest energy level will be 10^{10} times greater than that for rotation about one of the perpendicular axes. Whereas kT is of the order of 100 times the energy of the lowest level for rotation about one of the axes perpendicular to the line joining the centres of the nuclei, the lowest energy state for rotation about the line joining the nuclei is of the order $10^8 kT$.

Applying eqn. (3.22) we see that a considerable number of molecules can occupy quite high rotational states for rotation about either of the perpendicular axes; at the same time it appears that there is a negligible probability of finding a molecule in even the lowest energy state, as far as rotation about the line joining the nuclei is concerned. Thus, under these conditions we are justified in asserting that no rotation takes place about this axis.

The essential point is that it is only when kT is large compared with a considerable number of possible energy levels that equipartition applies, and the average energy becomes $\frac{1}{2}kT$ for each degree of freedom. In the extreme case where the energy level of the lowest state is very much larger than kT, we can say there is no such rotation. In the intermediate conditions, a relation such as eqn. (3.22) must be used to calculate the number of molecules with a particular rotational energy.

The considerations of this section not only suggest why there is no energy associated with certain rotations, but also indicate how a quantum theory of heat capacities may be developed. Clearly as T increases, so does kT, and consequently the possibility of a particular higher energy level being occupied also grows.

In a somewhat similar manner application of the quantum theory leads to a number of possible energy levels as far as vibration of a molecule is concerned. Again we find that for many molecules the energy associated with the lowest vibrational state is large compared with kT at temperatures in the region of room temperature. So we would not expect to find molecules in these vibrational states.

A full investigation along these lines accounts for the variation of specific heat capacities and also for the changes in the value of γ which occur at the higher temperatures.

QUESTIONS

1. An ideal gas is heated under such conditions that the product of its pressure and its absolute temperature is maintained constant. Calculate the difference between this specific heat capacity and that measured at constant volume.

2. A vessel contains a mixture of hydrogen and oxygen at atmospheric pressure and temperature 300 K, with exactly twice as many hydrogen molecules as there are molecules of oxygen. The molecules react with the release of 2.4×10^5 J for a mole of steam produced in an explosive manner. Calculate the temperature and pressure of the steam immediately after the explosion before any warming up or expansion has occurred. Heat capacities at constant volume of oxygen and hydrogen 20 J mol^{-1} K^{-1}; for steam 30 J mol^{-1} K^{-1}.

3. Calculate the ratio of the atmospheric pressure at a height of 10 km to that at ground level on the assumption that the temperature at ground level is 15 °C, and that the temperature falls by 10 °C for each km of ascent. Assume the molecular weight of air to be 29.

4. An ideal gas is enclosed in a cylinder with a frictionless piston, and the force on the piston is adjusted so that the ratio of pressure to volume remains constant. Find the difference between the specific heat capacity under these conditions and that at constant volume.

5. A hair dryer has a nozzle of radius 6.0 cm and it blows out air at 1.5 m s^{-1} and 67 °C when the atmospheric temperature is 17 °C. If the electrical energy consumed is 1 kW, calculate the fraction used in heating the air.

6. If the density of hydrogen at s.t.p. is 8.99×10^{-5} g cm^{-3} and its specific heat capacity at constant pressure is 16.3 J g^{-1} K^{-1}, what is its specific heat capacity at constant volume? Assume standard atmospheric pressure = 10^5 N m^{-2}.

7. A mole of oxygen at 300 K is liquefied and cooled to the temperature of liquid nitrogen by passing it at atmospheric pressure into a bottle immersed in liquid nitrogen, also at atmospheric pressure. The pipes carrying the incoming oxygen and the evaporating nitrogen are strapped together in good thermal contact so that the nitrogen emerges at 300 K. Estimate how many moles of nitrogen are evaporated in the process. (Assume that C_p per mole is $3.5R$ for a diatomic gas and $6R$ for a diatomic liquid, and that the latent heat of evaporation per mole of any liquid is $10RT_B$, where T_B is the boiling point. T_B is 90 K for oxygen and 78 K for nitrogen.

8. A small particle of mass 8×10^{-16} kg exhibits Brownian motion in air at 40 °C. Assuming it attains its equipartition energy, calculate its root mean square speed. Assume $R = 8.3$ J K^{-1} mol^{-1} and $L = 6.02 \times 10^{23}$.

9. Explain why the specific heat capacity of a gas is greater when measured at constant pressure than at constant volume.

Derive an expression for the difference in these specific heat capacities for an ideal gas.

Suggest a reason why the difference might be greater for a real gas.

10. Use the basic assumptions of the kinetic theory of gases to obtain the value of γ, (C_p/C_v) for an ideal monatomic gas.

Explain why this ratio would be less for a gas of diatomic molecules.

The First Law of Thermodynamics

4

We have so far considered three variables which define the state of an ideal gas; its pressure, volume and temperature. However, since these three quantities are related by the fundamental ideal gas equation

$$PV = RT$$

the state of the ideal gas must be precisely defined as soon as two of these variables are fixed. This suggests that the condition of the gas can be represented by a point on the diagram showing the pressure and volume for a particular gas. Such a diagram is sometimes referred to as an *indicator* diagram, and we now make use of it to consider some of the changes to which a gas may be subjected.

1 ISOTHERMAL CHANGES

In Fig. 4.1(a) the point Q corresponds to a mole of an ideal gas at a pressure P_1 and occupying a volume V_1; from the gas equation it must represent gas at a particular temperature T_1, where

$$P_1 V_1 = RT_1.$$

A change in temperature means a change in the *internal energy* (U) of the gas; for an ideal gas the internal energy includes possible rotational and vibrational energy of the molecules themselves in addition to their kinetic energy of translation.

If the gas is not ideal and there are forces of attraction between the molecules, this energy could also include potential energy arising from the work done against this attraction as the separation of the molecules increased. However, we are considering the case of an ideal gas so we will not be concerned with this form of energy.

Every point on the indicator diagram represents a particular internal energy (U) and this quantity is related to the absolute temperature (T) for a mass m of gas, by the relation

$$\Delta U = m\, c_v\, \Delta T \tag{4.1}$$

from the definition of c_v – see eqn. (3.1).

If the state of a gas changes, but its temperature and hence its internal energy remains constant, the change is an *isothermal.* In this case P and V vary according to the relation

$$PV = mrT = \text{constant.} \tag{4.2}$$

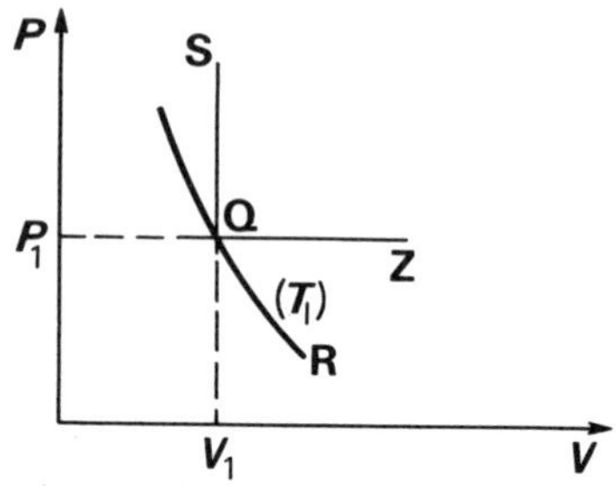

Fig. 4.1(a)

The change represented by QR in Fig. 4.1(a) is an isothermal change which involves expansion of the gas and consequently the performance *by it* of work *against* the external pressure acting upon it. It is important to appreciate that in order to maintain the temperature constant, there must be an input of energy into the gas.

The energy could be provided by an external agency such as a spring doing work on the gas; this would be a *mechanical* transfer of energy into the gas system, followed by a further mechanical transfer out of the system as work is done in the expansion. We are, however, concerned with the case where there is no such external agency to bring about a transfer of this nature, but where energy is transferred into the gas by a flow of *heat.* By this we mean a *non-mechanical* energy transfer. It is brought about as a result of the system being in contact with another body at a slightly higher temperature. We can imagine that the molecules of the gas use some of their internal energy in doing work against the external pressure, i.e. in transferring energy *out* of the system by mechanical means. Consequently the temperature of the gas falls below that of its surroundings and so heat flows into the gas. It is important to realize that we cannot normally make any direct observation of this heat flow; we only infer it from its effect on the temperature.

Heat may conveniently be defined as *energy transferred by means of a temperature difference.* It is occurring on a microscopic scale and involves forces and displacements on this scale, as opposed to the macroscopic forces and displacements involved in the performance of work.

If the change is carried out in the reverse direction from R to Q, the gas is compressed; thus mechanical energy is transferred into it as this change takes place. Some external agency is doing work *on* it; thus, if its internal energy is to remain constant, a non-mechanical transfer of energy out of the system occurs in the form of a heat flow.

If ΔQ represents the heat flow into the system, and ΔW the work done on the system, the essential condition for an isothermal change is

$$\Delta Q + \Delta W = 0. \tag{4.3}$$

2 FIRST LAW OF THERMODYNAMICS

The isothermal change considered in the last section is only one of many changes in the state of a gas which can take place and may be represented by lines on the P–V diagram. For example QS in Fig. 4.1(a) is a change at *constant volume*, sometimes known as an *isovolumetric* or *isochoric* process; for an ideal gas it is represented by

$$\frac{P}{T} = \text{constant.} \tag{4.4}$$

If in such a process the temperature changes by ΔT, the change in internal energy, ΔU, for the case of unit mass is given by (cf. eqn. 3.1),

$$\Delta U = c_v \, \Delta T. \tag{4.5}$$

The change QZ is occurring at *constant pressure*, an *isobaric* process, and the corresponding change in internal energy is given by

$$\Delta U = c_p \, \Delta T. \tag{4.6}$$

These and all other changes are governed by the *first law of thermodynamics*, which states that

> *The total change in internal energy of the system is the sum of the energy transfers into the system, in mechanical and non-mechanical forms.*

Thus, if ΔQ is the heat flow *into* the system and ΔW is the work done *on* the system by an external agency,

$$\Delta U = \Delta Q + \Delta W. \tag{4.7}$$

If the heat flow is *out* of the system, or work is done *by* the system, then the respective quantities, ΔQ and ΔW are negative.

Eqn. (4.7) is a general relation which reduces to the simpler special forms of eqns. (4.3), (4.5) and (4.6) for those particular changes.

It is important to appreciate that the change from one point to another on the P–V diagram may be carried out by any number of paths, but the change in internal energy is always the same; each path represents different quantities of work performed and of heat flow. The total energy transfer is the same, but it includes varying proportions of the mechanical and non-mechanical type.

Thus the change from Q to S in Fig. 4.1(b) can be carried out simply by adding a quantity of heat $c_v \, \Delta T$ to the gas.

However, the same change may be brought about by taking it from Q to Z, and subsequently from Z to S along the isothermal for $T + \Delta T$. In the first part of this change, the heat added is $c_p \, \Delta T$, which we have already seen to be $(c_v + r) \, \Delta T$.

The extra amount of heat supplied is transferred out of the gas as it

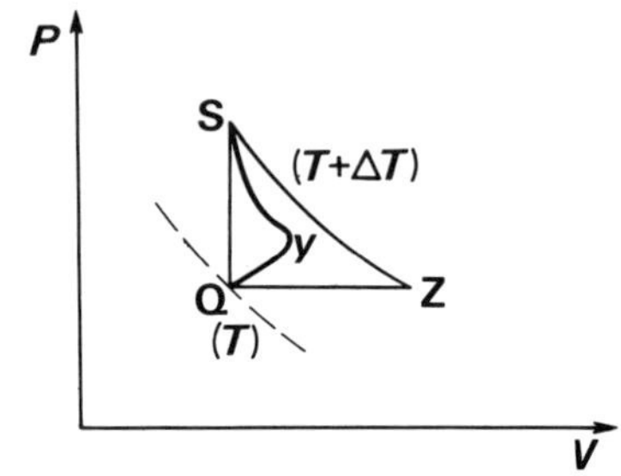

Fig. 4.1(b)

performs work in the expansion from Q to Z. In the final stage from Z to S, the gas is being compressed, i.e. work is done on it, but an equal loss of energy occurs in the form of heat flowing out of the system, since the change is isothermal.

If we choose another path such as that represented by the curved line QYS, the heat supplied is different from either of the other cases, but so also is the work done, and the net change in internal energy remains exactly as before.

3 WORK DONE IN AN ISOTHERMAL CHANGE

The gas in Fig. 4.2 is confined in a cylinder by a frictionless piston so that as soon as there is the slightest pressure difference on the two sides of the

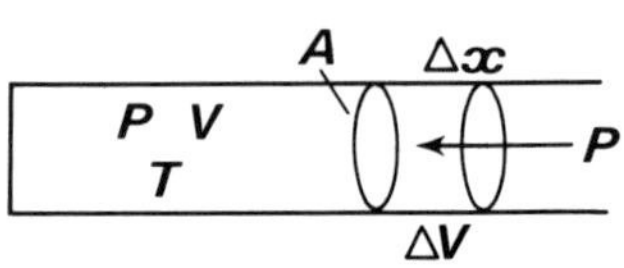

Fig. 4.2

piston, it moves. If the area of the piston is A and it moves Δx, the work done by the gas (see Chapter 3, Section 1) is

$$PA \, \Delta x \quad \text{or} \quad P\Delta V$$

where ΔV is the volume change occurring.

In an expansion, where work is done by the gas, ΔV is positive; in a compression the negative value of ΔV indicates that a negative amount of work is done by the gas, i.e. positive work is done on the gas.

In all cases,

$$\text{work done } on \text{ the gas} = -P\,\Delta V.$$

If at every stage of the process there is only an infinitesimal difference in pressure on the two sides of the piston, P can represent both the pressure of the gas and the external pressure. A change taking place under these conditions is said to be *reversible*, since the slightest change of pressure in the correct direction reverses the motion. It follows that the piston moves slowly from one position to another and never acquires kinetic energy. We shall often use this idea of ideal reversible changes; practical changes rarely fulfil exactly the conditions for reversibility, and from time to time it is important to consider how nearly they do approximate to the ideal. It was necessary to consider a change of this nature in Section 1 of Chapter 3, when dealing with the difference in the principal heat capacities of a gas.

If a change is to be isothermal, it is necessary that at each stage as work is done by the expanding gas, the inflow of heat is sufficient to keep the temperature constant. If the change is from A in Fig. 4.3, where the volume is V_1 and the pressure P_1, to B, where the corresponding values are V_2 and P_2, the work done by the gas against the external pressure is

$$\int_{V_1}^{V_2} P\,\mathrm{d}V.$$

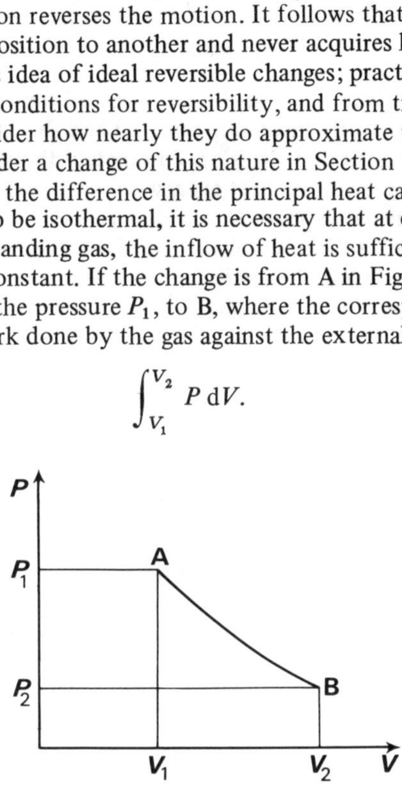

Fig. 4.3

For a mole of ideal gas at a constant temperature T, this becomes

$$\int_{V_1}^{V_2} \frac{RT}{V}\,\mathrm{d}V$$

$$= RT \log_e (V_2/V_1). \qquad (4.8)$$

Since for this particular change AB is an expansion, $V_2 > V_1$, and the work done *by* the gas is positive. This quantity is also the heat flowing into the system during the isothermal change. When the change takes place in the opposite direction, a negative quantity of work is done by the gas, and an equal amount of energy flows out of the system as heat.

4 REVERSIBLE ADIABATIC CHANGES

We now consider a rather different type of change to which an ideal gas may be subjected.

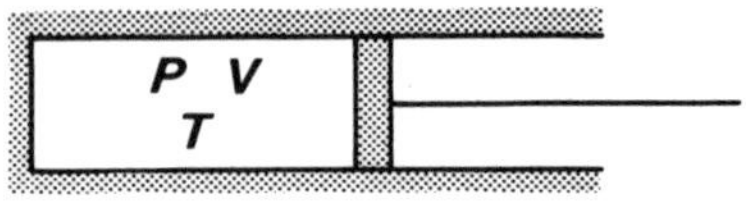

Fig. 4.4

The gas is again confined in a cylinder with a piston, but in this case the piston is made of perfectly insulating material and the cylinder is surrounded with lagging, so that the gas is completely thermally isolated from its surroundings; thus no heat energy can enter or leave the system. It follows that if the gas expands the work necessary for the expansion must come solely from the internal energy of the gas, which consequently cools. If on the other hand the gas is compressed, the work done on the system must increase the internal energy with a consequent rise in temperature. Such a change, which in terms of the first law of thermodynamics is characterized by

$$\Delta Q = 0,$$

is an *adiabatic* change.

In this case, eqn. (4.7) becomes

$$\Delta U = \Delta W. \qquad (4.9)$$

It is again necessary to make the further stipulation that the change be completely reversible, i.e. there is no friction and the piston moves slowly from one position to another so that the pressures on the two sides of the piston are only infinitesimally different.

Since ΔW is work done on the gas, we must write

$$\Delta W = -P\,\Delta V$$

and thus eqn. (4.9) becomes, for a mole of gas

$$C_v\,\Delta T + P\,\Delta V = 0.$$

If we consider infinitesimal changes in the variables, we obtain the differential equation,

$$C_v\,dT + P\,dV = 0. \qquad (4.10)$$

Since we are dealing with a mole of an ideal gas

$$PV = RT. \qquad \text{(i)}$$

Eqn. (i) must remain true whatever changes occur in P, V and T,

$$\therefore\ P\,dV + V\,dP = R\,dT. \qquad \text{(ii)}$$

Eliminating $\mathrm{d}T$ between (4.10) and (ii),

$$\frac{P\,\mathrm{d}V + V\,\mathrm{d}P}{R} = \frac{-P\,\mathrm{d}V}{C_v}$$

or

$$P\,(C_v + R)\,\mathrm{d}V = -\,C_v\,V\,\mathrm{d}P$$

which by eqn. (3.4) becomes

$$C_p P\,\mathrm{d}V = -\,C_v\,V\,\mathrm{d}P$$

or

$$\gamma\,\frac{\mathrm{d}V}{V} = \frac{-\mathrm{d}P}{P}. \qquad \text{(iii)}$$

Integrating (iii) we obtain if $\gamma \log_e V = -\log_e P + A$
where A is a constant

$$\therefore\ \log_e\,(PV^{\gamma}) = A$$

or

$$PV^{\gamma} = \text{constant.} \qquad (4.11)$$

If eqn. (4.11) is combined with (i), two further relations are obtained.

$$T\,V^{\gamma - 1} = \text{constant} \qquad (4.12)$$

$$\frac{T^{\gamma}}{P^{\gamma - 1}} = \text{constant.} \qquad (4.13)$$

The three equations (4.11, 12 and 13) enable us to determine how pressure, volume and temperature vary in any adiabatic change, as is illustrated below.

Example 1. Air at 15 °C is compressed reversibly and adiabatically so that it occupies one-third of the volume it originally occupied at a pressure of 760 mm of mercury. If γ for air is 1.4, calculate the final temperature and pressure at the end of the compression.

If V is the original volume and P the final pressure

$$P\left(\frac{V}{3}\right)^{1.4} = 760V^{1.4}$$

or

$$P = 760 \times 3^{1.4}$$

$$= 3\ 540 \text{ mm of mercury.}$$

Substituting this value in the ideal gas equation

$$\frac{760 \times V}{288} = \frac{3\ 540 \times V}{T \times 3}$$

where T is the final temperature.

$$\therefore\ T = \frac{288 \times 3\ 540}{3 \times 760} = 447\ \text{K}.$$

This result could also have been obtained by direct substitution in eqn. (4.12), i.e.

$$T\left(\frac{V}{3}\right)^{0.4} = 288\ V^{0.4}.$$

Thus the final pressure at the end of the compression is 3 540 mm of mercury and the final temperature 447 K or 174 °C.

This worked example shows the considerable rise in temperature produced by the adiabatic compression. It also shows that the pressure increases to considerably more than the 2 280 mm, which is the pressure which would be reached in the corresponding isothermal compression.

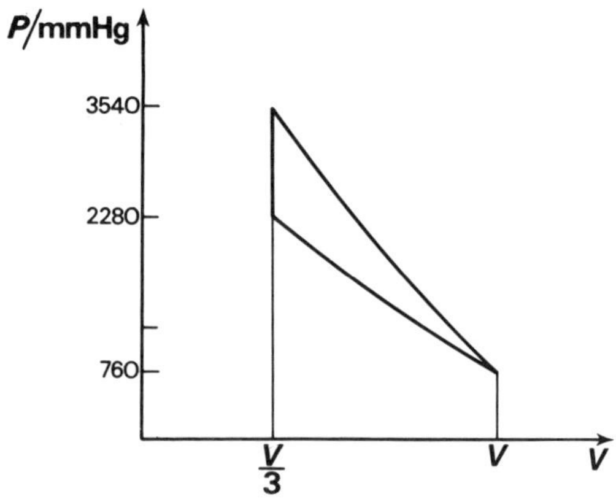

Fig. 4.5

These two changes, adiabatic and isothermal are shown in Fig. 4.5, and it is evident that the adiabatic curve rises more steeply than the isothermal.

Energy is transferred into the gas in each of the isothermal and adiabatic compressions; in both cases the gas molecules move more rapidly as a result, and consequently exert an increased pressure. However, in the case of the isothermal change the extra energy is transferred out of the gas as a flow of heat. At the conclusion of the isothermal change the speed of the molecules is the same as it was initially; the greater pressure is a consequence of the molecules being confined in a smaller volume and therefore hitting the walls more often. In the case of the adiabatic change the molecules are travelling more rapidly; thus the pressure is also greater on this account.

The gradients of the respective curves for isothermal and adiabatic compressions can be obtained. For the isothermal,

$$PV = A$$

where A is a constant.

$$\therefore\ P = \frac{A}{V}$$

and

$$\frac{dP}{dV} = \frac{-A}{V^2} = \frac{-P}{V}. \tag{4.14}$$

For the adiabatic,

$$PV^{\gamma} = B$$

where B is a constant.

$$\therefore\ P = BV^{-\gamma}$$

and

$$\frac{dP}{dV} = -\gamma BV^{-\gamma-1}$$

$$= \frac{-\gamma P}{V}. \tag{4.15}$$

From this we see that at their point of intersection, the gradient of the adiabatic is always numerically γ times as great as that of the isothermal.

The investigation of adiabatic changes provides a method of determining γ for any particular gas, but it is important to realize that eqns (4.11), (4.12) and (4.13) will only be accurately obeyed if the change is adiabatic and reversible. We therefore proceed to consider where such changes are found in practice.

5 ADIABATIC CHANGES IN PRACTICE

The escape of air from a tyre when the valve is released is a change which will normally take place without any appreciable quantity of heat passing into the gas, and it is therefore accompanied by considerable cooling; however, it can only be considered as a reversible change if all the work that the gas is called upon to do is in pushing back a piston which has a pressure acting upon it equal to or slightly less than that of the gas. This is not so for the escaping air and the emergent flow has appreciable kinetic energy; thus work has been done in accelerating the gas. It would therefore be expected that the gas cools more than the equations of the last section would indicate. But if the change in pressure is small, it is approximately true to consider a change of this nature to be a reversible adiabatic, and the experiment of Clément and Désormes described in the next section uses such an expansion.

In the case of air being pumped into a tyre, although work will certainly be done against friction, this energy is not passed on to the gas, and provided the process is carried out reasonably slowly so that little acceleration of the gas results, and at the same time it is not so slow that there is much opportunity for heat to escape from the gas, the change can be considered a good approximation to a reversible adiabatic, as far as the gas itself is concerned.

However, the best example of reversible adiabatic changes which occur in nature are the variations in pressure, volume and temperature which take place in a medium through which a sound wave is passing. The piston effectively confining any particular mass of gas is here provided by the surrounding gas, and the poor thermal conductivity of the gas normally ensures that little exchange of heat with the surroundings occurs during the compressions and expansions which take place. The speed of propagation of longitudinal waves can be shown to be given by

$$\sqrt{\frac{\text{Elastic modulus}}{\text{density}}}.$$

In the case of a gas such as air the appropriate modulus is the *bulk modulus* (K) under adiabatic conditions. This modulus is defined by the relation

$$K = -\Delta P \Big/ \frac{\Delta V}{V} = -V\frac{\Delta P}{\Delta V}.$$

For infinitesimal changes of pressure this can be written

$$K = -V\frac{\mathrm{d}P}{\mathrm{d}V}$$

and by equation (4.15) for the gradient of the adiabatic, it follows that

$$K = \gamma P$$

and thus c, the speed of sound waves in the gas, is given by

$$c = \sqrt{\frac{\gamma P}{\rho}}. \tag{4.16}$$

Thus a determination of the speed of propagation of sound at a measured pressure and density, enables γ to be deduced.

In the case of nitrogen at standard temperature (273 K) and pressure (1.01×10^5 N m^{-2}) the speed of sound waves is 337 m s^{-1}. Under these conditions of temperature and pressure the density of nitrogen is 1.25 kg m^{-3}; thus substituting in eqn. (4.16) and re-arranging,

$$\gamma = \frac{1.25 \times 337^2}{1.01 \times 10^5}$$

$$= 1.41.$$

For a gas of molecular weight M, the ideal gas equation can be written in the form

$$\frac{PM}{\rho} = RT.$$

Substituting for P/ρ from this eqn. in eqn. (4.16), we obtain

$$c = \sqrt{\frac{\gamma RT}{M}}. \tag{4.17}$$

This relation has the advantage of showing more explicitly how the speed of a sound wave depends on both the temperature and the molecular weight of the gas; it also shows that change of pressure, without alteration of temperature, has no effect on the speed of propagation.

6 CLÉMENT AND DÉSORMES' DETERMINATION OF γ

The air is contained in a large globular vessel, frequently of the type used for the storage of large quantities of acid; as is shown in Fig. 4.6, the neck is closed by a bung carrying three tubes. A bicycle pump is used to pump air into the vessel through one tube; another tube is connected to a manometer containing a low-density liquid (e.g. a light oil or concentrated sulphuric acid) and the third tube contains a tap or cock V through which the air can escape. It is also convenient to have a small quantity of concentrated sulphuric acid at the bottom of the vessel in order to ensure dryness of the air.

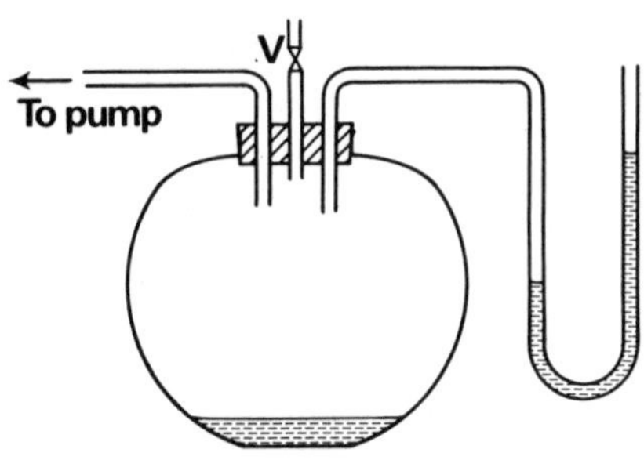

Fig. 4.6

Initially air is pumped into the vessel until a suitable difference in manometer levels is obtained, and the apparatus is then left so that the temperature of the air returns to the normal temperature in the laboratory as a result of exchanging heat with its surroundings. When this process is complete the steady difference in levels of the manometer (h_1) is read. In effect, the air in the globe at this stage has undergone an isothermal compression to a pressure P_1 at the temperature T_0 of the laboratory.

The cock is now opened for a short time, allowing the air to expand to atmospheric pressure. During this expansion there is little opportunity for heat to enter the air, and the conditions can be considered to be adiabatic. The temperature of the air therefore falls to T_1; there are difficulties in determining T_1 directly, and the cock is now closed and the air allowed to warm up to the laboratory temperature. This final change is at constant volume and the rise in temperature will be accompanied by an increase in pressure from the atmospheric pressure P_0 to a pressure P_2, which corresponds to the final difference in levels (h_2) when they are again steady.

Thus
$$\frac{P_0}{P_2} = \frac{T_1}{T_0}$$
and also
$$P_2 = P_0 + h_2 .$$

The two changes, one adiabatic and a subsequent warming-up at constant volume are represented by Fig. 4.7.

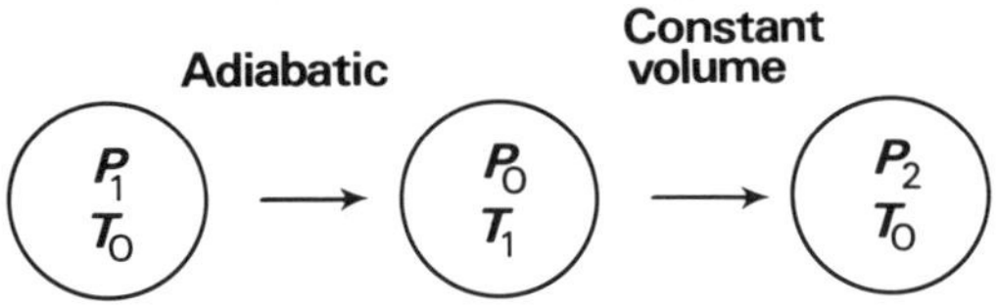

Fig. 4.7

For the adiabatic expansion,

$$\frac{P_1^{\gamma-1}}{T_0^{\gamma}} = \frac{P_0^{\gamma-1}}{T_1^{\gamma}}. \tag{ii}$$

Combining (i) and (ii), we obtain

$$\left(\frac{T_0}{T_1}\right)^{\gamma} = \left(\frac{P_1}{P_0}\right)^{\gamma-1} = \left(\frac{P_2}{P_0}\right)^{\gamma} \tag{iii}$$

and since $P_1 = P_0 + h_1$, (iii) becomes

$$\left(\frac{P_0 + h_1}{P_0}\right)^{\gamma-1} = \left(\frac{P_0 + h_2}{P}\right)^{\gamma}. \tag{4.18}$$

The complete experiment can be represented by the P–V diagram shown in Fig. 4.8. The initial compression is represented by AB, and it is likely that this change is one similar to an adiabatic; however, its precise nature is of no consequence, as it is immediately followed by the cooling at constant volume, represented by BC. CD is the adiabatic expansion, and DE the subsequent warming-up at constant volume. It can be seen that the three points A, E and C must all lie on the isothermal (shown dotted) for T_0 the temperature of the laboratory.

In order to ensure that the change is reversible – or at least a good approximation to this ideal – it is essential that the pressures are very

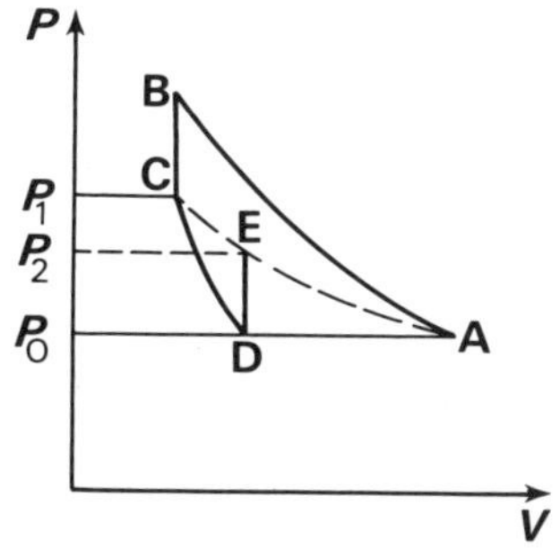

Fig. 4.8

little different from atmospheric; in a typical experiment the the two differences in levels measured on the manometer, h_1 and h_2 will probably be of the order of 15 cm for a liquid with a density such that atmospheric pressure would be of the order of 1 000 cm. Thus the ratios h_1/P_0 and h_2/P_0 are sufficiently small that the squares of these quantities can be neglected.

Eqn. (4.18) can be written

$$(1 + h_1/P_0)^{\gamma-1} = (1 + h_2/P_0)^{\gamma}$$

which can be replaced by the approximate relation

$$1 + (\gamma - 1)\frac{h_1}{P_1} = 1 + \frac{\gamma h_2}{P_0}$$

or

$$\gamma h_1 - h_1 = h_2$$

or

$$\gamma = \frac{h_1}{h_1 - h_2}. \qquad (4.19)$$

Thus this simple relation of eqn. (4.19) may be used to evaluate the ratio of the heat capacities.

In practice the expansion does not cease when the pressure reaches atmospheric; the air continues to expand until the pressure reaches a lower value, and then oscillations of pressure occur. The amplitude of these oscillations can be reduced by careful design of the orifice through which the gas expands, but there always remains some doubt as to the precise moment at which the vessel should be closed. This difficulty is most important for accurate measurements, but for simple determinations an investigation of the effect of varying the time for which the air expands between one and four seconds may serve to indicate whether the oscillations are big enough to affect the result significantly; if necessary they can then be reduced by alterations in the orifice. It is sometimes suggested that it is necessary to lag the vessel; however, the very short duration of the expansion renders this unnecessary and any lagging would certainly be an inconvenience in retarding the warming and cooling which take place at constant volume.

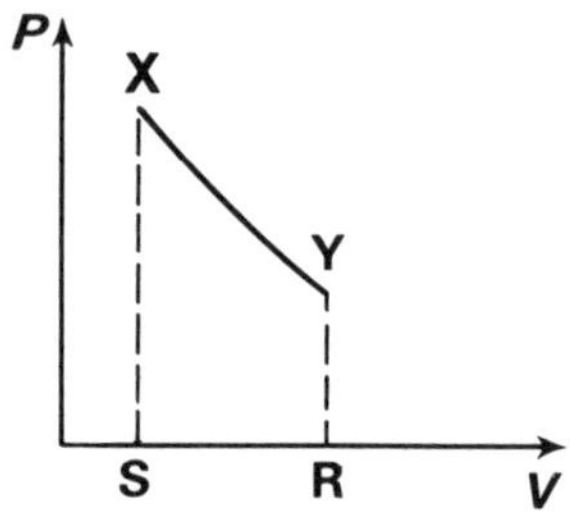

Fig. 4.9

If in the expansion, the pressure of the gas falls from that represented by X to that at Y in Fig. 4.9, the energy available from the gas is

$$\int_X^Y P\,dV$$

i.e. the area XYRS on the graph. However, the work done against the atmosphere is

$$\int_S^R A\,dV = A\,(V_R - V_S)$$

where A is the atmospheric pressure.

If the expansion terminates at atmospheric pressure, more energy is clearly available from the gas than is needed to do work against the atmosphere, and this balance provides kinetic energy of the emerging gas stream. Thus the energy transferred from the gas is equal to that which would have been required in a reversible adiabatic, although some has been transferred to kinetic energy of the gas stream.

Lummer and Prinsheim, and also Partington, used a similar expansion, but attempted to measure the temperature (T_1) reached at the end of the expansion in a direct manner. This can only be done with a very sensitive and quick-acting thermometer which is placed in the middle of the vessel containing the air. A special low-heat-capacity platinum resistance thermometer was used in conjunction with a modified Wheatstone bridge incorporating a very short period string galvanometer: in this way Partington was able to study the pressure oscillations by the resulting temperature variations they produced, and subsequently to design an orifice where there was very little oscillation. The accurate balancing of the bridge took some time and it was necessary to set the bridge circuit so that it corresponded to a particular final temperature, and then to discover by trial and error the original pressure needed to produce this final temperature.

7 RUCHHARDT'S METHOD FOR γ

In 1929 Ruchhardt developed an interesting method of measuring γ from the oscillations of a small metal ball-bearing in a long tube attached to a large vessel as shown in Fig. 4.10. It is necessary for the bore of the tube to be accurately uniform, and the fit between ball and tube to be excellent in order to ensure that they give a gas-tight seal; at the same time both

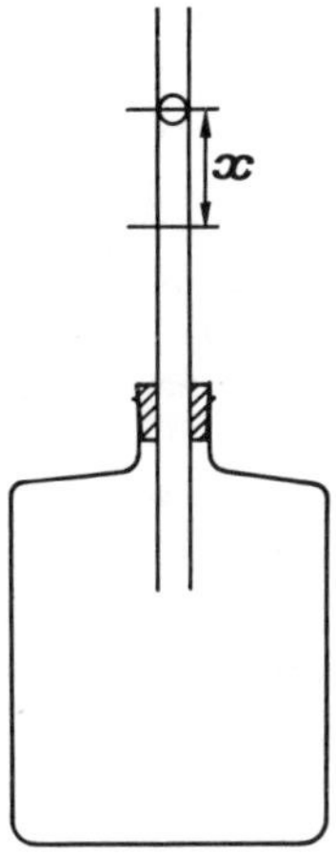

Fig. 4.10

must be smooth so that frictional effects are negligible. Under these circumstances the gas in the vessel may be considered to undergo adiabatic expansions and compressions.

If A is the area of cross-section of the tube and m the mass of the ball, it is in equilibrium when the pressure p in the tube is given by

$$p = p_0 + mg/A \tag{i}$$

where p_0 is the atmospheric pressure.

Any displacement from this position leads to pressure changes, producing a resultant force on the ball restoring it to its equilibrium position, and so oscillations will ensue. If V is the volume of the air below the ball-bearing, when in the equilibrium position

$$p\,V^\gamma = \text{constant}$$

and, on differentiating,

$$\gamma p V^{\gamma-1} \Delta V + V^\gamma \Delta p = 0$$

or

$$\Delta p = \frac{-\gamma p\,\Delta V}{V}.$$

For a small displacement x, the consequent small volume change is Ax, and the restoring force $A\Delta p$ is given by

$$\frac{-\gamma p A^2 x}{V} \tag{4.20}$$

which is proportional to the displacement x, so the oscillations are simple harmonic, with a period T given by

$$T = 2\pi\Big/\sqrt{\left(\frac{\gamma p A^2}{mV}\right)}$$

$$= 2\pi\sqrt{\left(\frac{mV}{\gamma p A^2}\right)}. \tag{4.21}$$

Of the quantities appearing in eqn. (4.21), m, V and A can be measured directly and a number of oscillations may be timed in order to obtain a mean value for T; if p is known, γ may thus be calculated. Eqn. (i) can be used to calculate p, but for most determinations little significant error will be introduced by replacing p by p_0.

Using a vessel of volume approximately 10 litre and a ball-bearing of diameter 2 cm, a period of oscillation of the order of 1 second is obtained, although it may be impossible in a simple apparatus to obtain more than 20 oscillations. The relatively small number of oscillations shows that considerable frictional damping is present, and this is the main cause of error. It is possible to increase the number of oscillations by an impulse given regularly to the ball to help maintain the oscillations, and the use of a ground glass cylinder as an alternative to the steel ball-bearing tends to give a larger number of oscillations.

A further development uses a steel piston which is held suspended by a magnet in order to reduce friction; the piston is in a cylinder closed at both ends and is set in oscillation by the magnetic field produced by alternating current in suitably placed coils. The frequency of the current is then adjusted until resonance occurs at the natural frequency of the air in the cylinder.

8 WORK DONE IN ADIABATIC CHANGE

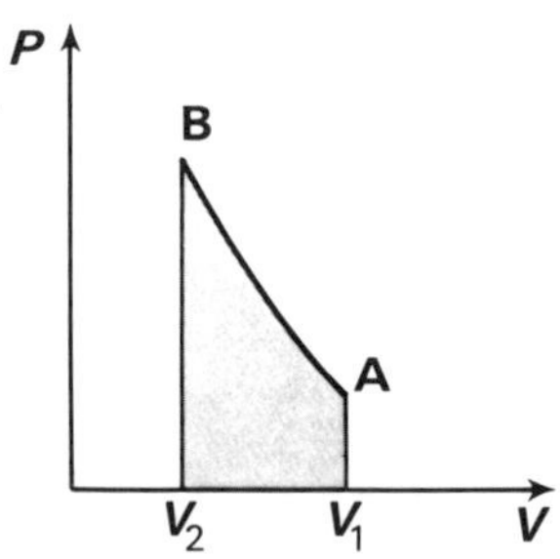

Fig. 4.11

The work done in an adiabatic compression such as that from A to B in Fig. 4.11 is

$$-\int_{V_1}^{V_2} P\,\mathrm{d}V$$

or the area between the adiabatic curve and the volume axis. However, it is instructive to calculate this work by considering what happens to it in the compression.

Since no heat can enter or leave the system all the work performed is converted into internal energy of the gas. Thus if as a result of the compression the temperature of the gas rises from T_1 to T_2, the work done

$$= C_v (T_2 - T_1)$$

if we are considering a mole of gas.

Although the volume is not remaining constant during this change, it must be remembered that the internal energy of an ideal gas does not depend on its volume and thus the increase in internal energy is exactly the same as would occur for an equal temperature rise with the volume remaining constant.

Since $C_p - C_v = R$, this amount of work may be written

$$\frac{R}{(C_p - C_v)} C_v (T_2 - T_1)$$

$$= \frac{R (T_2 - T_1)}{\gamma - 1}. \tag{4.22}$$

Using the ideal gas equation, this result may be expressed as

$$\frac{P_2 V_2 - P_1 V_1}{\gamma - 1}. \tag{4.23}$$

It is readily verified that these results may be obtained by direct integration, using $\int P \, \mathrm{d}V$.

Since the volume decreases in the compression, the work done on the gas

$$= -\int_{V_1}^{V_2} P \, \mathrm{d}V$$

$$= -\int_{V_1}^{V_2} \frac{A}{V^\gamma} \mathrm{d}V \qquad \text{where } A = P V^\gamma$$

$$= -\left[\frac{A V^{1-\gamma}}{1-\gamma}\right]_{V_1}^{V_2}$$

$$= \frac{A}{\gamma - 1}\left[\frac{1}{V_2^{\gamma-1}} - \frac{1}{V_1^{\gamma-1}}\right]$$

$$= \frac{P_2 V_2 - P_1 V_1}{\gamma - 1}$$

since $A = P_1 V_1^\gamma = P_2 V_2^\gamma$.

Consider a mole of ideal gas in the state represented by $P_1 V_1 T_1$, i.e. A in Fig. 4.12; let it be subjected to an adiabatic compression so that its final state is P_2, V_2, T_2, i.e. B.

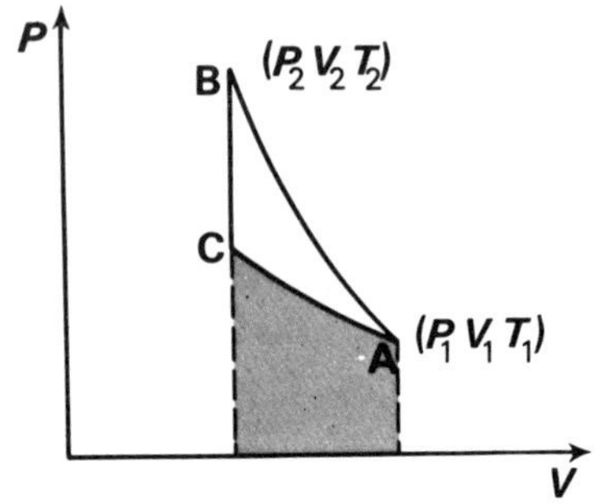

Fig. 4.12

In this process $C_v (T_2 - T_1)$ of work is done on the gas, and all this energy becomes increased internal energy of the gas, since no heat flows in or out of the system.

The same change from A to B could be brought about by the isothermal change AC followed by heating at constant volume along CB in the diagram.

During the isothermal change work is done on the gas, but this energy flows out of the gas in the form of heat, so that the temperature and internal energy remain constant.

In the change from C to B, energy of amount $C_v (T_2 - T_1)$ in the form of heat is supplied; this example shows clearly that the internal energy changes by the same amount whichever route is taken; this must be so since this quantity is a property of the state of the gas.

On the other hand, the work done in the second case is clearly less, since it is $-\int P \, dV$, which is equal to the area between the appropriate path in the $P - V$ diagram, and the volume axis; the diagram clearly shows this quantity to be greater for the adiabatic change.

Rinkel used an apparatus similar to Ruchhardt (See Fig. 4.10), but employed a static method instead of observing oscillations. He measured the distance dropped by a ball-bearing on its first fall before oscillations began. Initially the ball was held at the top of the tube so that the air up to this point was at atmospheric pressure, and was compressed adiabatically as the ball fell. When the ball comes to rest and subsequently begins its upward journey, it has lost *mgh* of potential energy, and this energy has been transferred to the compressed gas. We cannot, however, equate this to the work done in the compression – given by eqn. (4.22) – since much of this work has been done by the atmospheric pressure. The work done by by the ball, i.e. its loss in potential energy, has been done against the *excess* pressure of the gas above atmospheric. By the result in eqn. (4.20), the force arising from this excess pressure is

$$\frac{\gamma p_0 A^2 x}{V}$$

when the ball has descended a distance x.

Thus for a fall h, we have

$$mgh = \frac{\gamma p_0 A^2}{V} \int_0^h x \, dx$$

where p_0 and V, being the initial pressure and volume of the air, are constants.

Thus
$$mgh = \frac{\gamma p_0 A^2 h^2}{2V}$$

or
$$\gamma = \frac{2Vmg}{p_0 A^2 h}. \qquad (4.24)$$

It is important to ensure that the appropriate conditions apply before using the relations for a reversible adiabatic change. This is illustrated by the following example, where the conditions are not reversible.

Example 2. An ideal gas is pumped into an evacuated container of volume V, until the pressure reaches atmospheric. Work is done on the gas in this process and if the whole arrangement is thermally isolated from its surroundings, calculate the rise in temperature.

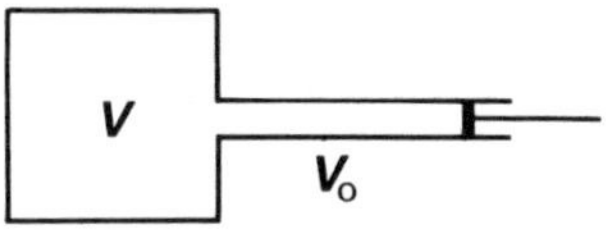

Fig. 4.13

We can imagine that the gas is pushed in by a piston, sliding in a long cylinder, as in Fig. 4.13. The volume swept out by the piston is V_0, the volume occupied by the air at atmospheric pressure A and T_0, the temperature of the atmosphere.

Thus the work done $= A\ V_0$

$$= n\,RT_0. \qquad \text{(i)}$$

if n moles enter the vessel.

However, this work is also equal to the change in internal energy brought about, since the system is thermally isolated; this change is

$$nC_v\,(T - T_0) \qquad \text{(ii)}$$

where T is the final temperature in the vessel.

Since
$$C_p - C_v = R$$

division by C_v gives
$$\gamma - 1 = R/C_v$$

or $$C_v = \frac{R}{\gamma - 1}. \tag{4.25}$$

Therefore, equating the work done (i) to the change in internal energy brought about (ii), and substituting for C_v,

$$\frac{nR\,(T - T_0)}{\gamma - 1} = nRT_0$$

or $$nRT - nRT_0 = \gamma nRT_0 - nRT_0$$

$$\therefore\ T = \gamma T_0.$$

Thus, although there is no heat exchange with the surroundings, the temperature is not given by eqn. (4.12), because the change is not taking place under reversible conditions. The problem below provides a further example.

Example 3. A container of gas of volume V at a pressure P and temperature T is connected by a closed stopcock to a deflated rubber balloon; the cock is opened for a short time so that the pressure in both the container and the balloon reaches atmospheric pressure A, and is then closed. Calculate the temperature of the air, assuming that the pressure difference across the fabric of the balloon is negligible compared with all other pressures. Calculate also the volume of the balloon at this time.

In view of the assumption concerning the negligible pressure difference across the balloon, external work is being performed in this case against the constant external pressure A.

Thus the work done in blowing the balloon up to a volume v

$$= Av.$$

It is this performance of work against a constant pressure which makes it invalid to apply the results for a reversible adiabatic expansion.

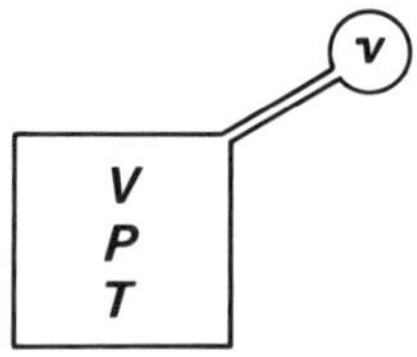

Fig. 4.14

If the whole gas corresponds to n moles, and the temperature falls to T', by the first law of thermodynamics, since $\Delta Q = 0$,

$$Av = nC_v\,(T - T'). \tag{i}$$

Originally this gas occupied a volume V at a temperature T and a pressure P,

$$\therefore\ PV = nRT. \tag{ii}$$

Substituting from $$C_v = R/(\gamma - 1)$$

for C_v in (i), and then substituting for R from (ii), we obtain

$$AvT(\gamma - 1) = (T - T')\,PV$$

or

$$PVT' = PVT - AvT(\gamma - 1). \tag{iii}$$

Applying the gas equation to the pressure, volume and temperature of the gas before and after the change,

$$\frac{PV}{T} = \frac{A(V + v)}{T'}$$

or

$$PVT' = AVT + AvT. \tag{iv}$$

Combining this with (iii),

$$AvT = PVT - AVT$$

or

$$v = \frac{(P - A)}{A\gamma}.$$

Substitution of this result in (iv) leads to

$$T' = T\,\frac{P + (\gamma - 1)A}{\gamma P}.$$

It should be noted that these results are different from those obtained by the application of the equation for a reversible adiabatic change; however, it is easily verified that when v is small compared with V the results are the same. This fact prompts the thought that under the conditions normally applying in Clément and Désormes' experiment, the changes should be thought of as corresponding to this problem, rather than those of a reversible adiabatic change.

9 ENTHALPY

When a gas is heated at constant volume, its internal energy alone is changing, but when the heating takes place at constant pressure it is convenient to consider the quantity $(U + PV)$ which is altering. This quantity is known as the *enthalpy*, and normally represented by H. Thus for a mass m, if

$$H = U + PV \tag{4.26}$$

$$c_p = \frac{1}{m}\frac{\Delta H}{\Delta T}. \tag{4.27}$$

Since U, P and V are all properties of any particular state of the gas, it follows that the enthalpy change between two states of a substance is independent of the particular path taken for the change.

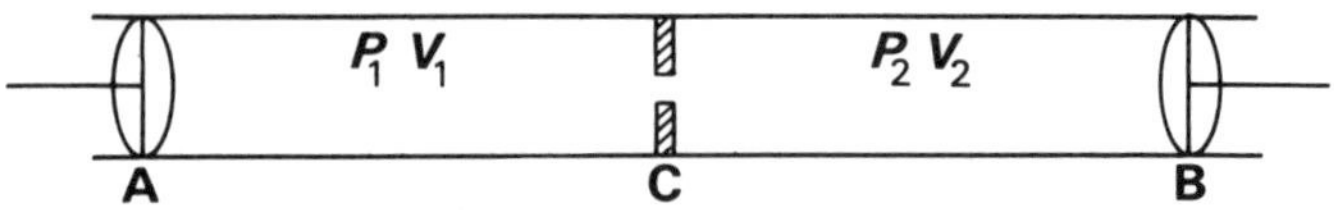

Fig. 4.15

Enthalpy is of considerable importance in considering a *throttling* process such as that indicated schematically in Fig. 4.15.

The cylinder shown is constructed of a perfect heat insulator and the two parts of it are separated by a wall with an aperture through which the gas can pass, under the influence of the difference in pressures maintained in the two parts. The pressure on the left is P_1 and a mass of gas occupies a volume V_1, on that side of the aperture; the same mass of gas occupies a volume V_2 at a pressure P_2 on the other side. We are considering the passage of this mass of gas from one side to the other. Thus the pistons, which must also be perfectly heat-insulating, move respectively towards and away from C.

In this process the net work done on the gas is

$$P_1 V_1 - P_2 V_2 .$$

Because of the heat insulation no heat can enter or leave this mass of gas, and thus if U_1 and U_2 represent the internal energies of the gas before and after passing through the orifice, by the first law of thermodynamics,

$$U_2 - U_1 = P_1 V_1 - P_2 V_2$$

or

$$U_2 + P_2 V_2 = U_1 + P_1 V_1. \tag{4.28}$$

Thus in a throttling process of this nature, there is no net change in enthalpy, but it is important to realize that such processes must take place slowly, or there will be changes in the kinetic energies of the gas streams on the two sides of the orifice.

10 THE SECOND LAW OF THERMODYNAMICS

The first law of thermodynamics (page 63) enables us to calculate the change in internal energy of a system as a result of simultaneously performing work on the system and allowing heat energy to flow into it; in each case work done *by* the system or a flow of heat *out* of the system is represented by a negative quantity in eqn. (4.7) which states the law. It is concerned with the overall effect of mechanical and non-mechanical transfers of energy into or out of the system.

A system with a particular quantity of internal energy is able to transfer part of this energy out of it, i.e. to perform some mechanical work. For example, steam is able to do work as a consequence of the considerable kinetic and potential energies of its molecules. As it cools in doing this work, the kinetic energy of the molecules decreases, and when it changes to the liquid state they lose potential energy in respect of the attractions between them,

The second law of thermodynamics provides us with information concerning how much of the internal energy of a system can be converted into mechanical work under ideal conditions. We can consider it with reference to an *ideal heat engine E* which utilizes the energy available in a hot body, frequently referred to as the *source*, and represented by H in the schematic diagram of Fig. 4.16.

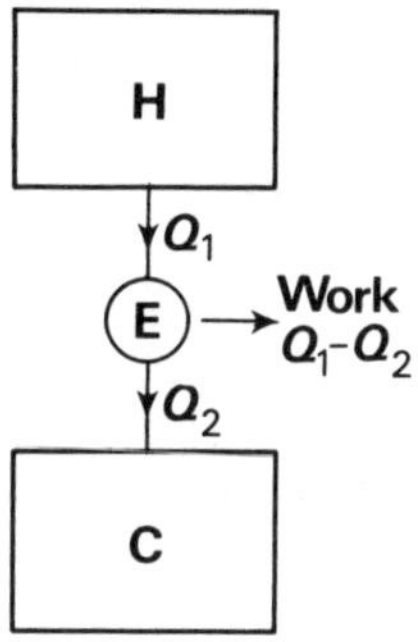

Fig. 4.16

On each cycle the engine takes Q_1 units of energy from H, performs work and subsequently rejects Q_2 of energy to a cold body, usually referred to as the *sink*, and represented in the diagram by C.

At the end of a complete cycle the working substance in the heat engine returns to its original state and thus has an unchanged internal energy. It follows by a simple application of the first law of thermodynamics that the work done in the cycle is $Q_1 - Q_2$.

The second law of thermodynamics has been stated in a number of forms; Kelvin's formulation was:

It is impossible to derive a continuous supply of work by cooling a body to a temperature lower than that of the coldest of its surroundings.

Applying this to the heat engine, it implies that we must have a cold sink to which some energy is rejected. This suggests an alternative statement, perhaps more directly relevant to the ideal heat engine.

It is not possible in a cyclical process to convert heat into work without transferring heat from a hot body to a colder body.

It follows that since Q_2 is always positive and greater than zero, the work done is always less than Q_1. If the efficiency of the engine as a convertor of energy input into work is η,

$$\eta = \frac{Q_1 - Q_2}{Q_1}. \tag{4.29}$$

The second law asserts that even under ideal conditions 100 per cent efficiency cannot be obtained.

Using arguments based on the second law of thermodynamics it is possible to show that, provided all the changes occurring are reversible, the efficiency of an ideal heat engine depends only on the temperatures of the hot and cold bodies involved in its operation. *The thermodynamic scale of temperature* is then defined so that the temperature θ_1 and θ_2 of the hot and cold bodies are given by

$$\frac{Q_1}{Q_2} = \frac{\theta_1}{\theta_2}. \tag{4.30}$$

By considering a reversible heat engine which uses an *ideal gas* as the working substance it can be shown that a scale of temperature defined by eqn. (4.30) is at all temperatures identical with the ideal gas scale of temperature, provided the two scales agree at a fixed point (the triple point of water) and have degrees of the same size (the kelvin). It therefore follows that if T_1 and T_2 are the temperatures of the source and sink respectively, measured on the ideal gas scale,

$$\eta = \frac{T_1 - T_2}{T_2}. \tag{4.31}$$

Eqn. (4.31) indicates the importance of a large difference in temperature for obtaining a high efficiency; it also shows that 100 per cent efficiency could only be obtained by using a body at the absolute zero to receive the rejected energy. The unattainability of the absolute zero of temperature is sometimes referred to as the *third law of thermodynamics.*

A heat engine utilizes the energy associated with the random motion of molecules by converting it into harnessed, directed kinetic energy in its moving piston; it is obtaining ordered energy from a more disordered form. The second law of thermodynamics shows how the temperatures of the bodies used as source and sink control the efficiency of this process.

Transfer of heat takes place under a temperature gradient from a hotter to a colder body; this is the natural direction of heat flow, and common sense tells us that heat will not, of its own volition, flow in the opposite direction. However, if we reverse the individual processes involved in the operation of a heat engine we can, as a consequence of an input of mechanical work, make heat flow from a cold body to one at a higher temperature. Such a device tends to increase the difference in temperature between the two bodies, in contrast to the heat engine which is tending to make the temperatures of source and sink more nearly equal. We can think of an arrangement of this nature either as a *heat pump* which is reversing the normal direction of heat flow, or as a *refrigerator* which is further cooling the colder of two bodies by the expenditure of work. We return to a consideration of a refrigerator in Section 1 of Chapter 8, but it is appropriate at this point to consider a further statement of the second law, which was made by Clausius.

It is impossible to cause heat to flow from a cold body to a hotter one without the use of an external supply of energy.

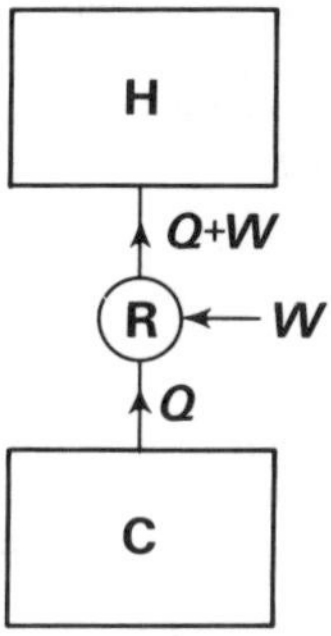

Fig. 4.17

Referring to Fig. 4.17 we see that this implies that more heat reaches the hot body than is extracted from the cold body. If we consider the refrigerator as an engine in reverse, we see that this is equivalent to the statement that $Q_1 > Q_2$ in Fig. 4.16; and is therefore equivalent to the earlier statement of the law.

The second law of thermodynamics is concerned with the restrictions on the conversion of random energy into more ordered forms, and we return briefly to this point in Section 8 of Chapter 5.

QUESTIONS

1. A gas which is originally at atmospheric pressure and 290 K has its volume reduced to one-fifth of its original value, under adiabatic reversible conditions; calculate the resulting pressure and temperature. Assume $\gamma = 7/5$.

2. A gas which is originally at a pressure of two atmospheres, a temperature of 300 K and occupies a volume of 800 cm^3, expands until its pressure is half atmospheric. Calculate the temperature and its volume if the change takes place under reversible adiabatic conditions. Assume $\gamma = 5/3$.

3. A gas at 280 K and atmospheric pressure, occupying a volume V, is compressed until the pressure is 6 atmospheres, under reversible adiabatic conditions. If γ for the gas is 5/3, calculate the volume of the gas and its temperature after compression.

4. A gas with a ratio of its specific heats of 7/5 undergoes a reversible adiabatic expansion which cools it from 290 K to 260 K. If the final pressure is atmospheric, calculate what it must have been prior to the expansion.

5. A gas with a value of $\gamma = 7/5$ expands adiabatically and reversibly so that its volume increases ten fold. Calculate its final pressure and temperature if initially it was at atmospheric pressure and a temperature of 285 K.

6. A bicycle pump of heat capacity 83 J K^{-1} contains a mole of air at 27 °C. Calculate the final temperature of the pump when the air is rapidly compressed to one-quarter its original volume. Assume that the heat capacity of air at constant volume is 8.3 J $mole^{-1}$ and that the ratio of its specific heats is 1.4. Discuss the other assumptions you made in arriving at your result.

7. An internal combustion engine has a compression ratio of 10:1 and the volume before compression is 1 litre. Assuming the cylinder contains gas at s.t.p. at the beginning of the stroke, calculate the pressure and temperature at the end of each stroke on the assumption that the compression is reversible and adiabatic. Assume γ for the gas is 7/5.

8. Calculate the ratio of the work done in compressing a gas to one-tenth of its volume under (a) isothermal conditions, (b) adiabatic conditions, if the gas is originally at atmospheric pressure and 280 K.

9. A horizontal cylinder which is made of material impervious to heat is divided into two halves by a piston which is also a perfect insulator for heat. Initially each half contains a mole of ideal gas at 300 K. Heat is supplied to one side until the volume on the other side is reduced by 1 per cent. Assuming the piston to be frictionless, calculate the temperatures produced in the two compartments and the total heat supplied. Assume $R = 8.3$. J K^{-1} mol^{-1} and $\gamma = 1.4$.

10. A hollow cylinder of length 2 m and internal cross-section 1 cm^2 is closed at each end and divided into two halves by a frictionless piston of mass 0.2 kg. Both halves of the apparatus contain an ideal gas at a pressure of 10^5 N m^{-2}. With the cylinder horizontal, the piston is displaced slightly and then released; it is found to oscillate with a period of 0.52 s. Show that the oscillations are of a simple harmonic nature and calculate γ for the gas.

11. A large localized mass of air at ground level is heated to a temperature of 27 °C whilst the temperature of the atmosphere remains constant at all heights at 17 °C. Assuming that γ for air is 7/5, and that the molecular weight of air is 29, estimate the height to which the mass of hot air rises if it does not mix with the surrounding air.

12. An ideal gas expands from a volume V_1 at a pressure P_1 to a final volume V_2, under conditions such that the temperature always varies so that P^2V = constant. Calculate how much heat has to be added to the gas, and sketch a graph to show the relation between P and V during the change.

13. An ideal monatomic gas slowly expands from a volume V to a volume $2V$ under conditions where the temperature is varied so that (a) P^2V = constant, and (b) PV^2 = constant. Calculate the work done in each case if the initial pressure of the gas is P_1. Discuss whether heat is added to or substracted from the gas under these circumstances.

14. 5 g of ideal monatomic gas of molecular weight 28 expands adiabatically and reversibly from a temperature 290 K and a pressure 10^5 N m^{-2} until it occupies double its initial volume. Calculate (a) final pressure, (b) final temperature, and (c) work done by the gas. How much heat would have to be supplied to the gas to bring about the same expansion under isothermal reversible conditions; Assume γ for the gas is 5/3 and $R = 8.3$ J K^{-1} mol^{-1}.

15. In an internal combustion engine a mixture of air and fuel is drawn into each cylinder in turn and compressed before the cylinder is fired. The ratio of the volumes before and after this compression is known as the *compression ratio.* Assuming that the compression before ignition is perfectly adiabatic and raises the temperature of the fuel/air mixture from 50 °C to 500 °C, calculate the compression ratio in the cylinder. (Take the value of γ for the mixture to be 1.4.)

16. What is meant by a reversible adiabatic change? How can the rise of temperature during an adiabatic compression by explained on the kinetic theory?

A cylinder of negligible thermal capacity with non-conducting walls is fitted with a frictionless piston. The cylinder contains 2.24 litres of nitrogen at s.t.p. A small explosion is fired inside the cylinder, producing 1 000 J of heat; the gas is then allowed to expand reversibly and adiabatically to atmospheric pressure. Calculate the final temperature of the gas.

In the final state, is all the energy of the explosion present as heat in the gas? If not, what has happened to any difference?

(C_V for nitrogen = 20.6 J mol^{-1} K^{-1}; C_p/C_v for nitrogen = 1.40)

17. 7.5 litres of air at 17 °C and standard atmospheric pressure are compressed isothermally to 2.5 litres and the air is then allowed to expand adiabatically to its original volume. Calculate the final temperature of the gas and show the process on a p–v diagram. Assume γ for air = 1.4.

18. A fixed mass of an ideal gas whose principal specific heats have a ratio γ of 1.67, occupies 200 cm^3 at 31 °C and at one atmosphere pressure. It is then allowed to expand adiabatically until the volume is 300 cm^3, after which it is kept at constant pressure until the temperature returns to 31 °C. Calculate (a) the pressure and temperature after the adiabatic expansion, and (b) the final volume.

19. A cylindrical tube of length 1 metre and cross-sectional area 4.0 cm^2 is held vertically with its lower end closed; a closely-fitting glass stopper of mass 30 g is inserted into the open end and pressed down until its lower surface is within 10 cm of the bottom of the tube. Calculate the height to which it will rise when it is suddenly released, assuming that the compressed air has time to reach room temperature before the stopper is released, but expands adiabatically thereafter. Ignore friction with the tube and any leakage of air past the stopper. Assume γ for the air to be 7/5, atmospheric pressure = 10^5 N m^{-2}, and g = 10 N kg^{-1}.

20. A simple air gun consists of a uniform tube of cross-sectional area a and length l, to one end of which is attached a closed chamber of air under pressure p(> atmospheric pressure P_0). A close-fitting pellet lies in the tube immediately adjoining the chamber, and the gun is discharged by opening a connection between the tube and the chamber of compressed air. Assuming a complete absence of leakage or friction, calculate the value of l for which the greatest kinetic energy is imparted to the pellet, and the value of this energy.

21. A vessel of 1 litre capacity is filled with a perfect gas at 300 K and a pressure of five atmospheres; the ratio of the principal specific heat capacities of the gas is 5/3. Calculate the final pressure and temperature of the gas if it is expanded to twice its volume (a) suddenly by opening a tap connecting with an evacuated vessel, and (b) very slowly by pushing back a piston. The whole vessel is perfectly heat-insulated so that no heat enters or leaves the gas, and the heat capacity of the vessel may be neglected.

22. A horizontal cylinder of length 300 cm and cross-sectional area 100 cm^2 contains equal volumes of hydrogen and helium at a pressure of 10^5 N m^{-2}. The gases are separated by a thin frictionless piston. The cylinder is then turned until it is vertical. If the piston has then moved 2.5 mm from its original position, calculate its weight. Assume that the cylinder and piston are perfect thermal insulators, and neglect the mass of each gas.

(C_p/C_v for hydrogen = 1.40; C_p/C_v for helium = 1.67)

23. 3.9 g of a gas occupies 3.0 litres at 15 °C and 76 cm of mercury pressure. It is supplied with 250 J of heat energy. What is its new pressure and temperature if its volume is kept constant? If it is now allowed to expand adiabatically back to its original pressure, what is its volume and temperature?

Specific heat capacity of gas at constant volume = 0.71 J g^{-1} K^{-1}.
Specific heat capacity of gas at constant pressure = 1.08 J g^{-1} K^{-1}.

Vaporization 5

An ideal or perfect gas consisting of molecules of a negligible size which exert no forces on each other could never condense to the liquid phase. Any increase of external pressure would reduce its volume until this applied pressure is balanced by the increased pressure from the rapidly moving molecules. Cooling would reduce both the volume and the pressure as the kinetic energy of the molecules was decreased; at the absolute zero of temperature the product of pressure and volume would be zero, and the molecules would have no translational kinetic energy.

In a real gas this would not occur because as the molecules become close enough together, the forces between them become sufficiently important to produce the characteristics of the liquid phase. This chapter will be concerned with the transitions between the liquid and gaseous phases, and the properties of gases as they approach the point of liquefaction.

1 EVAPORATION

The molecules in a liquid are in a state of continual motion; those very near to the surface possess – in addition to their kinetic energy – potential energy, represented by the work done against inter-molecular attractions in attaining this position from the general body of the liquid. In order that they escape from the liquid surface a further large amount of work has to be done against these forces – it will be appreciated that these are the very forces which give a liquid its characteristic surface tension. Unless the molecules in the surface have a large kinetic energy they will be unable to escape from the surface into the vapour phase; *evaporation* therefore only involves the faster-moving molecules, and it is apparent that a rise in temperature will increase the number of molecules able to evaporate.

Thus a particular molecule changing from the liquid to the vapour phase increases its potential energy at the expense of its kinetic energy; as a vapour molecule it has less kinetic but more potential energy than it had in the liquid phase; on the other hand, only the more energetic molecules are able to evaporate. Thus these more energetic molecules change some of their kinetic into potential energy in the process of escaping, and when constituting a group of vapour molecules they have the same average kinetic energy as molecules in the liquid at the same temperature.

The difference between molecules in the two phases lies in the *greater potential energy* of those in the vapour phase; it is this energy which has to be supplied as *latent heat* to the liquid in order to produce evaporation without any fall in temperature of the remaining unevaporated liquid. It is the continual removal of the faster-moving molecules which tends to bring about the fall in average energy of the remaining liquid molecules, if no heat is supplied from an external source. This fall in average energy of the liquid molecules means a drop in temperature, and produces the phenomenon of cooling by evaporation which is responsible for the strong sensation of 'cold' when a volatile liquid such as ether is placed on the skin. If the rate of evaporation is increased by blowing a jet of air through the ether in a metal can the effect is very much greater, and can be sufficient to freeze a film of water between the bottom of the can and a wood board on which it is standing.

In a similar manner it is the evaporation of water from the surface of a muslin bag and the consequent cooling produced which enables such a bag to be used to keep milk cool.

This process of cooling by evaporation is utilized in many refrigerators. A volatile liquid such as ammonia flows through a spiral tube, is caused to evaporate and draws its latent heat of evaporation from a bath of liquid in which it is immersed; the cooling of this liquid is then used to cool the refrigerator compartments themselves. It is necessary to ensure the continuation of the evaporation process and the subsequent return of the vapour to the liquid phase. There are a number of ways in which this can be achieved, but in the commonest type an electrically-driven pump maintains pressure differences throughout the system so that circulation continues. The operation of refrigerators is considered in greater detail in Section 1 of Chapter 8.

2 DETERMINATION OF LATENT HEAT OF VAPORIZATION

The apparatus shown in Fig. 5.1 can be used to measure the specific latent heat of vaporization (L) of a liquid. The immersion heater (H) heats the liquid to its boiling point, and then vaporizes it. Once the whole apparatus has reached a steady temperature, the liquid changes into vapour at a constant rate which can be determined by collecting the outflow of liquid from the condenser C. It is important to take a number of successive weighings to ensure that a steady state has been reached.

If I is the current through the heater and V the potential difference across it, electrical energy is being converted into heat at a rate of IV watts. However, some of this energy is escaping from the outer surface of the apparatus; if this is h watts, we have

$$IV = mL + h \tag{5.1}$$

where m is the mass of liquid vaporized per second.

The flask F can be in the form of a specially constructed double-walled vessel with a vacuum between the two walls, and it may then be possible to neglect h. Otherwise the effect may be eliminated by repeating the

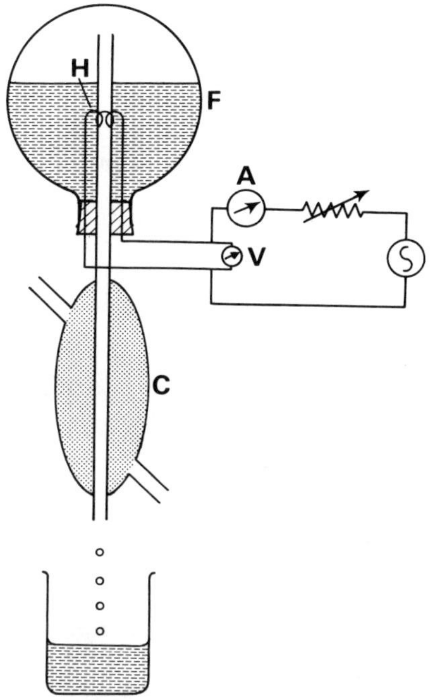

Fig. 5.1

experiment with a different rate of supply of energy, using a current I' and a potential difference V'; if the new mass vaporized per second is m',

$$I'V' = m'L + h \tag{5.2}$$

Since the temperature of all parts of the apparatus remains the same as before, the rate of heat loss is unchanged. The value of L is then obtained after subtraction of eqn. (5.1) and (5.2).

Specific latent heats of vaporization should be expressed in J kg^{-1}, and values for some common substances are given below.

Specific latent heat/J kg^{-1}			
Water	22.6×10^5	Turpentine	2.93×10^5
Ethanol	8.4×10^5	Carbon tetrachloride	1.93×10^5
Ether	3.77×10^5	Methanol	11.1×10^5
Mercury	3.01×10^5		

The increase in potential energy referred to earlier represents the major part of the energy required for a phase change, but under normal conditions some further energy is required. This can be seen by considering the liquid to be contained in a cylinder fitted with a frictionless piston as indicated in Fig. 5.2 (overleaf). In order to accommodate the large volume change resulting from vaporization, work has to be done in pushing the piston back against the external pressure. This work can be calculated, as in the case below of water vaporizing at its normal boiling point.

If A is the area of the piston, P the external pressure and x the distance moved by the piston when unit mass of liquid becomes vapour, the external work done is

$$PAx = P(V - v)$$

where V and v are the volumes of unit mass in the vapour and liquid phases respectively.

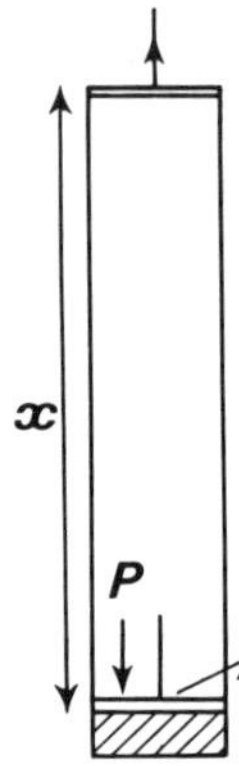

Fig. 5.2

Under normal conditions, $P = 10^5 \text{ N m}^{-2}$ and, for 1 kg, $V = 1.7 \text{ m}^3$, whilst $v = 10^{-3} \text{ m}^3$.

Thus external work done $= 1.7 \times 10^5 \text{ J kg}^{-1}$.

Under these conditions the specific latent heat is of the order of $2.3 \times 10^6 \text{ J kg}^{-1}$, so the external work done therefore represents slightly less than 8 per cent of the total energy needed; the balance represents the work done against inter-molecular forces in increasing the potential energy of the molecules in the vapour phase.

Referring back to eqn. (4.26) we see that the latent heat represents the change in enthalpy associated with the phase change.

It is well known that the surface tensions of liquids fall with increasing temperature, so the work done on this account would be expected to decrease as the temperature rises. On the other hand the work done against the external pressure increases with the temperature, but this is not usually sufficient to make the total latent heat become larger.

3 SATURATED VAPOURS

If a very small quantity of liquid is introduced into a space, evaporation continues until no liquid remains; cooling of the apparatus provides the latent heat required and normally heat from the surroundings flows into the apparatus. As the concentration of vapour molecules increases the chance of such a molecule hitting any remaining liquid surface and being captured by the attractive forces of the liquid molecules increases. At any stage the observed evaporation is a net effect, resulting from a rate of vaporization which is greater than that of re-condensation.

If all the liquid evaporates, the resulting vapour is *unsaturated*; these conditions can be obtained in the apparatus shown in Fig. 5.3. The space

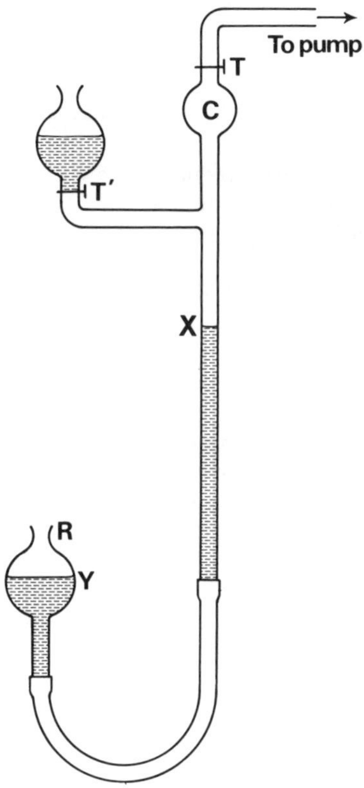

Fig. 5.3

C is evacuated by the pump drawing air through the tap T. This tap is then closed and T′ opened to allow a small quantity of liquid to drop through and evaporate. Provided it is arranged that a small enough quantity of liquid enters the evacuated part of the apparatus, the resulting vapour is an unsaturated one.

The reservoir R can be raised or lowered, thereby changing the volume of the vapour; its pressure can be obtained from the difference between the pressure represented by the height of the liquid between X and Y, and atmospheric pressure. The results obtained are of the form shown in Fig. 5.4.

For the larger volumes Boyle's law is obeyed, but as the volume is reduced the pressure does not increase as much as the law would predict. At a certain value no further increase occurs provided the temperature is

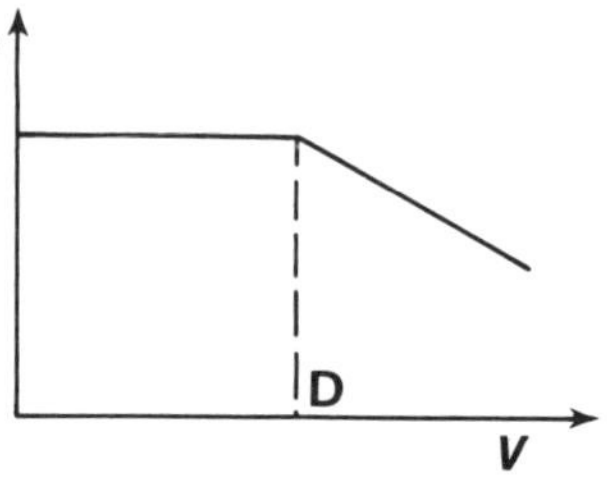

Fig. 5.4

kept constant. As the volume is reduced below that at D the pressure remains constant, but it becomes apparent that vapour is condensing.

A constant temperature implies a constant mean kinetic energy of the molecules, and since $P = \frac{1}{3} mn\overline{c^2}$, constancy of pressure must imply that the concentration of molecules in the vapour phase is remaining unchanged. Clearly D corresponds to the stage where the concentration of vapour molecules has reached its maximum possible value.

At any state beyond that represented by the area to the left of D, both liquid and vapour are present and the vapour is *saturated.*

However, molecules are continuing to escape from the liquid and the equilibrium must result from a *dynamic equilibrium*, where an exactly equal number are returning from the vapour to the liquid state, as a result of coming within range of the forces exerted by those molecules near the surface of the liquid.

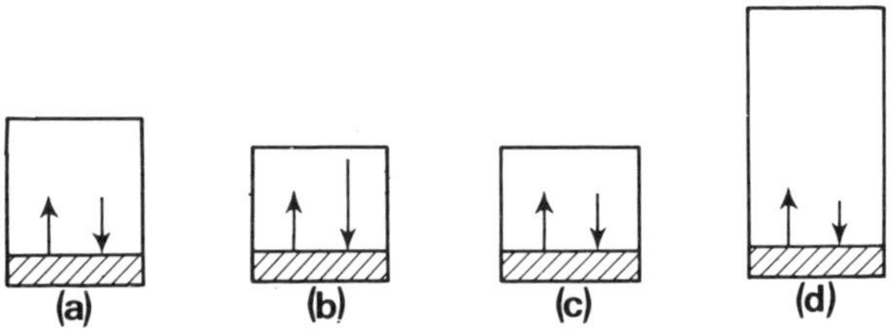

Fig. 5.5

In Fig. 5.5(a), a saturated vapour is shown in a closed container in equilibrium with its liquid. The two arrows represent by their equal lengths the rates of flow of molecules between the two phases.

In (b) the volume available to the vapour has been reduced so that the concentration of vapour molecules is temporarily increased and there is a greater chance of a vapour molecule hitting the surface and condensing; this is shown by the greater length of the downward arrow. The rate at which molecules are evaporating is unchanged since it depends only on the temperature and the particular nature of the molecules. So in these conditions more molecules are returning to the liquid than are escaping from it, so the concentration of vapour molecules falls. This continues until in (c) the two rates of flow are again equal; the number of molecules hitting the liquid surface in any time is now the same as it was originally. Since the temperature and hence the mean velocity of the molecules is unchanged, the pressure is unaltered.

If the volume is increased as in (d), there is an initial fall in the rate of condensation – and hence a net evaporation – until a new equilibrium is established with the same rates of flow of molecules.

In this way we see how it comes about that as a result of the dynamic equilibrium, the saturated vapour pressure at a given temperature is independent of the volume.

If the temperature of the liquid is increased the number of molecules escaping per second from unit area also increases, and thus the concentration of vapour molecules rises until a new dynamic equilibrium is reached. When this occurs the pressure exerted by the saturated vapour will be greater than previously.

4 MEASUREMENT OF SATURATED VAPOUR PRESSURE

The variation of saturated vapour pressure with temperature may be investigated with the apparatus shown in Fig. 5.6. A small quantity of

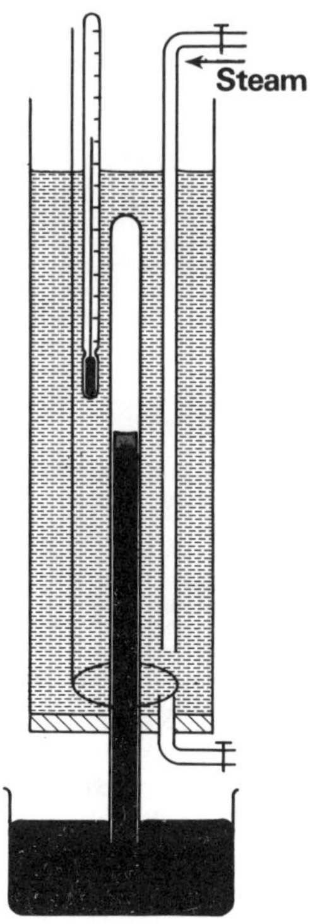

Fig. 5.6

liquid is introduced into the space above the mercury in the barometer tube, using a bent pipette; the consequent evaporation produces a fall in the mercury level so that only a height h is now supported, whereas the corresponding height was h_0 before the introduction of the liquid. Thus the saturated vapour pressure of the liquid is equal to a pressure represented by a height $(h_0 - h)$ of mercury.

The mercury column and the vapour above it is now heated by passing steam into the surrounding water bath; at a suitable time the steam flow is cut-off and the apparatus allowed to reach thermal equilibrium. The saturated vapour pressure at the temperature read by the thermometer is then measured as before.

In assessing the likely accuracy of the results obtained, a number of points must be considered. As the mercury column is heated its density falls and thus the measured heights must be corrected to 0 °C in all cases. At the lower temperatures there must be an appreciable quantity of liquid on top of the mercury and this exerts a pressure; however, if there was as much as 15 mm of liquid with a density of the order of that of water, the error on this account would only be of the order of 1 mm of mercury so that, with care, the effect of such liquid will be of little significance.

Although the bath may be left for some time and stirred thoroughly before attempting to take a reading, it is very difficult indeed to obtain constancy of temperature throughout the bath; this can be readily established by raising and lowering the thermometer. It therefore becomes necessary to consider the effect of a temperature gradient in the vapour.

Fig. 5.7

If the vapour at B in Fig. 5.7 is hotter than that at A, it would seem that evaporation would lead to a greater vapour pressure at B. However, the consequence of this would be to make vapour flow from B to A in an effort to equalize the pressures; this must lead to condensation in the upper parts of the tube. It follows that the only possible pressure in the space which is consistent with equilibrium is that corresponding to the saturated vapour pressure of the coldest part of the vapour.

The fact that the pressure of vapour in a closed system which contains only vapour is the vapour pressure of its coldest part is of considerable importance in an arrangement such as that shown in Fig. 5.8, for measuring the vapour pressure at low temperatures. The whole apparatus has previously been completely evacuated and when vapour is admitted to the bulb X, some condenses on account of the low temperature. Although the vapour in Y is at room temperature, the pressure recorded on the mercury manometer is the saturated vapour pressure corresponding to the temperature in X; this will normally be well below room temperature because of the freezing mixture with which it is surrounded.

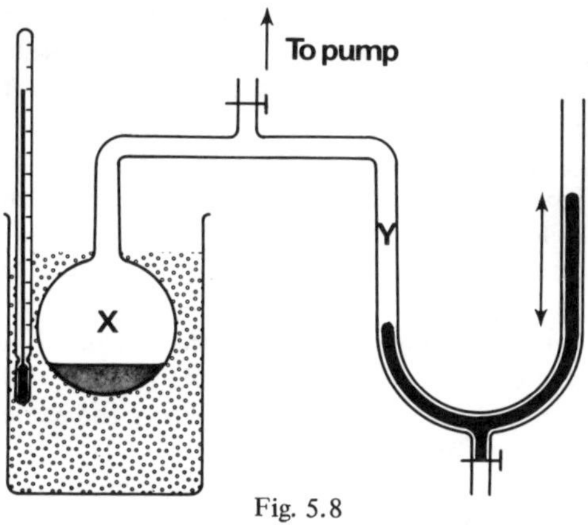

Fig. 5.8

The apparatus of Fig. 5.9 is a convenient means of measuring saturated vapour pressures over a considerable range of temperatures. The closed U-tube at the left, which is in a bath whose temperature can be varied, contains mercury. A small quantity of the liquid under test floats on the mercury and above it there is the corresponding saturated vapour. By means of the pump and the air vent at Y, the pressure in the right-hand part of the apparatus is adjusted until the mercury levels in the U-tube are

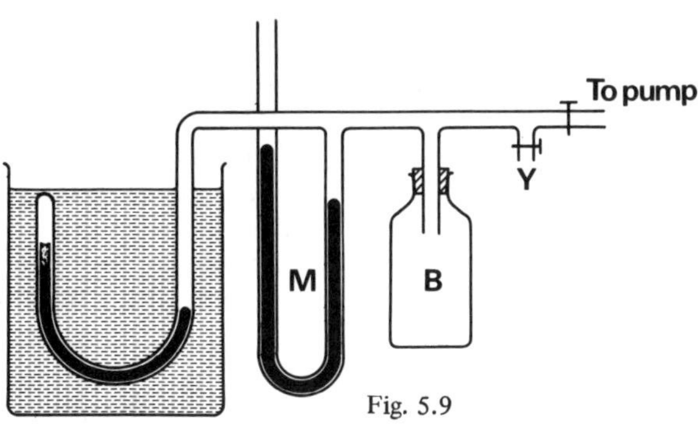

Fig. 5.9

equal; the pressure of the saturated vapour can then be read directly from the mercury manometer M. The large bottle B serves as a reservoir and provides better pressure control.

This apparatus avoids any difficulties arising from change in the density of the mercury as its temperature alters. For measurements at low temperatures the apparatus can also be modified by using an exhaust pump, and if necessary a closed manometer tube.

5 BOILING

When a liquid boils, small vapour bubbles form in the body of the liquid, then rise to the surface as they grow. The maximum possible pressure inside such a bubble is the saturated vapour pressure, and if the bubble is to be in equilibrium, this pressure has to balance the sum of the external pressure and a small pressure arising from the surface tension forces in the liquid surface. This latter quantity is equal to $2\gamma/r$, for a bubble of radius r in a liquid of surface tension γ, and will only be important for very small bubbles. The external pressure is, of course, atmospheric pressure plus that due to the appropriate depth of liquid. It follows that for bubbles that are not too small, *boiling occurs when the saturated vapour pressure equals the external pressure.* Unless a particularly deep vessel is being considered the external pressure is approximately the atmospheric pressure.

If a vessel of water is heated, the first bubbles observed are air bubbles but, as the temperature rises, and in a few small regions, reaches the boiling point, vapour bubbles may form around air bubbles as nuclei; in this way the need for a small extra pressure to balance the forces of surface tension is avoided since the original bubbles are quite large. When such bubbles pass into the cooler parts, slight condensation occurs and they collapse. It is this collapse which produces the familiar 'singing' of a kettle just before it 'boils'. When water is boiled in an electric kettle it will be observed that the first bubbles always come from the hotter water immediately in contact with the surface of the heating element.

If there are no edges, impurities or insoluble solid particles on which the bubbles can form, it is necessary for the temperature to be considerably above the boiling point before the vapour pressure inside the tiny bubble is great enough to overcome the surface tension effect so that the bubble may grow. This is the phenomenon of *super-heating* or *delayed boiling*; once the bubbles are able to form and begin to grow the effective external pressure rapidly decreases as the radius increases, so the bubble grows very rapidly indeed as it rises into a region or slightly smaller pressure – the phenomenon of *bumping.* A few pieces of broken china or porcelain provide edges around which the bubble may form with a sufficiently large radius to render the surface tension effect negligible.

When there are no artificially-provided nuclei and the liquid itself is very pure, the bubbles form in the first instance on roughnesses and cracks on the surface of the vessel; in some cases such cracks may contain minute quantities of air which also can serve as nuclei for bubble formation. However, under these circumstances there will certainly be a degree of super-heating before boiling occurs.

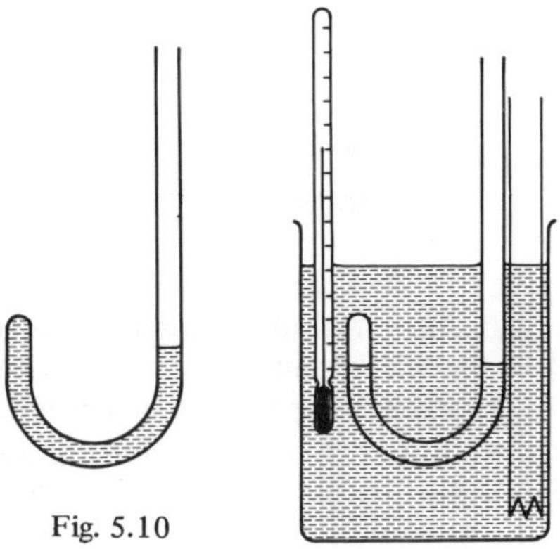

Fig. 5.10

The arrangement shown in Fig. 5.10 may be used to show that, in the absence of super-heating, the liquid boils when the saturated vapour pressure equals the external pressure. The left-hand limb of the J-tube is initially full of liquid, and is then immersed in a bath of the same liquid. As the temperature of the bath is raised, evaporation takes place and the pressure of the vapour above the liquid in the left-hand limb depresses the surface level; when the liquid in the bath is boiling the levels in the two limbs are seen to be equal.

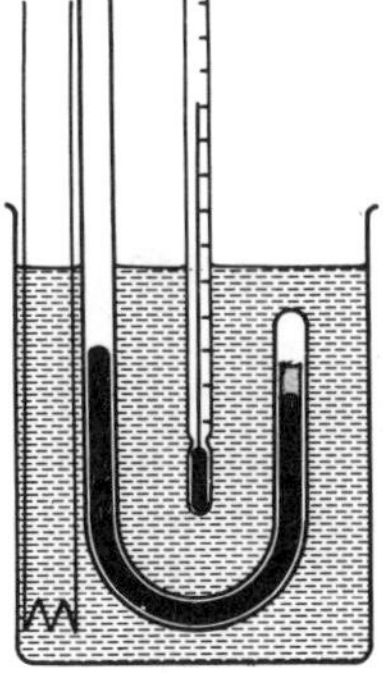

Fig. 5.11

Fig. 5.11 shows a variant of this experiment where the liquid floats on mercury in the J-tube; initially the tube contains mercury and the liquid, all the air having been previously removed from the apparatus. When the boiling point is reached the mercury levels will be seen to be equal. This apparatus is useful for determining the boiling point of a liquid when only a small quantity of it is available. It is inserted into the J-tube, and the surrounding bath of a different liquid is heated until the mercury levels are equal. The temperature of the bath then gives the boiling point of the liquid directly.

6 VARIATION OF VAPOUR PRESSURE WITH TEMPERATURE

The apparatus of Fig. 5.12 is very convenient for determining the saturated vapour pressure at temperatures approaching the normal boiling point. The pressure in the whole apparatus is reduced by the pump attached at X, and the large flask R prevents large fluctuations of pressure in the apparatus. The pressure is reduced to a suitable value which is read from the difference in levels of the mercury manometer M, and the liquid in the flask F is slowly heated until it boils; the boiling point can then be read from the thermometer in the vapour. The condenser C turns the vapour into liquid so that it returns to the flask. With pure liquid it is important to place a few bumping stones in the liquid in order to prevent delayed boiling.

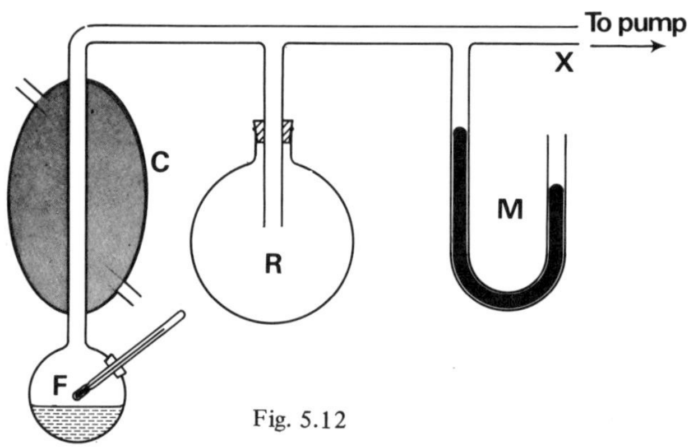

Fig. 5.12

The range of temperatures over which this experiment can be carried out for a particular vapour depends on the pump available. In the case of water vapour a good rotary pump makes it relatively easy to obtain water boiling at temperatures near 50 °C, and it is in the interval between this temperature and the normal boiling point that the experiment is more convenient and more accurate than the barometer tube type of experiment previously described.

If the arrangement is modified by replacing the exhaust pump by a compressor we can obtain boiling under pressures in excess of atmospheric, and thus determine saturated vapour pressures at temperatures above the normal boiling point.

It is instructive to consider the distribution of partial pressures in the various parts of the apparatus of Fig. 5.12. Above the liquid in the flask there is only pure vapour and this exerts the saturated vapour pressure appropriate to its temperature. The total pressure in the condenser will also have this same value, but here some of the vapour has condensed because of the lower temperature, and there is a considerable partial pressure exerted by the air which is present. In the closed limb of the manometer the temperature is so low that there can be little pressure from the vapour, and most of the pressure arises from the partial pressure of the air. However, in an equilibrium situation the total pressure is the same for all parts of the apparatus.

Example 1. A capillary tube of uniform cross-section, closed at one end, has a small water index whose lower end is 15.4 cm from the closed end of the tube when the temperature is 20 °C. On heating the tube and contents to 70 °C the length of the air column below the water index increases to 25.6 cm. If the atmospheric pressure is 760 mm of mercury and the s.v.p. of water at 20 °C is 17 mm of mercury, calculate the s.v.p. at 70 °C.

The presence of the water index ensures that there is a mixture of saturated water vapour and air between the index and the closed end of the tube.

Initially the pressure of the water vapour = 17 mm mercury, and thus the pressure of the air = 760 − 17 = 743 mm, ignoring the tiny pressure due to the water index.

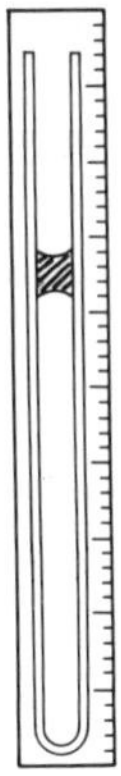

Fig. 5.13

On heating to 70 °C, this air exerts a pressure P, where

$$\frac{743 \times 15.4}{293} = \frac{P \times 25.6}{343}$$

and thus $$P = 523 \text{ mm.}$$

Since the sum of the partial pressures of the air and the water vapour must still be 760 mm, the water vapour is exerting a pressure of 760 − 523 = 237 mm.

Thus the saturated vapour pressure at 70 °C is 237 mm of mercury. Such a tube mounted on a ruler in a beaker of water may easily be used to plot a graph of length of air column against temperature. The tube and ruler can be used as a stirrer to obtain a uniform temperature throughout the water in the beaker, and as a result of the low heat capacity of the tube a true thermal equilibrium is readily obtained. If the length of air column is now read from the graph at various temperatures the corresponding saturated vapour pressures may be calculated as above.

It is important to realize the effect on the result of a slight error in the measured length.

If each of the two lengths used in the calculation is subject to an error of ± 1 mm, these represent percentage errors of 2/3 and 2/5 per cent respectively. These lead to a total possible error in the air pressure at the higher temperature of approximately 1 per cent, if we ignore any errors in the temperatures. This represents in the particular case of the calculation above, a pressure error of about 5 mm of mercury, which is some 2 per cent cent of the vapour pressure.

In calculating the vapour pressure at a rather lower temperature the actual error in the air pressure would be of a similar size – or slightly larger, on account of the larger partial pressure of the air; a similar *absolute error* would, however, represent a much greater *percentage error* in the smaller vapour pressure. Thus an appreciably larger percentage error would occur in using this method to determine the saturated vapour pressure at 40 °C.

As the temperature of a liquid rises, an increasing proportion of its molecules have sufficient energy to escape from the action of the surface tension force. Further rise of temperature produces a disproportionately large increase in the rate at which these molecules escape and consequently the concentration of molecules in the vapour state increases rapidly.

At the same time, the average speed of these molecules in the vapour rises, so that the gradient of the pressure–temperature curve increases rapidly. This can be seen from Fig. 5.14 which shows the variation of saturated vapour pressure with temperature for water. Some corresponding values are shown in the table below.

S.V.P. of Water

Temperature °C:	0	20	40	60	70	80	90	100	102	105
S.V.P. in mm mercury:	4.6	17.5	55	149	234	355	526	760	816	906

It follows from eqn. (3.20) that the number of molecules with energy greater than E is proportional to $\exp(-E/kT)$ and it is readily established that this expression increases rapidly with T; on the other hand the number returning to the liquid surface is proportional to the mean speed $\bar{c}$, which is in turn proportional to $T^{\frac{1}{2}}$

By equating the two rates of flow it is possible to determine the molecular concentration required in the vapour for a dynamic equilibrium at any temperature and thus deduce a theoretical expression for the variation of saturated vapour pressure with temperature.

7 PHASE DIAGRAMS

The curve in Fig. 5.14 shows the precise values of pressure and temperature at which the transition from liquid to vapour occurs; since pressure, volume and temperature for any particular mass of gas are related by an equation, each point on the graph represents a particular state of the substance. Points below the curve correspond to states in the vapour phase whilst those above the curve represent the vapour phase.

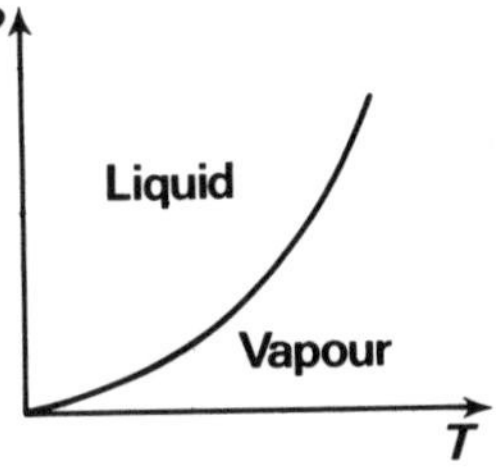

Fig. 5.14

At any point on the vapour–pressure curve the two phases can co-exist in equilibrium, but for all other states only one phase is stable; molecules in the other phase would immediately change to the stable phase. It should also be realized that a transition from one side of the vapour pressure curve to the other is accompanied by either the absorption or evolution of heat – the latent heat of vaporization.

Gases and vapours present in the same space always mix completely as a result of diffusion. The whole space is therefore absolutely homogeneous in composition; a sample removed from any region would always contain the various constituent gases. We therefore say that we have *one gaseous phase.* This is not so in the case of liquids and solids. There are circumstances in which two solids, or two liquids, can exist in equilibrium without mixing; each constitutes a separate phase. Both the solid and liquid phases can be regarded as *condensed phases.* A solution is a single condensed phase, but a mixture of oil and water – or of water and sand – represents two separate phases, no matter how much they are stirred.

Whereas a system may contain any number of condensed phases it can only contain one gaseous phase.

Since Fig. 5.14 shows the transition curve between the gaseous and liquid phases, it is usually referred to as a *phase diagram.* However, it is a very incomplete phase diagram as it shows nothing of the solid phase. At any particular pressure there is a temperature, the melting point, at which the solid melts. In Fig. 5.15, the line TS shows the transition curve between the liquid and solid phases in the case of water.

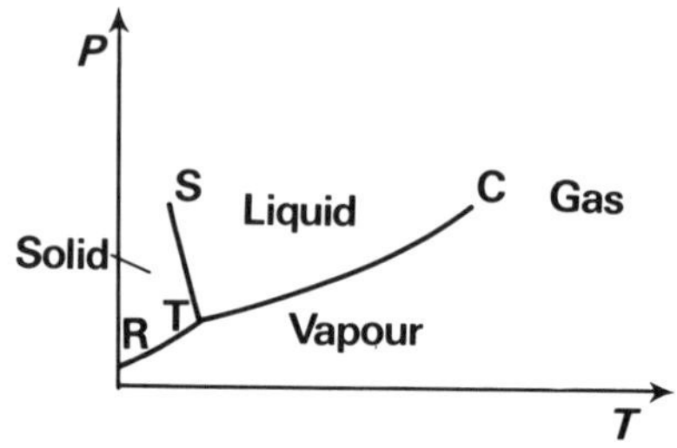

Fig. 5.15

The backward slope of TS indicates a fall in melting point with increasing pressure, and in this respect the behaviour of water is unusual. For the majority of substances, increase in pressure raises the melting point and the curve slopes in the opposite direction as shown in Fig. 5.16.

The curve TC is the vapour-pressure curve, and the areas corresponding to the various stable phases are labelled on the phase diagrams. C is the *critical point*, above which temperature the gas cannot be liquefied by the application of pressure (See Chapter 6, Section 1). Above this temperature the liquid and gaseous phases cannot co-exist, so the vapour pressure curve terminates at C. It is usual to refer to *vapour* below the critical temperature and *gas* above it.

It is well known that molecules in the solid phase can escape to form a vapour. Therefore at any temperature there is an equilibrium saturated vapour pressure for the solid-vapour transition, represented by TR, The solid-vapour transition or *sublimation* as it is known, is particularly evident in the case of solid carbon dioxide (dry ice).

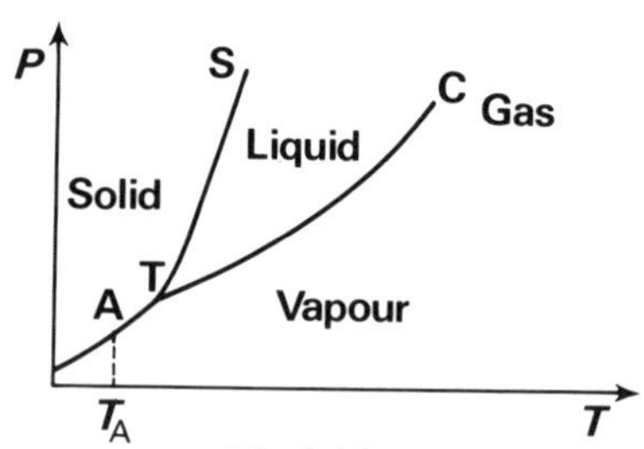

Fig. 5.16

Fig. 5.16 shows a phase diagram for carbon dioxide, and at the point A the pressure is atmospheric; at the corresponding temperature T_A, the solid phase is stable at pressures greater than atmospheric and the vapour at lower pressures. This diagram also shows that the liquid form cannot exist at any temperature at atmospheric pressure; it is only a stable phase at considerably greater pressures.

The point of intersection (T) of the three transition curves corresponds to the one set of conditions under which the three phases, solid, liquid and gas are able to exist together; this is the *triple point.* The triple point of water was referred to in Chapter 1, Section 10, in connection with the definition of a scale of temperature. It is 0.01 K above the melting point under normal atmospheric pressure, and corresponds to a pressure of 4.6 mm of mercury.

8 SATURATED VAPOUR PRESSURE OVER CURVED SURFACES

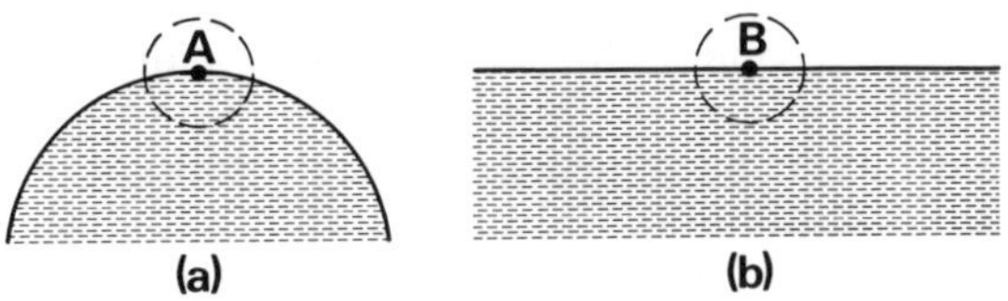

Fig. 5.17

A molecule at A in Fig. 5.17(a) is near a sharply-curved surface, and experiences a smaller force binding it to the surface than does the corresponding molecule at B, close to the flat surface of Fig. 5.17(b). The circles in the diagrams represent the spheres of molecular action for the particular molecules, i.e. the volumes within which the molecular attractions can be considered significant (see Chapter 7, Section 1). It is apparent that the number of liquid molecules exerting significant attractions on A is smaller than for B. It follows that at a given temperature a larger number of molecules escape per second from a convex surface than from a plane one. Consequently the equilibrium vapour pressure over such a surface is greater than over a flat surface. Similar considerations of the forces acting on a molecule near a concave liquid surface show that the equilibrium vapour pressure is reduced in this case.

It can be established that this pressure change is

$$2\gamma\sigma/r\rho$$

where γ is the surface tension of the liquid, σ and ρ are the densities of the vapour and liquid respectively, and r is the radius of curvature of the surface.

This effect is small unless the curvature of the surface is very great indeed, i.e. r is very small. In the case of a water drop of radius 10^{-3} mm, the pressure change is only 1 part in 800 of the normal vapour pressure, but for a drop of 10^{-6} mm radius, the saturated vapour pressure is doubled. Thus if a drop when first formed has a radius of the order of 10^{-6} mm, it will immediately re-evaporate unless there is a very high degree of super-saturation. It is thus apparent that if there are no dust particles or other nuclei present, condensation does not normally occur when the state of saturation is reached.

However, the situation is altered considerably by the presence of ions; the minute drop formed around the ion is charged and has a tendency to expand, which to some extent counter-balances the tendency of the drop to contract its surface area due to its surface tension. In effect the surface tension of the liquid is reduced so that a smaller degree of super-saturation is required than is the case for uncharged drops; thus condensation does occur with the ions serving as nuclei.

The Wilson cloud chamber contains dust-free air saturated with vapour. As a result of an adiabatic expansion the temperature falls so that a super-saturation is produced which is sufficient to allow condensation on ions, but not without them. Any ionizing particle entering the chamber leaves a trail of ions on which condensation occurs, and its path is thus rendered visible.

A more recent technique of making visible the paths of such small charged particles is used in the bubble chamber, in this arrangement the chamber contains a liquid in a super-heated condition, so that although above its boiling point there are no vapour bubbles forming in the body of the liquid. A charged particle passing through the liquid gives up part of its energy to a small number of fast-moving electrons which produce a localized rise in temperature along the ionization path. This, together with the presence of charged nuclei, enables boiling to occur and thus the particle's trail is marked by a train of minute bubbles. The pressure on the liquid is arranged so that no boiling takes place until a charged particle passes through it. Liquid pentane and propane have both been used in such chambers, but it is more common to use liquid hydrogen; in one recently-developed chamber the hydrogen was in a large coffin-shaped stone vessel six feet long.

9 VAPORIZATION AND ENTROPY

We have already emphasized that the energy supplied to a liquid in order to vaporize it increases the potential energy of the molecules; since there is no temperature change there is no increase in the kinetic energy of the molecules. However, we can view the change from the liquid to the gaseous phase from a different point of view. Whereas in the liquid phase the molecular separation is more or less constant, the distance between these same molecules in the gaseous phase is continually changing. There is also a much greater spread of speeds in the gas than in the liquid. The short-range order which prevails in the liquid is replaced in the vapour by thorough disorder and the molecular motion is completely random. This reduction of order or a corresponding increase in randomness is a characteristic of the phase change from liquid to vapour. A similar change occurs in the transition from the highly ordered arrangement of the solid to the less ordered conditions in a liquid.

The *entropy* (S) of any system is a quantity which measures the degree of randomness of disorder which is present. Entropy increases with the randomness of the arrangement, and a liquid thus has a greater entropy than a solid; similarly a gas has a greater entropy than a liquid.

The entropy is related to the *probability* of the arrangement. In the absence of any external controlling agency an ordered arrangement is always less probable than a more disordered one. Considering the two extreme phases of matter, the ordered lattice of the solid is a much less probable arrangement in which to find the molecules than is the random distribution in the gas. We can draw an analogy with the shuffling of a pack of cards; we are most unlikely by chance to produce the cards in sequence in their respective suits.

Changes in entropy can be defined by the relation

$$\Delta S = \Delta Q/T \tag{5.3}$$

where ΔS is the entropy change resulting from the absorption of ΔQ units of heat at a temperature T, where it is also necessary that the energy flow is perfectly reversible; this means that it takes place slowly under an infinitesimal temperature difference. Eqn. (5.3) defines changes of entropy but gives no absolute definition of the quantity. As with potential energy any convenient zero level may be used in order to give a value to the quantity itself. It is, however, usual to consider a perfect crystal at the absolute zero of temperature as representing the state of zero entropy. In such a crystal all motion and randomness has disappeared and there is the maximum possible degree of order.

If we consider a pack of cards with the cards in an ordered arrangement any shuffling is likely to increase the randomness of the arrangement. Likewise, a definite arrangement of coloured balls on a tray becomes disordered as a consequence of shaking. In each of these cases it is extremely unlikely – but just possible – that an ordered arrangement could be brought about; this possibility can be envisaged on account of the relatively small number of cards or balls involved. When we consider the vast number of particles which make up even a tiny quantity of matter, we can see that the possibility of an ordered arrangement coming about by chance can be ignored. Considerations of this nature lead to the conclusions that all processes which occur spontaneously involve an increase in randomness or entropy. There are certainly cases where a local increase in order – and hence a decrease of entropy – occurs, but it will always be associated with a larger increase in entropy elsewhere. The general principle that

the total entropy never decreases

can be shown to be equivalent to the second law of thermodynamics considered in Chapter 4, Section 10.

It is readily confirmed that the ideal reversible heat engine considered in that section could operate under ideal conditions without any change in entropy. However, any imperfections and any irreversibility that arise in practice do involve an increase in entropy.

The increase in entropy accompanying vaporization is L/T, where L is the specific latent heat and T the boiling point. When this quotient is evaluated for a mole it is remarkably constant for a large number of gases, as indicated below.

ΔS_{vap}/ J K^{-1} mol^{-1}			
Oxygen	75.7	Benzene	88.8
Hydrogen chloride	85.9	Water	108.7
Hydrogen sulphide	87.7	Ethanol	112.5
Chloroform	88.2	Hydrogen	44.1
Diethyl ether	88.1	Helium	21.4
Sodium	84.4		

The constancy of L/T is often referred to as *Trouton's rule.* The cases where the entropy change is particularly high seem to correspond to the vaporizing of liquids which are known to be particularly ordered, even when near their boiling points. These results do seem to suggest that the increases in entropy are at any rate of the same orders of magnitude, even when the individual temperatures and energy changes are greatly different.

QUESTIONS

1. A space contains air and a small quantity of liquid. When the pressure is reduced from 760 mm of mercury to 400 mm, it is observed that the volume is doubled, while the pressure has to be reduced to 280 mm in order to treble the volume. Assuming the temperature to remain constant throughout, calculate the saturated vapour pressure, explaining the steps in your calculation.

   Discuss the effect of a further reduction in pressure.

2. A vessel contains water and air saturated with water vapour at 20 °C and 760 mm of mercury pressure. Calculate the pressure if the vessel is sealed and heated to 100 °C ignoring the expansion of the vessel and any change in volume of the water. Assume the s.v.p. of water at 20 °C = 17 mm. Would the water boil under these circumstances?

3. A vessel containing air, water vapour and a small quantity of water is maintained at 45 °C; the total pressure is found to be 150 mm of mercury. The vessel is then connected to another identical vessel which has been evacuated, and the whole apparatus maintained at 45 °C; when the final equilibrium is established it is observed that there is water present. Calculate the final pressure in the apparatus.

   (S.v.p. of water at 45 °C = 72 mm of mercury.)

4. A narrow uniform capillary tube, closed at the lower end and open at its upper end, contains a short water index trapping a volume of air between itself and the closed end. When the tube stands vertically immersed in a bath maintained at 30 °C, the length of the enclosed space is 15.5 cm. When the temperature of the bath is raised to 60 °C the length of the air space becomes 20.0 cm. If the saturation vapour pressure of the water at 30 °C is 31.7 mm of mercury, determine the s.v.p. at 60 °C assuming the atmospheric pressure to be 765 mm of mercury.

5. A mixture of air and saturated water vapour is contained in a closed vessel under a total pressure of 121 cm of mercury and a temperature of 75 °C. Calculate the pressure if (a) the temperature is reduced to 30 °C, and (b) at the new temperature the volume is halved.
(S.v.p. water at 75 °C = 289 mm of mercury; at 30 °C = 32 mm of mercury.)

6. A uniform capillary tube closed at its lower end has a column of air 16.5 cm long between the bottom of the tube and a short water index, when the temperature is 20 °C. Calculate the length of this column of air when the temperature of the tube is raised to 55 °C.
(S.v.p. water at 20 °C = 17 mmHg; at 55 °C = 118 mmHg; atmospheric pressure = 760 mm Hg.)

7. On a day when the atmospheric pressure is 10^5 N m^{-2}, a tube of length 1.00 m and cross-sectional area 10^{-4} m^2, which is closed at one end, is filled with air saturated with water vapour at 15 °C. A piston is now inserted into the tube and forced in until the pressure is doubled; the length under the piston is found to be 49.5 cm if the temperature is maintained constant. Estimate the saturated vapour pressure of water and the mass of water which condenses during the compression.

8. Moist air exerting a pressure of 750 mm of mercury at 50 °C is cooled in a closed vessel of constant volume, condensation commencing at 30 °C. What will be the pressure in the vessel at 10 °C ?
(S.v.p. of water at 50 °C = 92 mm of mercury; at 30 °C = 31 mm; at 10 °C = 9 mm. Assume that water vapour obeys the ideal gas laws up to the point of saturation.)

9. The vessel shown in the diagram contains a mixture of water and water vapour but no air. Explain why, if the sphere B is surrounded with a bath of liquid air, all the water in the sphere A freezes after a time.

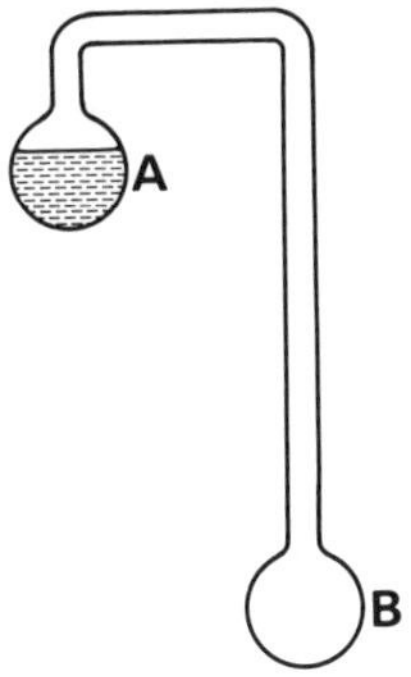

Fig. 5.18

The Properties of Real Gases

6

In Chapter 5 we investigated the properties of the vapours arising from those liquids which were, for the most part, stable under normal laboratory conditions of pressure and temperature. Ether, alcohol and water vapour are typical examples; at room temperatures an increase in pressure on any of these vapours leads to liquefaction.

We now proceed to consider how the properties of real gases differ from those of the ideal gas, and this is most conveniently carried out by investigating how accurately these gases obey Boyle's law. The vapours we have already considered showed marked deviations from this law, mainly as a consequence of inter-molecular attractions, and our investigations should indicate to what extent these attractions are important in the behaviour of real gases such as air. Many of the experiments to be described need very large pressures; not only are these difficult to produce and apply, but their measurement poses very difficult problems indeed. For these reasons it is almost impossible to carry such out investigations in the school laboratory, and we must be content with a historical survey of the various experiments.

We begin with a series of experiments carried out on carbon dioxide, a gas which can be condensed at room temperature if a sufficiently large pressure is applied to it. Subsequently we shall be concerned with the so-called 'permanent' gases such as air. It was early apparent that they could not be readily liquefied by pressure and this fact gave rise to the misnomer.

1 ANDREWS' EXPERIMENTS ON CARBON DIOXIDE

In 1863 Andrews carried out a series of experiments to measure the compressibility of carbon dioxide at various temperatures. The gas was contained in a glass tube of the shape shown in Fig. 6.1; the upper part was a narrow capillary whilst the wider central portion had a bore of 2.5 mm. At its lower end the gas was confined by a mercury thread, and the tube was inserted in the H-shaped copper vessel, which was filled with water as shown. An exactly similar tube in the other part of the apparatus contained air; equal pressures were applied to the tubes by screwing in the two plungers at the bottom. The capillary portions had previously been accurately calibrated using a mercury thread of known volume, and thus the volumes of carbon dioxide and air under the various pressures applied could be measured.

Pressures up to 100 atmospheres were applied and calculated on the

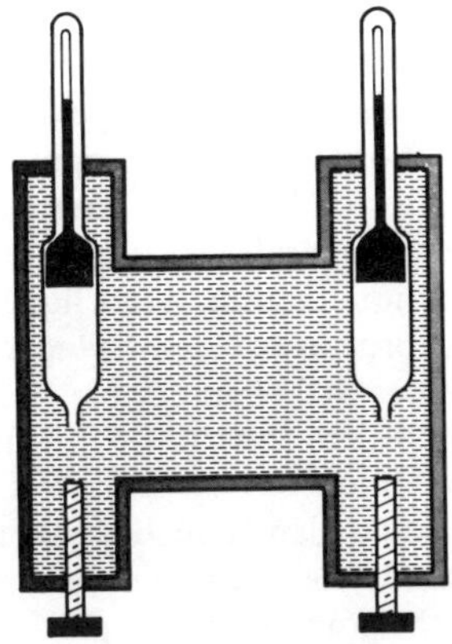

Fig. 6.1

assumption that the air was behaving as an ideal gas and thus obeying Boyle's law exactly. Since the deviations of carbon dioxide from the ideal are so very much greater than those of air over the same range the error introduced by this assumption was of little significance. The upper part of the carbon dioxide tube was inserted in a water bath, and experiments were carried out at various temperatures below 50 °C. The results obtained are shown in Fig. 6.2 where pressure is plotted against volume for a number of temperatures giving a series of isothermals.

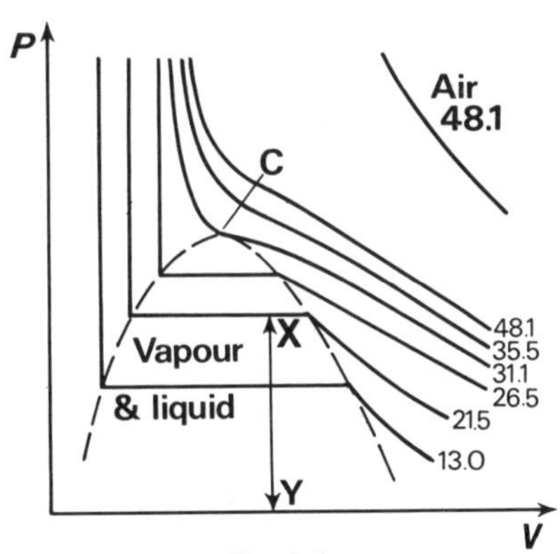

Fig. 6.2

The curves for the lower temperatures show a horizontal portion where the volumes decrease suddenly at a constant pressure, and this represents the process of liquefaction. Above 31.1 °C there is no sign of any such horizontal region although the curves depart from the rectangular hyperbolae to be expected for an ideal gas. Comparison of the isothermal for carbon dioxide at 48 °C with that for air at a similar temperature shows that the carbon dioxide curve is less steep except at the higher pressures, indicating that the gas is easier to compress than air. This is also true in those parts of the isothermals for lower temperatures which correspond to the smaller pressures, i.e. those in the lower right-hand part of the diagram. This greater ease of compression becomes more marked with increasing pressure and for the lower temperatures culminates in the sudden decrease in volume associated with liquefaction. After liquefaction the curves are very nearly parallel to the pressure axis, showing that considerable further increases of pressure produce little appreciable change in volume.

As the temperature increases, the change in volume between the liquid and gaseous phases becomes less but up to 31.1 °C there are clear signs of the change of phase. It should also be realized that the constant pressure during the change of phase is the saturated vapour pressure for that temperature, i.e. XY on the graph is the s.v.p. of carbon dioxide at 21.5 °C.

Above 31.1 °C there is no sign of liquefaction although there is a region where the volume of carbon dioxide changes rapidly with increase of pressure. As the temperature rises further this region of very easy compression becomes less noticeable, although the gas is still somewhat more easily compressed than air. This temperature above which there is no sign of liquefaction, 31.1 °C in the case of carbon dioxide, is defined as the *critical temperature.*

It would seem that above the critical temperature, no matter how large a pressure is applied to the gas, no liquefaction occurs. The dotted curve in Fig. 6.2, which passes through the ends of the horizontal sections of the isothermals, therefore bounds the region in which liquid and vapour can exist together; to the left of the curve the liquid is the stable phase, and to the right of it only the vapour is found. The maximum of this dotted curve at C is the point where the isothermal for 31.1 °C seems to flatten out but does not quite do so; in mathematical terms C is a horizontal point of inflection. The pressure and volume in respect of unit mass, corresponding to C, are known as the *critical pressure* and *critical volume*; some typical values are shown in the table on page 113.

The term *gas* is normally reserved for a gaseous substance *above* its critical temperature, whilst *below* this temperature we refer to the *vapour.* Gases such as oxygen, nitrogen and hydrogen were at one time referred to as 'permanent gases' because attempts to liquefy them by the application of pressures up to 2 000 atmospheres had failed; this was simply because their critical temperatures happened to be below the ordinary laboratory temperatures at which these attempts were made.

2 CONTINUITY OF LIQUID AND GASEOUS PHASES

The existence of a critical temperature had also been indicated by experiments carried out many years earlier by Cagniard de la Tour in 1822. He confined a small quantity of liquid (e.g. water or ether) in a bulb which previously had been thoroughly evacuated. As shown in Fig. 6.3 the liquid floated on mercury, whilst the region above the mercury in the other, closed limb contained air. The whole apparatus was heated in an oil bath, and as the temperature rose more liquid evaporated so that it exerted an

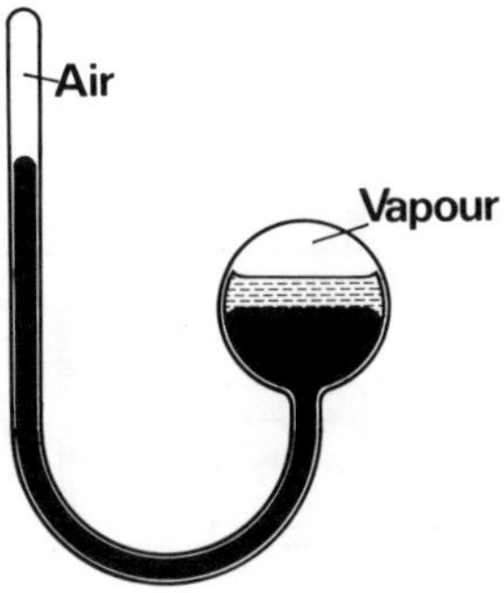

Fig. 6.3

increasing vapour pressure. The liquid was unable to boil since it was always under its own vapour pressure; thus the pressure inside bubbles in the body of the liquid could not exceed the pressure outside the bubble in the liquid, as is necessary for the growth of a bubble. However, as the temperature increased the meniscus became flatter, indicating a lower surface tension of the liquid phase, and at a certain temperature the meniscus completely disappeared, the whole contents of the tube appearing homogeneous. It thus appeared that above this temperature there were no longer the two phases, liquid and vapour, in the tube and it was de la Tour who first referred to this temperature as the *critical temperature.* Cooling of the tube from above the critical temperature brought a reappearance of the meniscus at precisely the critical temperature. The critical temperature of water is approximately 374 °C, and a number of other values are given in the table below. This also shows values of critical

Table of critical constants

Substance	Critical Temperature °C	Critical Pressure Atmospheres	Critical Density kg $m^{-3} \times 10^{-3}$
Water	374	219	0.4
Ether	197	36	
Sulphur dioxide	155	79	0.52
Ammonia	130	115	0.24
Freon 115	80	31	
Carbon dioxide	31.1	73	0.46
Oxygen	−118	50	0.43
Nitrogen	−146	33	0.31
Hydrogen	−240	13	0.03
Helium	−268	2.3	0.07

pressures which de la Tour estimated from the compression of the air in the closed limb: it will be noticed that these are very high pressures, and it is this fact which is responsible for the difficulty of carrying out the experiment in the school laboratory for most gases.

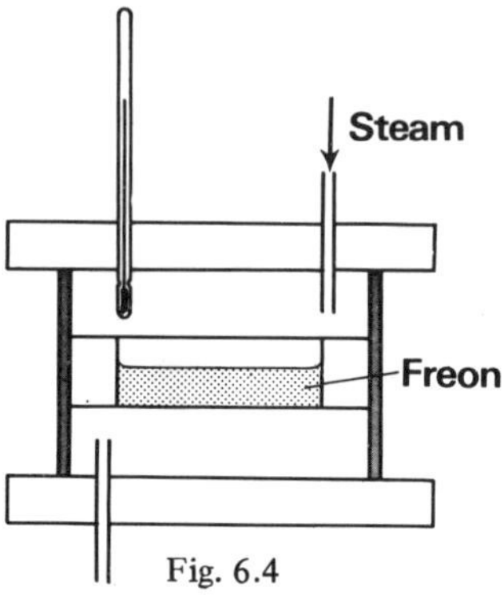

Fig. 6.4

The arrangement of Fig. 6.4 can, however, be used in the laboratory to show the critical temperature of Freon, which is about 87 °C, so that the sealed container can be heated by a steam bath. An image of the meniscus is is focused on the screen so that the sudden disappearance and subsequent re-appearance of the meniscus can be clearly seen.

The existence of surface tension is the essential characteristic of the liquid phase. As a result of the molecular attractions responsible for this property, only the more energetic molecules are able to escape into the vapour phase with its associated greater potential energy. As the temperature rises a larger proportion are enabled so to escape and eventually the cohesive forces are unable to maintain the molecules within a liquid meniscus; the absence of the meniscus implies that the liquid phase has ceased to exist. The rise in temperature decreases the density of the liquid and at the same time the pressure – and hence the density of the vapour – increase until at the critical temperature the two densities are equal.

Although an experiment such as that described does give a clear indication of the existence of the critical point, a difficulty in understanding the results arises when one considers them in detail in the light of the isothermals of Fig. 6.5. If we start with a volume per unit mass corresponding to the point L, and heat it at constant volume, the proportion in the liquid phase increases and the meniscus moves up the tube. When the state reached corresponds to M, the tube contains only liquid and the temperature is certainly less than the critical temperature. On the other hand if there are initially a much smaller number of molecules in the tube, the volume per unit mass at the original temperature is greater than previously; this implies a greater proportion of molecules in the vapour phase and corresponds to a point such as N. On heating the meniscus would move down the tube, and at O the tube would be completely full of vapour at a temperature which is also below the critical. It would seem that the sudden disappearance of the meniscus at the critical temperature only occurs when exactly the appropriate number of molecules are originally in the tube, so that the overall density is exactly equal to the critical value.

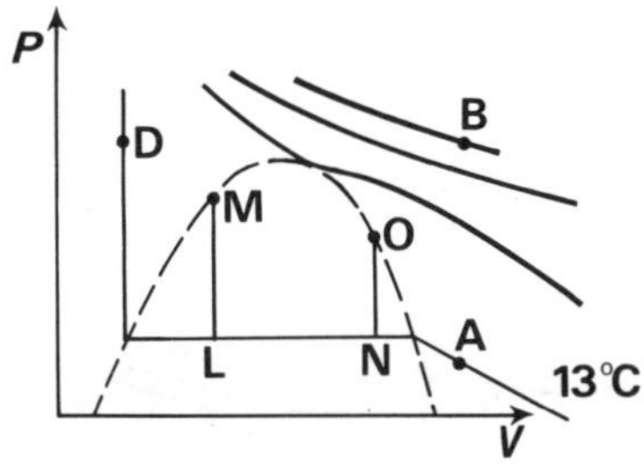

Fig. 6.5

At the critical point the densities of the liquid and vapour are equal, but a careful investigation has shown that the meniscus separating the two phases disappears over a wide region where there is a considerable difference in the density of the two phases. Experiments have been carried out using small glass spheres suspended on a sensitive quartz spiral so that the difference between their weight and the fluid upthrust acting on them could be measured in various parts of the liquid and vapour by moving the spiral. In experiments with propylene it was established that density differences existed at as much as 6 °C below the critical temperature although there was no sign of a meniscus.

The point A in Fig. 6.5 clearly corresponds to the state of an unsaturated vapour. If it is heated and at the same time the pressure increased so that the volume is kept constant, the vapour rises through the critical temperature, and at B is a gas, although it is under a high pressure. Cooling at a constant pressure from B eventually brings the substance to the state represented by the point D on the isothermal for 13 °C, and this certainly corresponds to conditions where all the substance is in the liquid phase. At no stage of the transformation from vapour at A to liquid at D did the state of the substance pass through the region bounded by the dotted curve on the graph; it is only within this region that liquid and vapour can co-exist, so at no time was there a meniscus in the vessel. There has therefore been a steady change from one phase to the other, and this suggests the essential *continuity of the two phases.*

3 *PV–P* ISOTHERMALS

The results of experiments such as those of Andrews on carbon dioxide are often represented by graphs of the product of pressure and volume, PV, against P. These have the advantage of showing more clearly smaller deviations from the ideal. ABDE in Fig. 6.6 is an isothermal for a gas well below its critical temperature. The isothermal for an ideal gas would be a straight line parallel to the P axis, and the downward trend of AB shows that with increasing pressure PV decreases below the value expected for an

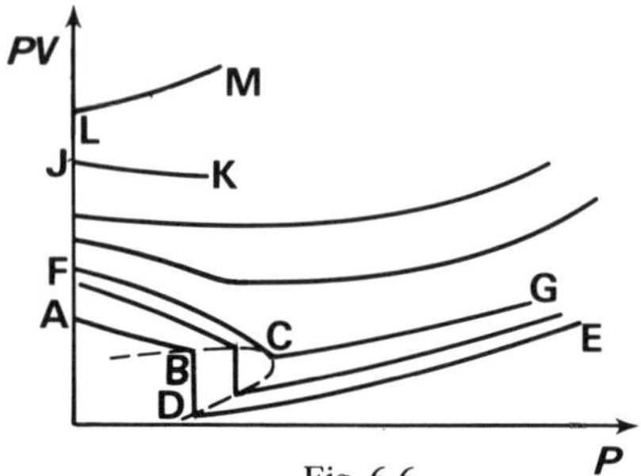

Fig. 6.6

ideal gas. Thus, for a certain increase in pressure, the volume decrease is greater than that of an ideal gas. This means that the gas is more readily compressible than the ideal.

The vertical portion BD represents the process of liquefaction with its large sudden volume change at a constant pressure – the saturation vapour pressure appropriate to the temperature. The subsequent steady rise of PV corresponds to the liquid state, where the volume changes little as the pressure increases.

As the temperature increases, the vertical part of the isothermal becomes shorter and eventually disappears completely in the curve FCG for the critical temperature. Several isothermals are also shown for higher temperatures and it is evident that both the regions of greater and less easy compressibility remain, although there is no liquefaction.

In order to obtain information about the behaviour of gases at temperatures above the critical, it is useful to consider the so-called 'permanent' gases whose critical temperatures are considerably below room temperature and the next section is concerned with compressibility experiments on these gases.

4 EXPERIMENTS OF REGNAULT AND AMAGAT

The first systematic attempts to detect any deviations from Boyle's law for air and the other 'permanent' gases were carried out by Regnault, who in 1847 measured the volumes of gases subjected to pressures up to about 15 atmospheres. The gas was confined over mercury in a vessel of accurately known volume at a pressure measured on a mercury manometer consisting of a very long tube whose upper end was open to the air. The pressure was increased until the volume was precisely halved and then the pressure was measured again. The experiment was repeated after admitting more gas to the vessel so that it was initially full of gas at the higher pressure.

His results showed that the product PV decreased with increasing pressure for air, nitrogen and carbon dioxide, but increased in the case of hydrogen. Thus a typical isothermal for air would be JK in Fig. 6.6, while that for hydrogen could be represented by LM.

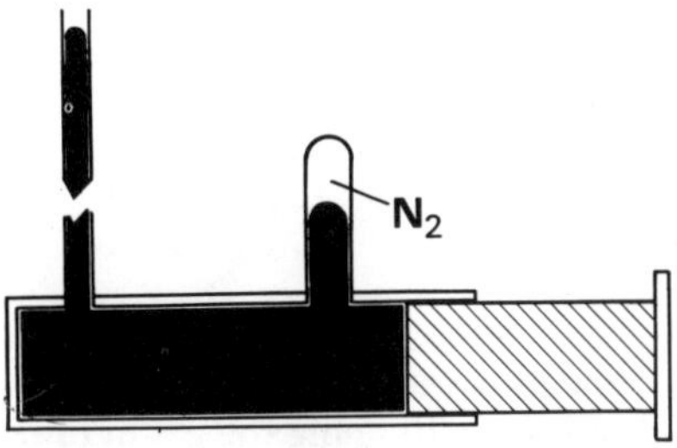

Fig. 6.7

A much more comprehensive series of experiments were carried out by Amagat between 1869 and 1893. Nitrogen was the first gas to be investigated using pressures up to 300 atmospheres, which were obtained by a screw plunger arrangement as shown in Fig. 6.7, and then measured by an open air manometer similar to that used in Regnault's investigations. The great length required was obtained by constructing the manometer tube from a very large number of rifle barrels screwed together and supported inside a tower some 65 feet high. Later the whole apparatus was placed at the bottom of a coal mine so that a much higher column could be conveniently supported. Once he had obtained detailed information concerning the behaviour of nitrogen, he was able to extend his experiments with other gases without the use of the open-air manometer. Equal pressures were applied to the gas under test and to nitrogen, and the pressure was calculated from the change in volume in nitrogen using the compressibility data obtained for nitrogen in the first series of experiments using nitrogen.

It was possible to measure pressures up to 400 atmospheres by the method just indicated, but in order to extend the range of his experiments Amagat used a pressure balance of the type shown in Fig. 6.8. The double piston is in equilibrium between the high pressure to be measured, which is applied to the small end X, and a much smaller pressure which is applied to the larger end Y, as indicated in the diagram. The major problems were the prevention of leaks and the avoidance of any tendency for the piston to stick; treacle was used to overcome the former difficulty and the piston was kept rotating continuously to remove the latter trouble. The sizes of the pistons were chosen so that even at pressures of the order of 3 000 atmospheres the pressure on the low pressure side could be easily measured with a mercury manometer.

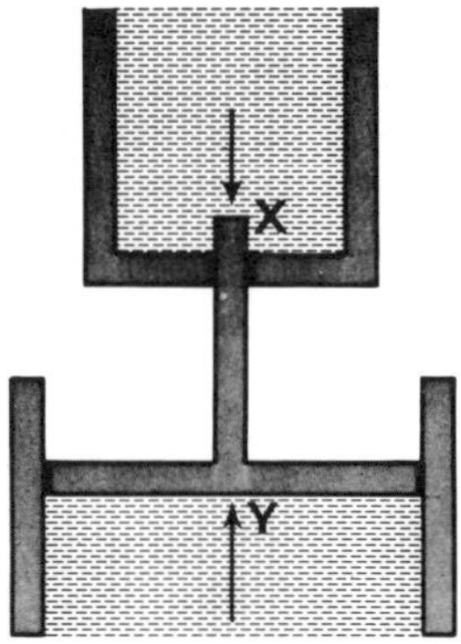

Fig. 6.8

Above 400 atmospheres it was necessary to apply an equal pressure to the outside of the glass tube containing the gas in order to prevent it bursting; this necessitated enclosing the tube in a steel cylinder S and it was no longer possible to observe the mercury meniscus directly in order to measure the volume occupied by the gas. A number of platinum wires were sealed into the capillary part of the tube as indicated in Fig. 6.9; as the mercury rose in the tube it completed a different electrical circuit as it reached each wire. The pressure was transmitted through water onto the surface of the mercury, initially by a force pump and subsequently by screwing in the plunger P at the top.

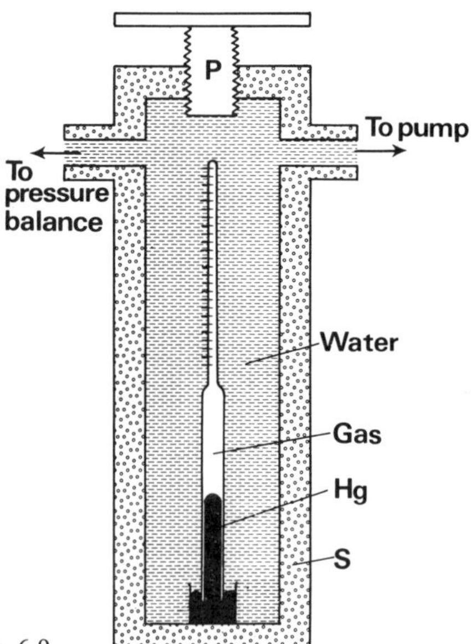

Fig. 6.9

5 THE EXPERIMENTS OF HOLBORN

At the high pressures reached by Amagat the volume of the gas becomes exceedingly small, and in fact Amagat's apparatus was even longer and thinner than is indicated in Fig. 6.9. The accurate measurement of such a small volume presents increased difficulties; in the earlier experiments of Regnault the difficulty was avoided by varying the mass of gas under investigation, and in the series of experiments he carried out in 1915 Holborn chose to measure the *mass* of gas required to fill a *fixed volume* at various high pressures.

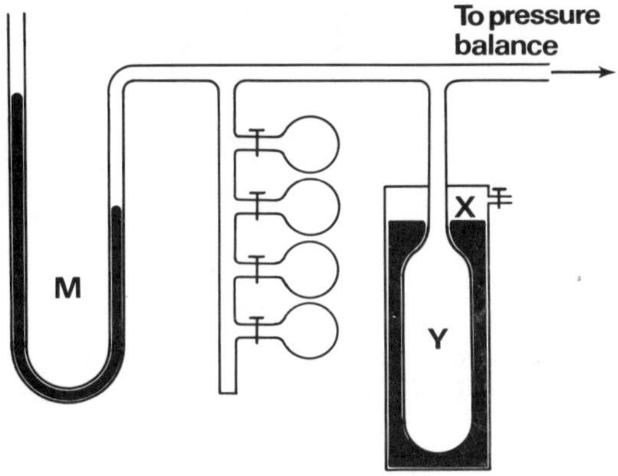

Fig. 6.10

Holborn used a glass vessel Y of volume about 200 cm^3; this was surrounded by mercury which was in a steel container so that by applying compressed air to X the pressures inside and outside the vessel could be kept equal. The arrangement is indicated schematically in Fig. 6.10. This part of the apparatus was then placed in an oil bath (which is not shown in the figure) so that it could be maintained at any required temperature. After the vessel had been filled at a particular high pressure – which was measured – the gas was allowed to expand into a large number of graduated containers indicated by the four shown in the diagram; taps to the containers of various volumes were opened until the pressure had fallen to a value near atmospheric, which was then measured on the mercury manometer M; in the actual set-up these containers had a very much greater volume than is indicated on the diagram. Since the density of the gas at pressures near atmospheric is accurately known, this last volume reading at a known low pressure and temperature enables the mass of gas to be calculated; this is the mass which originally filled the cylinder at a high pressure.

This high pressure was measured by a balance of the type indicated in

Fig. 6.11. The tube at A was connected to the gas under pressure, and the oil transmitted this pressure to the under surface of the rod B, which fitted into a channel in the metal block C which was itself firmly clamped in a fixed position. The upward force on the rod was balanced by weights

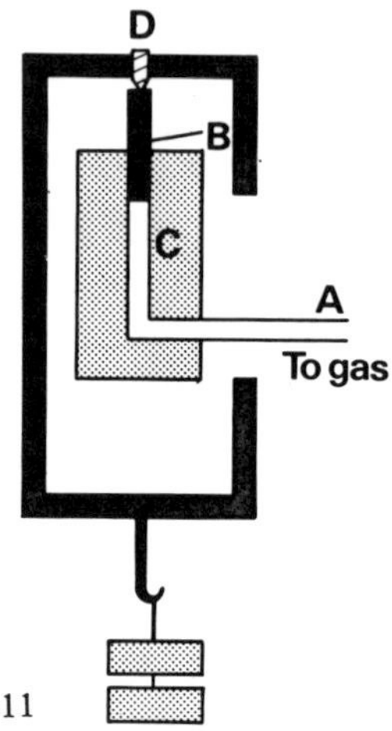

Fig. 6.11

hung from the framework, so that the pressure was applied to B through the end of the screw D. The effect of friction was reduced by suitable lubrication between B and C by means of a slow stream of liquid continuously issuing from the top of C, and also by arranging for B to rotate slowly throughout the experiment.

More recent investigations such as those of Bridgman have used pressures up to 100 000 atmospheres and special techniques have been developed to prevent leakage and damage to the containing vessels under these pressures. In many cases the volumes have been measured using mercury and electrical contact wires in the manner previously employed by Amagat. The change in electric resistance of a wire subject to pressure has often been used to measure these huge pressures instead of a direct form of pressure balance.

6 THE GENERAL BEHAVIOUR OF GASES

The isothermals shown in Fig. 6.12 represent the behaviour of all gases; in each case the curves at the top of the page represent higher temperatures, but the actual temperature corresponding to any particular curve varies from gas to gas. No scales are shown because, provided the scales of pressure and volume are suitably chosen, the one set of curves will represent the behaviour of any particular gas.

At temperatures below the critical temperature C, there is a clear indication of liquefaction. Above C, all gases show an initial drop in the

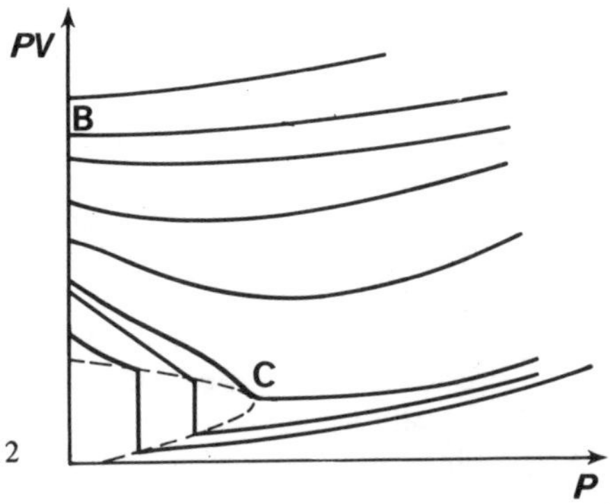

Fig. 6.12

product PV as the pressure increases, but this effect decreases with increasing temperature, until it disappears completely at the *Boyle temperature* B. The isothermal for B begins parallel to the P axis, and at this temperature there is little departure from Boyle's law over a considerable range of pressures. Whereas the Boyle temperature of nitrogen is 323 K (50 °C), for hydrogen it is 109 K, and for helium 23 K.

The downward trend of the PV isothermals, indicating that the gas is easier to compress than an ideal gas, is a consequence of the inter-molecular attractions which below the critical temperature are sufficiently powerful to bring about liquefaction. At higher temperatures the greater kinetic energy of the molecules prevents them from cohering in such a manner as to lead to the liquid phase but, nevertheless, any increase of pressure brings about a larger change in volume than would be the case with an ideal gas.

The resistance of a liquid to compression indicates that at a sufficiently small separation the molecules exert very great repulsive force on one another. On a simple picture of the molecules as solid spheres, this repulsion is the force brought suddenly into existence as the molecules make contact with each other; such forces become important as soon as it is no longer permissible to ignore the size of the molecules themselves. Later in the next chapter we will consider in some detail the nature of this repulsive force between molecules.

The various experiments so far considered in this chapter show the deviations from the ideal gas equation that are found in practice for real gases. These deviations can be explained in a general manner in terms of forces between molecules, and thus suggest looking for more direct evidence of the existence of these forces.

7 DIRECT EVIDENCE FOR INTERMOLECULAR ATTRACTIONS

When a gas confined by a piston in a cylinder expands, it does work against the force pressing on the other side of the piston. However, if there is a vacuum on this other side, the only work it can be called upon to do is against forces of internal attraction between its molecules. If such attractions exist, an increase of the distance between molecules entails an increase in potential energy. If the container is perfectly lagged so that no heat can flow into the gas, this increased potential energy can only come from the kinetic energy of the molecules, and any decrease in this represents a fall in temperature. Thus a gas of attracting molecules undergoing such a free expansion in an insulated container cools.

In 1845 Joule carried out an experiment hoping to show such a cooling as direct evidence of the existence of inter-molecular attractions. His apparatus, indicated schematically in Fig. 6.13 consisted of two metal containers connected by a pipe, fitted with a stop-cock.

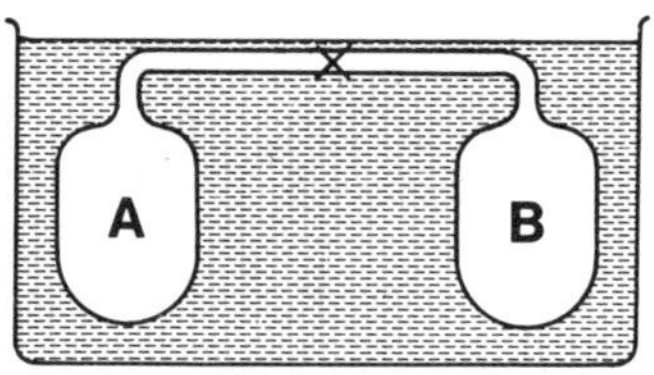

Fig. 6.13

One of the vessels, A, was filled with dry air at a pressure of 22 atmospheres, whilst the other, B, was thoroughly evacuated. The whole apparatus was immersed in water in a vessel with a thermometer which enabled the temperature to be read to 0.005 °F.

When the stop-cock was opened, air expanded from A into B until the pressures in A and B became equal. No external work was performed in this process. The first small quantity of air entering B expands into a vacuum. Thereafter the air passing into B does work in compressing the air already in this container, and as a result heat is generated. The energy for this work is provided by the cooling of the gas in A; in the absence of any inter-molecular forces the heating and cooling effects are equal. Thus if the two containers are enclosed in the same bath, which is thoroughly stirred, no change in temperature would result on this account.

However, if there are forces of attraction between the molecules, the increased average separation of the molecules resulting from the expansion requires the performance of work; this work increases the potential energy of the molecules, and does so at the expense of their kinetic energy. Thus such a gas should show a cooling.

Joule was unable to detect any temperature change, but this was a consequence of the large thermal capacity of this apparatus. He did not, however, conclude that these inter-molecular attractions did not exist, but rather that they were too small to be detected by his apparatus, and in 1853 in collaboration with William Thomson (later to become Lord Kelvin) designed a more sensitive apparatus which we now consider.

8 THE POROUS PLUG EXPERIMENT

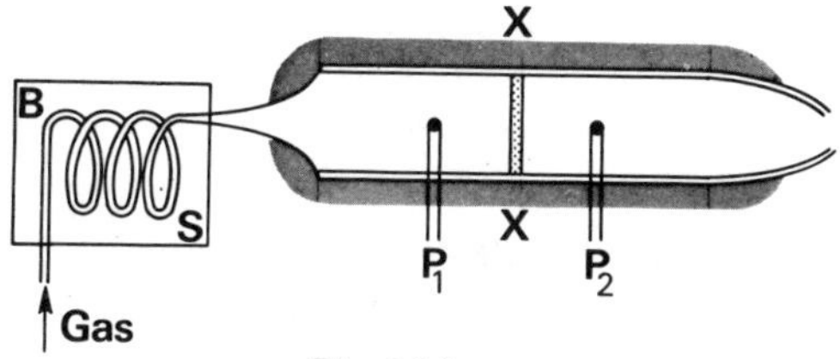

Fig. 6.14

The essentials of the apparatus are shown in Fig. 6.14. The gas from a compressor passed through a spiral tube S in a water bath B so that is was cooled to the required temperature, and then it was allowed to expand through the large number of holes in a wad of cotton wool, represented by X in the diagram. Platinum resistance thermometers P_1 and P_2 measured the temperature of the gas just before it reached the plug and also immediately after it emerged on the other side. The cotton wool plug was in a wooden tube which was surrounded by a vessel containing a large quantity of lagging so that the gas was effectively completely thermally isolated. It will be shown later that provided the gas obeys Boyle's law there is no net expenditure of external work in the expansion through the plug; the work done by the gas in pushing that ahead of it through the plug is exactly balanced by the work done on it by the gas behind it. On the other hand, if there are inter-molecular forces against which work is done, i.e. if the internal potential energy of the gas is increased there will be a cooling as it expands, since the energy for this work can only come from the kinetic energy of the molecules.

Joule and Thomson carried out the experiment with a number of gases using initial pressures up to about six atmospheres. They found that oxygen, nitrogen and carbon dioxide all showed a cooling on expansion in this way, but that hydrogen showed a rise in temperature. The temperature change, which is known as the *Joule-Thomson* or *Joule-Kelvin* effect was found to be proportional to the pressure decrease during expansion; in the case of air at room temperature it was about 0.2 °C per atmosphere. Subsequent experiments have shown that helium exhibits a heating effect at room temperature, but that both in this case and that of hydrogen, the increase in temperature gets less as the initial temperature is reduced, and that in each case at a low enough temperature there is a cooling effect.

The results provide clear evidence of inter-molecular attractions for all gases except hydrogen and helium at room temperature, but seem to indicate a repulsion in the case of these two gases. However, a thorough consideration of the energy changes involved in the passage of the gas through the porous plug shows that the effect of external work must be taken into account.

Let unit mass of gas, initially at a pressure P_1, occupy a volume V_1

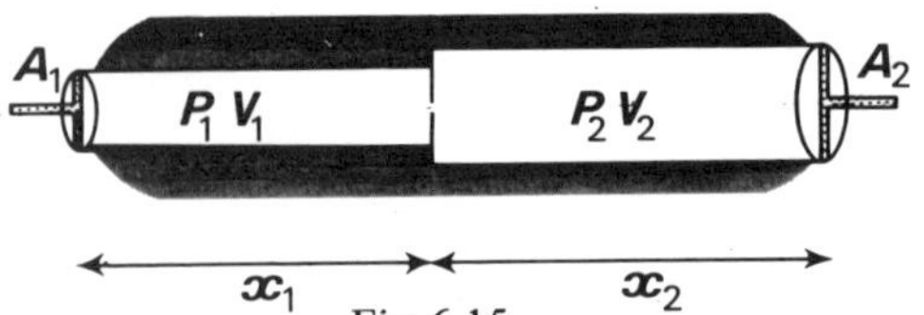

Fig. 6.15

before it expands, and a volume V_2 after it passes through the plug and its pressure has fallen to P_2, as indicated in Fig. 6.15.

Imagine the gas on the high pressure side of the apparatus to be in a cylinder fitted with a frictionless piston of area A_1. The force which acts on the piston in order to drive the gas through the plug is $P_1 A_1$, and if the piston travels a distance x_1 in forcing unit mass through the plug, the work done on the gas is

$$P_1 A_1 x_1.$$

Since $V_1 = A_1 x_1$, this work is

$$P_1 V_1.$$

In a similar way it can be shown that the work done *by* this gas as it emerges from the plug is $P_2 V_2$.

In the case of an ideal gas

$$P_1 V_1 = P_2 V_2$$

and thus no external work is done, but this will not be the case for any real gas.

When the gas is below the Boyle temperature, PV decreases with increasing pressure, as can be seen from Fig. 6.12 on page 121; thus $P_2 V_2 > P_1 V_1$, and more work is done by the gas than is done on it. It can only do this work at the expense of its molecular kinetic energy, and consequently it cools. So below the Boyle temperature this external work effect produces a cooling which augments that resulting from inter-molecular attractions.

Above the Boyle temperature, reference to Fig. 6.12 shows that

$$P_2 V_2 < P_1 V_1$$

so that the gas has more work done on it as it passes through the plug than it is called upon to perform, and consequently its temperature rises, as the extra energy is converted into kinetic energy of the molecules.

Thus *just* above the Boyle temperature this heating effect will tend to offset the cooling arising from inter-molecular attractions.

The external work effect becomes greater with increasing temperature; thus, as the temperature rises the over-all resultant cooling becomes less.

At the *temperature of inversion* the heating from the net external work done on the gas is exactly equal to the cooling from the effect of inter-molecular attractions, and there is no temperature change of the gas.

At higher temperatures the external work effect is the larger effect, and a resultant rise in temperature is observed.

Thus the resultant cooling below the *inversion temperature*, becomes a rise in temperature above it.

The apparent differences in the behaviour of gases arise because all the common gases except hydrogen and helium have inversion temperatures well above room temperature.

The cooling arising from the Joule-Kelvin effect is utilized in the Linde method for the liquefaction of gases, which is described in detail on page 145.

The table below shows the characteristic temperatures for a number of common gases. All temperatures are expressed on the absolute scale, i.e. they are measured from the absolute zero of – 273 °C. It will be noticed that the Boyle temperature is always considerably lower than the inversion temperature, as would be expected from the considerations of the Joule-Kelvin effect in the earlier part of this section.

Gas	*Critical Temperature* K	*Inversion Temperature* K	*Boyle Temperature* K	*Normal Boiling point* K
Helium	5	30	23	4.2
Hydrogen	32	190	109	20
Nitrogen	127	> 300	323	77
Oxygen	155	> 300	423	90
Argon	156	> 300	410	87
Carbon dioxide	304	> 500	> 600	195

QUESTIONS

1. Give a survey of experiments which suggest the existence of a critical temperature. Draw a number of P– V isothermals for a gas in the region of its critical temperature, and label clearly the particular isothermal corresponding to the critical temperature.

2. Explain what is meant by the 'continuity of the liquid and gaseous phases', and explain your answer by reference to a set of P– V isothermals for any gas you choose.

3. Give a summary of the experiments which show the deviations of gases such as air from Boyle's law. Draw graphs to show the deviations, and explain in general terms why they come about.

4. Explain the terms *critical temperature, Boyle temperature* and *inversion temperature.* Place them in order of increasing temperature and attempt to justify this order.

5. Describe an experiment or experiments which provide direct evidence of the existence of attractions between gas molecules.

Inter-molecular Forces 7

The experimental results of the last chapter can be explained in a general manner in terms of an attraction between molecules which are relatively close to one another, provided we bear in mind that as the molecules come even closer their finite size becomes significant. Thus their size prevents them approaching so that the distance between their centres is less than the molecular diameter.

The way in which the ideal gas equation can be modified to take into account these two effects was first investigated by van der Waals in 1873, and we now follow his method of analysis of the problem. We then proceed to consider the nature of the forces between molecules in more detail and discuss how they are brought into being.

1 VAN DER WAALS' EQUATION OF STATE

Whenever two molecules collide, the molecule moving in a particular direction 'gains' a distance of the order of a molecular diameter. If the collision is head-on, we can imagine that the colliding molecules exchange velocities. As far as an outside observer is concerned, they have effectively exchanged identities; as a result of the collision each has 'jumped' along its path a distance equal to the molecular diameter. As a consequence of the extremely small mean free path under normal conditions there is a very large number of collisions occurring in a small distance, and so a molecule travels across its container from one wall to the opposite one in a smaller time than would point molecules travelling with the same speed: thus collisions occur more rapidly. Alternatively, we may say that these molecules of finite size collide with the wall at the same rate as would point particles in a container of somewhat smaller size. The reduction in effective volume corresponds to the space which at any instant is occupied by other molecules, and which is consequently not available to the particular molecule.

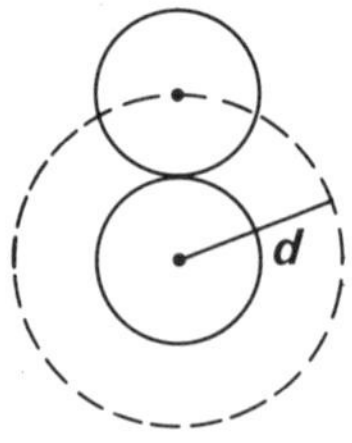

Fig. 7.1

Fig. 7.1 shows that this space is a sphere which surrounds each molecule and is of radius equal to the molecular diameter (d). Adding such spaces for all the n molecules in unit volume, we obtain

$$4\pi nd^3/3$$

for the total forbidden volume. However, in this enumeration each of the n molecules has been counted twice: once as the molecule at the centre of such a sphere of forbidden space, and once in the sphere surrounding another molecule. The correct forbidden volume is therefore

$$2\pi nd^3/3.$$

This volume is usually represented by b'. We can assert that a gas with molecules of finite size exerts the same pressure when in a container of volume V as would an ideal gas consisting of the same number of molecules having the same mass and at the same temperature in a volume $(V - b')$.

If we consider a mole of gas, the corresponding constant – which is frequently referred to as the *co-volume* – is represented by b. Thus for a mole of gas exerting a pressure P at a temperature T,

$$P(V - b) = RT. \tag{7.1}$$

Eqn. (7.1) suggests that the equation of state will be of the form

$$PV = RT + bP$$

leading to isothermals such as those indicated in Fig. 7.2, since b is necessarily positive.

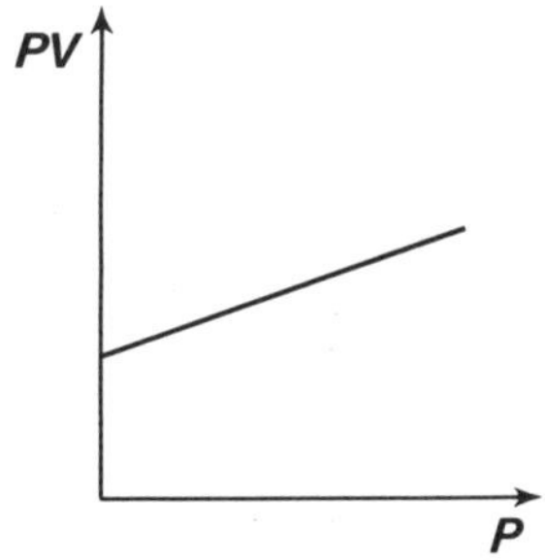

Fig. 7.2

This upward trend of PV with increasing P, suggests that the gas is more difficult to compress than the ideal.

As above, for a mole

$$b = \frac{2\pi L d^3}{3}.$$

The volume of each of the L molecules in a mole is

$$\frac{4}{3}\pi (d/2)^3 \text{ or } \pi d^3/6.$$

So b is seen to be four times the total volume occupied by these molecules.

It is evident, both from the near-ideal behaviour of many gases and from consideration of surface tension, that the attractions between molecules must fall off rapidly with distance. Later we will see that they obey an inverse seventh power law; doubling the separation between molecules thus reduces the force by a factor of 128. It is consequently reasonable to assert that molecules will only attract, or be attracted by, other molecules within a short distance of their centre. We can envisage each molecule surrounded by a *sphere of molecular action*, and it will only be attracted by other molecules whose centres lie within this sphere; the precise radius of this sphere is not important, but it will certainly only be equal, at most, to a few molecular diameters.

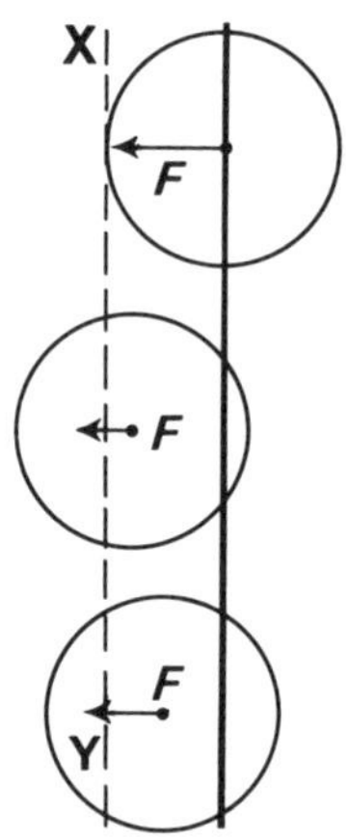

Fig. 7.3

In the case of a molecule in the interior of a gas these molecular attractions have no effect; it is surrounded by a complete sphere of action, and the uniform distribution of molecules within this sphere ensures that the forces of attraction balance out exactly. However, if XY in Fig. 7.3 is a plane at a distance from the wall of the container equal to the radius of the sphere of molecular action, any molecule between XY and the wall will have an incomplete sphere on the side facing the wall; it thus experiences a resultant attraction directed towards the interior of the gas as shown by the arrow F. The nearer the molecule to the wall the greater is this force, and it follows that as a molecule approaches the wall it is slowed down. In the same manner, after such a molecule has collided with the wall it is accelerated in its journey from the wall back to the line XY, and reaches it with exactly the speed it had when it reached XY previously.

Although the average velocity of the molecules in the general body of the gas is unaltered, each molecule hits the wall with a smaller velocity than it would if there were no inter-molecular attractions. As a molecule approaches the wall a small part of its kinetic energy is changed into a form of potential energy similar to that possessed by molecules near the surface of a liquid.

It might be thought that this slowing down would be compensated by an acceleration resulting from the attractions between a gas molecule and those of the walls. Molecules of gas will indeed be so accelerated, but at the same time each gas molecule exerts an equal and opposite force on the wall, and the impulse produced by this force exactly balances the extra impulse produced at the moment of contact as a result of this acceleration. Thus, over the whole interval in which a gas molecule interacts with those of the wall the net effect is zero. The collisions with the wall must not be thought of simply as occurring instantaneously, but rather as lasting over the whole period during which gas molecules and those of the wall interact.

The decrease in velocity arising from the attractions between gas molecules reduces the pressure exerted; the magnitude of this effect is proportional to the number of molecules hitting the wall in unit time, and this is in turn proportional to the density of the gas. The pressure reduction (ΔP) is also proportional to the magnitude of the effect on an individual molecule, and this is proportional to the number of molecules in any particular sphere of molecular action, which for a particular gas is also proportional to the gas density ρ. It follows that the total effect is proportional to ρ^2,

$$\therefore\ \Delta P = A\rho^2 = a/V^2$$

for a fixed mass of gas.

The pressure exerted by a gas with mutually attracting molecules is therefore less than that of an ideal gas occupying the same volume at the same temperature, by a/V^2; the constant a is a characteristic of the particular gas under consideration, and depends on the magnitude of the inter-molecular forces in the gas.

Thus,

$$P = P_i - a/V^2$$

or

$$PV = P_iV - a/V$$

where P_i is the pressure exerted by an ideal gas. Since we can write

$$P_iV = \text{k},$$

$$PV = k - a/V.$$

Since a is essentially positive this relation leads to isothermals of the form shown in Fig. 7.4, and it is clear that the gas is more easily compressible than an ideal gas.

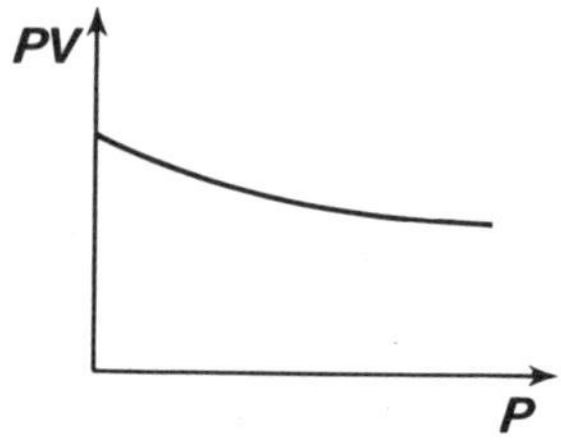

Fig. 7.4

Referring back to the discussion which led to Fig. 7.2, we see that the two correction terms proposed by van der Waals have opposing effects on the isothermals.

The observed pressure P and volume V of a van der Waals gas will not satisfy the ideal gas equation, but $(P + a/V^2)$ and $(V - b)$ will, so that the equation of state can be written

$$(P + a/V^2)(V - b) = RT \tag{7.2}$$

where a and b are the values of the constants appropriate to a mole of gas.

The constant a is in $(\text{N m}^{-2})(\text{m}^3)^2$, i.e. N m^4, whilst b is m^3, and some values for common gases are given in the table below.

Gas	$a/\text{N m}^4\ \text{mole}^{-1}$	$b/\text{m}^3\ \text{mole}^{-1}$
Hydrogen	0.25×10^{-1}	2.7×10^{-5}
Nitrogen	1.4×10^{-1}	3.9×10^{-5}
Carbon dioxide	3.6×10^{-1}	4.3×10^{-5}
Ammonia	4.2×10^{-1}	3.6×10^{-5}
Sulphur dioxide	6.8×10^{-1}	5.7×10^{-5}

2 VAN DER WAALS' ISOTHERMALS

The curves shown in Fig. 7.5 are obtained by plotting P against V, in accordance with eqn. (7.2) for a series of constant values of T; thus they represent isothermals for a gas which obeys van der Waals' equation of state. The isothermals for the higher temperatures exhibit a considerable similarity to those obtained experimentally for carbon dioxide by Andrews (Fig. 6.2, Section 1, Chapter 6), but those for the lower temperatures do not show the sudden changes in volume which are found in practice when liquefaction occurs. This is not surprising, however, for if we consider a vapour which is approaching saturation and is further compressed, we have seen that condensation only takes place if there are enough nuclei present for liquid drops to form around (see pages 105–6). In the absence of any such nuclei a very high degree of super-saturation can be reached without any change to the liquid phase taking place. This was seen to be a result of the surface tension of the liquid, which causes an increase in the equilibrium saturated vapour pressure over a convex surface (page 105). Thus without suitable nuclei the vapour would be expected to proceed along the part PQ of the isothermal.

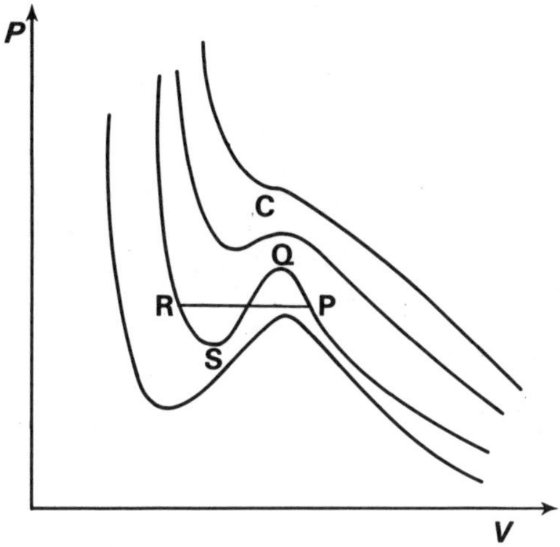

Fig. 7.5

A similar effect takes place in a liquid, the pressure on which is less than the saturated vapour pressure for the temperature. In this case, without suitable nuclei on which to form, vapour bubbles in the liquid are unable to grow and the change to the vapour phase does not take place at the expected temperature. Thus the liquid proceeds along the part RS of the isothermal. In practice there would always be a change from a state represented by some point on RS to a point on PQ as a result of the presence of nuclei. The conditions represented by points between Q and S are essentially unstable since the pressure and volume increase together, and such states cannot be realized experimentally.

The process of liquefaction can be represented by a straight line such as PR, which can only be drawn across isothermals which have maxima and minima. Thus at temperatures above that corresponding to C, liquefaction cannot take place. C is the critical point, and the corresponding isothermal has a horizontal point of inflection.

In order to calculate the values of P, V and T corresponding to the critical point, we use the conditions for a horizontal point of inflection

$$\frac{dP}{dV} = 0, \text{ and } \frac{d^2 P}{dV^2} = 0.$$

The equation of state can be written

$$P = \frac{RT}{V-b} - \frac{a}{V^2} \tag{i}$$

$$\therefore \frac{dP}{dV} = -\frac{RT}{(V-b)^2} + \frac{2a}{V^3}$$

and

$$\frac{d^2P}{dV^2} = \frac{2RT}{(V-b)^3} - \frac{6a}{V^4}.$$

Therefore at the critical point

$$\frac{RT}{(V-b)^2} = \frac{2a}{V^3} \tag{ii}$$

and

$$\frac{2RT}{(V-b)^3} = \frac{6a}{V^4}. \tag{iii}$$

Dividing these equations,

$$\frac{V-b}{2} = \frac{V}{3}$$

or

$$3V - 3b = 2V$$

$$\therefore V = 3b.$$

Substituting this value for V in (ii),

$$RT = \frac{2a(2b)^2}{(3b)^3}$$

$$= \frac{8a}{27b}.$$

Substituting for V and T in (i),

$$P = \frac{8a}{27b(2b)} - \frac{a}{9b^2}$$

$$= \frac{a}{27b^2}.$$

Thus the critical values of pressure, volume and temperature are given by,

$$P_c = \frac{a}{27\,b^2} \tag{7.3}$$

$$V_c = 3b \tag{7.4}$$

$$T_c = \frac{8a}{27\,Rb}. \tag{7.5}$$

It should be noted that the critical volume is three times the co-volume b and that $b = 2\pi LD^3/3$, which is $2\pi/3$ times the volume Ld^3 that the molecules would take up when packed closely together. Thus the critical volume is of the order of six times the volume occupied by the molecules when they are packed closely together.

3 THE CRITICAL AND BOYLE TEMPERATURES

A detailed analysis of the isothermals of a gas enables the constants a and b to be calculated; these results can then be used in eqn. (7.3), (7.4) and (7.5) to determine the critical constants. These values may then be compared with results obtained directly from experiment, but the most convenient way of assessing the correctness of van der Waals' values of the critical constants is by consideration of the expression

$$RT_c/P_cV_c.$$

Eqn. (7.3), (7.4) and (7.5) indicate that it should have the value 8/3 or 2.67.

The table below shows values of this expression calculated from experimental data for a number of gases.

RT/P_cV_c			
Oxygen	3.42	Carbon dioxide	3.57
Hydrogen	3.03	Water vapour	4.46
Nitrogen	3.42	Methyl alcohol	4.56
Argon	3.43	Hydrogen chloride	3.48
Helium	3.13		

In no case does the value agree precisely with the theoretical one; on the other hand, several of the values lie close together, and most of them are between 3.4 and 5.0, with the majority less than 4.0. Although the discrepancy from the 2.67 predicted by van der Waals is large, there seems some evidence for believing his approach to the problem to be substantially correct. It should be appreciated that the analysis is intended to apply to conditions where the effects of molecular attractions and the finite size of the molecules are small, whereas at the critical point this is certainly not so.

The molecular forces represented by the a/V^2 term give a certain residual cohesion to the gaseous phase; as V becomes smaller this factor becomes relatively more important and eventually so completely overcomes the tendency of the molecules to fly apart that the liquid phase becomes possible. This situation is first reached at the critical point, so that it is evident that we are here dealing with very significant forces between the molecules.

Van der Waals' equation would be expected to give a better representation of the behaviour of gases at higher temperatures, and it can be used to obtain a value for the Boyle temperature.

Eqn. (7.2) can be written

$$PV + \frac{a}{V} - Pb - \frac{ab}{V^2} = RT$$

or

$$PV = RT + Pb - \frac{a}{V} + \frac{ab}{V^2}.$$

If we now substitute RT/P for V in the last two terms as an approximation which will be valid if the deviations of the gas from the ideal are not large, we obtain

$$PV = RT + Pb - \frac{aP}{RT} + \frac{abP^2}{R^2T^2}.$$

At the Boyle temperature, the gradient of the graph of PV is zero for $P = 0$, and it follows that the coefficient of P in the expression obtained above must be zero. Thus the Boyle temperature is given by

$$b = a/RT$$

or

$$T_b = a/Rb. \quad (7.6)$$

Combining this with eqn. (7.5) for the critical temperature, we see that

$$T_b/T_c = 27/8 = 3.3 \text{ (approx.)} \quad (7.7)$$

In the case of hydrogen the ratio of these two temperatures is found to be about 3.4, but for helium it is 4.6, whilst for nitrogen it is 2.6, so that once again the predictions are somewhat inaccurate.

4 REDUCED EQUATION OF STATE AND LAW OF CORRESPONDING STATES

If the pressure, volume and temperature of a gas are expressed as multiples of the critical pressure, volume and temperature, the resulting variables are known as the *reduced* pressure, volume and temperature, respectively.

These reduced quantities are thus expressed in terms of different units for each gas, the unit in each case being the values appropriate to the critical point. Thus,

$$P_r = P/P_c,\ T_r = T/T_c, \text{ and } V_r = V/V_c.$$

On making these substitutions in eqn. (7.2) and using also the results of eqn. (7.3) to (7.5), we obtain

$$(P_r + 3/V_r^2)(3V_r - 1) = 8\,T_r. \quad (7.8)$$

This equation contains no constants which vary from gas to gas, and is referred to as the *reduced equation of state* derived from van der Waals' equation. It indicates that the behaviour of all gases is the same if their pressure, temperature and volume are considered relative to their appropriate critical values. This means that their behaviour can be represented by the same set of isothermals provided that the scales are adjusted according to the critical data of the gas; thus van der Waals predicts the law of corresponding states which was suggested by experiments such as those of Holborn.

5 OTHER EQUATIONS OF STATE

Van der Waals' equation achieves only limited success in explaining and accounting for the deviations of gases from the ideal, and since his time many attempts have been made to produce equations of state. Some fifty or sixty are recorded in the literature, but most are only of value over a very limited range of temperatures and pressures. We will only mention two modifications of van der Waals'.

Dieterici suggested the relation

$$(V-b)\,P\exp(a/RTV)=RT. \tag{7.9}$$

In general, this agrees more accurately with the experimental results than van der Waals'. It leads to a result of $2b$ for the critical volume and predicts a value slightly less than 3.7 for the expression RT/PV evaluated at the critical point.

Berthelot suggested modifying van der Waals' by introducing the absolute temperature into the term representing the attraction between the molecules, i.e.

$$\left(P+\frac{a}{V^2T}\right)\left(V-b\right)=RT. \tag{7.10}$$

This leads to the same value for the critical constants as does the simple form of van der Waals', but on the whole is rather more in accord with the experimental results.

6 THE NATURE OF INTER-MOLECULAR FORCES

In an isolated atom the electrons form a spherically symmetrical charge distribution, whose centre is the nucleus. In the case of diatomic molecules such as nitrogen the electron cloud is no longer spherically symmetrical but it does have a centre of symmetry which is half-way between the two nuclei. The situation is different for atoms such as hydrogen chloride, where the electron cloud is of the form shown in Fig. 7.6.

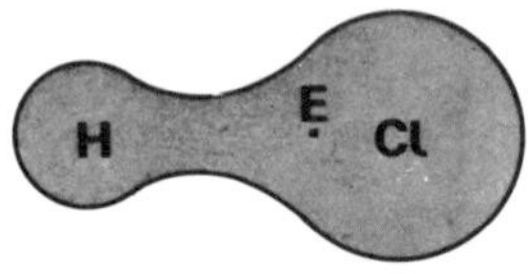

Fig. 7.6

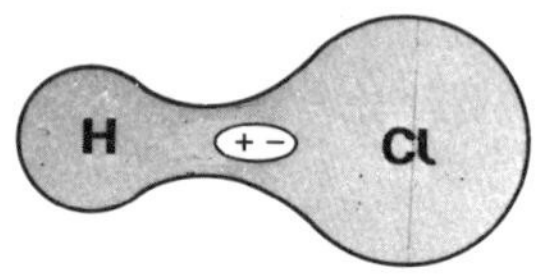

Fig. 7.7

The effective centre of the electron cloud is indicated by E, and is nearer to the chlorine nucleus. Since the centre of positive charge is half-way between the nuclei, there is an effective separation of the positive and negative charges which is represented schematically in Fig. 7.7. A charged doublet of this nature is known as a *dipole*. A number of polyatomic molecules possess a dipole moment, water being a common example.

A molecule with a permanent dipole moment produces an electric field intensity at a distance r, which is proportional to $1/r^3$. Any particular molecule is in the field of the neighbouring molecules, and clearly the force between any pair of molecules, is an attraction or a repulsion according to the relative orientation of the axes of the dipoles. It might be expected that all orientations would be equally probable and thus the resultant force zero, but it can be shown that the Maxwell-Boltzmann distribution law favours orientations which lead to an attractive force. Consequently there is an attractive force between pairs of polar molecules, which can be shown to vary with $1/r^7$.

However, attractions do exist between non-polar molecules, and it is only in the case of strongly polar molecules such as water that forces such as those discussed above are important.

If a molecule has no permanent dipole moment, there are changes taking place continually in the positions of the electrons within the molecule, and these can bring about instantaneous dipole moments. This asymmetry of the charge distribution is only momentary, and over any normal time-interval the net effect is zero; however each instantaneous dipole produces an electric field which in turn brings about a charge separation and hence an induced dipole moment in any neighbouring molecule as in Fig. 7.8.

Fig. 7.8

It is seen from Fig. 7.8 that a pair of dipoles of this nature will interact to produce an attraction between them, and it can be shown that this force also is proportional to $1/r^7$, where r is the separation of the two dipoles. Forces arising in this way from induction by instantaneous dipoles are referred to as *dispersion* forces. Although the mutual effect between any pair of dipoles is small, the forces are additive with little tendency to cancel each other, so that the total effect between a large number of neighbouring molecules becomes much greater; this additive nature is certainly not the case with the forces considered earlier between polar molecules. It should perhaps be mentioned that any molecule with a permanent dipole moment induces a dipole moment in a near-by molecule with a resulting attraction, but again the overall effect from this cause is found to be small.

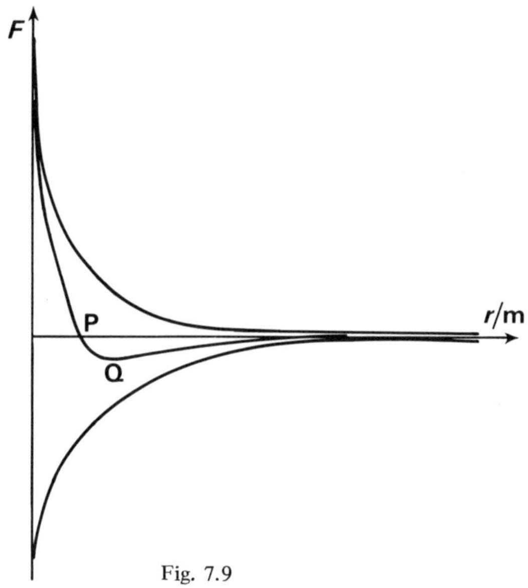

Fig. 7.9

These ideas may be summed up by saying that there is an attractive force, proportional to $1/r^7$, between any pair of molecules. Insignificant at large separations, the force rises as the distance between the molecules decreases. However, as the molecules become very close their electron distributions begin to intermingle and thereby bring about a repulsion. This repulsion can be shown to be proportional to $1/r^{13}$, so that for very small values of r the repulsion increases much more rapidly than does the attraction, as is indicated in Fig. 7.9 where the two separate forces are plotted on the same axes (repulsions positive, attractions negative) and the resultant for each separation is obtained by addition. The resultant reaches a maximum magnitude, indicated by the minimum of the curve, at Q; from there the attraction falls to zero at P, and then the resultant repulsion increases rapidly. Clearly, the normal equilibrium separation for a pair of molecules corresponds to P, where there is no resultant force acting.

If we are thinking of the molecules as solid spheres, this equilibrium separation represents the molecular diameter. Any attempt to get them closer together, is prevented by the finite size effect. So this molecular repulsion is simply a more sophisticated description of the 'finite size' effect of van der Waals.

7 INTER-MOLECULAR POTENTIAL ENERGY CURVES

Although the interactions between molecules can be understood in terms of forces, it is more convenient to consider the potential energies resulting from these forces.

The work done in bringing unit dipole moment from an infinite distance to a point which is r from the centre of the molecule, against the attractive force A/r^7 is

$$\int_{\infty}^{r} \frac{A}{r^7} \mathrm{d}r$$

$$= -\frac{A}{6\,r^6}. \tag{7.11}$$

This work is the potential energy, U, corresponding to the attractive force, and is plotted as the lower curve in Fig. 7.10.

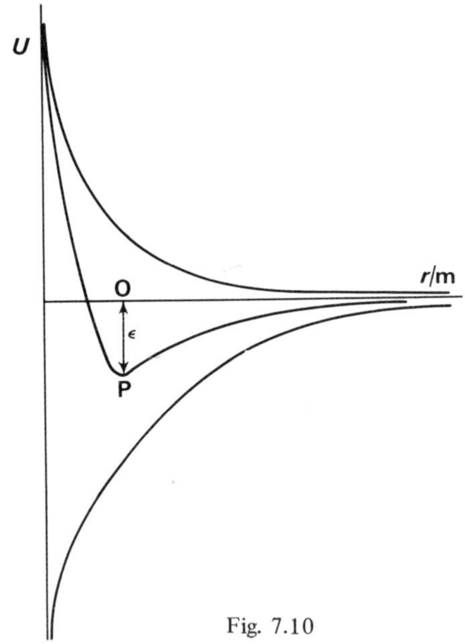

Fig. 7.10

The potential energy given by eqn. (7.11) is negative, indicating that work would be *done* in taking the molecule away from such a position.

Left to themselves the molecules would accelerate towards each other, continually gaining kinetic energy.

If the repulsive force obeys the relation B/r^{13}, a similar calculation establishes that the corresponding potential energy is

$$\frac{B}{12r^{12}} \tag{7.12}$$

and this is represented by the upper curve in Fig. 7.10.

The total energy is readily calculated and this is also plotted.

If U is the potential energy at any point in a field, and F the corresponding force

$$\mathrm{d}U = -F\,\mathrm{d}r$$

or

$$F = -\frac{\mathrm{d}U}{\mathrm{d}r}. \tag{7.13}$$

Eqn. (7.13) shows that the resultant force is represented in magnitude by the gradient of the potential energy curve. Thus the equilibrium position, where there is no resultant force, corresponds to a point where the potential energy curve has zero gradient. It follows that the minimum P in Fig. 7.10 is the equilibrium position.

At separations less than that for equilibrium, the resultant force is a repulsion, whereas at greater separations the force is of an attracting nature.

A direct measurement of the manner in which the attraction varies with distance has been carried out using a molecular beam. The beam was produced in an oven, and the molecules detected by a hot-wire detector in the same way as in the experimental investigation of the velocity distribution for molecules (Fig. 2.5, page 28). However, in this arrangement a number of molecules are introduced into the chamber between the oven and the detector in order to scatter those in the beam. The observed scattering varies with the speed of the molecules since a fast-moving molecule must pass very close to another in order to be deflected significantly by the inter-molecular attraction. It is possible to deduce the variation of force with distance from the form of the relation between angle of scattering and velocity; such experiments have provided a direct confirmation of the $1/r^7$ force law.

8 MAGNITUDE AND RANGE OF THE FORCES

At temperatures above that of the critical point molecules are unable to cohere into the liquid phase; presumably the inter-molecular attractions are not sufficiently strong to hold the molecules together. This suggests that at the critical volume the forces between molecules become particularly significant.

Many critical volumes are of the order of 90 cm^3/mole. Since Avogadro's number is approximately 6×10^{23}, each molecule at the critical point has an associated volume of the order of 15×10^{-23} cm^3.

This corresponds to a separation between neighbouring molecules of $(15 \times 10^{-23})^{1/3}$, or about 10^{-8} cm, which is often written as 0.1 nm.

The results of experiments on the compressibility of gases enables van der Waals' constant b to be calculated; the values obtained are frequently of the order of 30 cm^3/mole (see table on page 130), and if we envisage the molecules as solid spheres, we once again obtain values of the order of 0.1 nm for the molecular diameter. Further values of the same order of magnitude are obtained by considering the arrangement of the molecules in the solid state.

All these estimates therefore suggest that the minimum of the potential energy curve should be obtained for a molecular separation of the order 0.1 nm. It is possible to form an estimate of the 'depth' ϵ of the potential energy well, i.e. the negative potential energy at equilibrium.

Molecules in the solid and liquid phases clearly require energy to separate them completely from their neighbours, and this amount of energy controls the values of the specific latent heats of vaporization and sublimation. By making reasonable assumptions concerning the number of 'nearest neighbours' possessed by each molecule, the depth of the potential well can be calculated from the experimental values of these latent heats; in the particular case of the rare gases, values of the order of 10^{-21} J are obtained.

Similar values are obtained by considering the work done against the surface tension forces of the liquid when increasing the surface area of a liquid film.

If at some stage two molecules by chance find themselves close together, but possessing a kinetic energy which is less than ϵ, they will be unable to separate from one another, and will cohere to form a liquid. At an absolute temperature T the average energy of molecules is of the order of kT, and we would therefore expect that at the critical temperature, kT_c should be of the order of ϵ. If this argument is applied in the case of the inert gases, values for ϵ of the order of 10^{-21} J are again obtained.

QUESTIONS

1. Carbon dioxide has a molecular weight of 44, and at its critical temperature of 300 K is found to have a density of 450 kg m^{-3}; use this information to calculate the values of the constants a and b in van der Waals' equation of state for carbon dioxide.
   (R = 8.3 J mol^{-1} K^{-1}.)

2. A gas obeys van der Waals' equation, $(p + a/V^2)(V - b) = RT$ where $a = 1.4 \times 10^{15}$ N m^4 mol^{-2}, and $b = 32 \times 10^{-6}$ m^3 mol^{-1}. Calculate the work done when 1 mole is compressed from 20 litres to 0.1 litre at 0 °C. How does this work compare with that required to compress an ideal gas to the same extent?
   (R = 8.3 J mol^{-1} K^{-1}.)

3. A gas which obeys van der Waals' equation of state is expanded from a volume V_1 and a pressure P_1 to a volume V_2 and a pressure P_2.
(a) Calculate the work done against the inter-molecular forces represented by the a/V^2 term in the equation of state, in this expansion.
(b) Combine this result with that for the external work done by the gas in so expanding and use the equation of state to express the net work done in terms of the temperature, assuming that the deviations of the gas from the ideal are small.
In this way arrive at an estimate of the inversion temperature of the gas.

4. If the force of attraction F between gas molecules varies with their separation r according to the relation $F = A/r^7$, obtain the relation between r and the potential energy of a pair of molecules. Use this result to calculate this potential energy at separations between 1.0 and 5.0×10^{-10} m, and plot a graph to show how this energy varies with separation.

5. The repulsion between a pair of molecules can be expressed as

$$\frac{64 \times 10^{-60} A}{r^{13}}.$$

Determine the potential energy for a separation r, and thus calculate the potential energy for various separations less than 4.0×10^{-10} m. Plot a graph to show how this energy varies with r.

6. Assuming the constant A in the expressions in the two previous questions has the same value, use the two graphs obtained to plot the resultant energy of such a system of two molecules. If necessary improve the graph by plotting additional points, and then deduce the separation at which the potential energy is a minimum. Calculate the separate attractive and repulsive forces at this separation.

7. It is found that 6.3 kJ are required to vaporize a mole of Argon. Assuming that in the liquid form each argon atom has ten nearest neighbours, estimate the potential energy of a pair of atoms at their equilibrium separation.

8. The number of molecules per unit area of surface in the case of Argon is approximately 7.6×10^{18} m^{-2}. If the surface energy of argon is 13×10^{-3} J m^{-2}, estimate the depth of the potential energy 'well', on the assumption that those molecules in the surface have only five nearest neighbours.

Liquefaction of Gases 8

A liquid needs energy in order to evaporate into the gaseous phase. If no heat is supplied to aid this process, such a phase change can only be brought about by the liquid cooling itself and its immediate surroundings. The cooling of the hand produced when a few drops of a volatile liquid such as ether are placed on it is a simple example of this effect, and it was mentioned in Chapter 5, Section 1 that if the evaporation of ether is promoted by placing it in a can and blowing air through it, the cooling effect can be made great enough to solidify a film of water between the bottom of the can and a wooden base board. This *cooling by evaporation* is the principle of operation of the common refrigerator, which will now be considered in further detail.

1 THE REFRIGERATOR

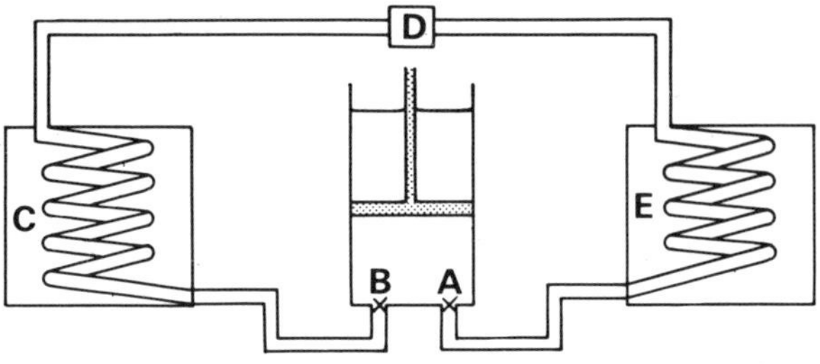

Fig. 8.1

The liquid circulates through the arrangement shown in Fig. 8.1; it evaporates in the low-pressure part on the right and subsequently condenses on the left. The circulation is maintained by the piston which in turn is driven by an electric motor. On the up-stroke vapour passes into the cylinder through the valve A; as the piston descends the vapour passes through valve B into the coiled tubes represented by C and there liquefies under pressure. The liquid passes through the throttle valve D into the tubes E, where the pressure is reduced and the liquid vaporizes cooling itself, the tubes and their immediate surroundings. In the domestic refrigerator these pipes are so arranged that heat passes to them from the refrigerating compartment, but in larger installations the tubes are immersed in a brine bath, and the cooled brine is subsequently used for refrigerating.

When the vapour condenses in C latent heat is evolved; in the domestic forms this heat is passed to the air at the rear of the cabinet, but in larger plants the tubes are surrounded by a cold water condenser.

In order to be suitable for use in a refrigerator a vapour should not require a very large pressure in order to liquefy at room temperature and should also have a large specific latent heat of vaporization; a low viscosity in the liquid state in another obvious advantage. Ammonia, sulphur dioxide and carbon dioxide may all be used in a refrigerator, but a number of compounds have been specially developed for this use, e.g. Freon in two forms, with chemical formulae CCl_2F_2 and $C_2Cl_2F_4$.

The operation of a refrigeration involves the transfer of heat from a lower to a higher temperature; this is a reversal of the normal direction of flow so a refrigerator can be considered to be a *heat pump.* This reversal of the direction of heat flow can only be achieved by the performance of mechanical work, and this is supplied by the motor driving the pump. If the heat withdrawn from the refrigerating chamber is Q_1, and subsequently Q_2 is given out at the higher temperature, the work done by the pump in the cycle is $Q_2 - Q_1$. The coefficient of performance of the refrigerator is defined as $Q_1/(Q_2 - Q_1)$.

Any refrigerator working normally thus gives out heat to the room through the heat-exchanging pipes at the back. Even if it were left working with the door open, so that it was apparently cooling the room, it would nevertheless have a net warming effect, since Q_2 is greater than Q_1.

Fig. 8.2 shows schematically another form of refrigerator which uses the evaporation of ammonia to remove heat from the object to be cooled, but has no pump to maintain the circulation. The gaseous ammonia from the evaporator E passes to the *absorber* A where it is dissolved in a weak aqueous solution of ammonia; the solution is thus strengthened and passes to the boiler B where some of its ammonia is evaporated. This gas now passes to the *condenser* C where it liquefies and returns to the *evaporator.* In order to maintain the evaporation of the ammonia in the evaporator a

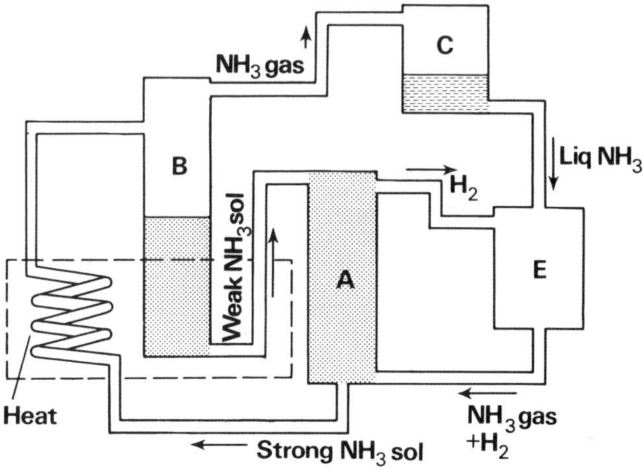

Fig. 8.2

stream of hydrogen circulates between the absorber and the evaporator; in the evaporator the presence of the hydrogen reduces the partial pressure of the ammonia. The sum of these two partial pressures must however equal the pressure of the ammonia in the condenser. Thus the pressure of the ammonia in the evaporator is less than the saturated vapour pressure at that temperature and evaporation continues. The ammonia solution in the boiler increases in density as it loses gas and consequently falls downwards and is returned to the absorber, where it absorbs the ammonia gas which has arrived from the evaporator. In this arrangement the energy input is in the form of the heat maintaining the temperature difference.

2 THE CASCADE PROCESS

Provided a gas can be cooled below its critical temperature it may be liquefied by the application of sufficient pressure; a liquid can then be used to cool itself or anything with which it is in contact, by evaporation. In this way sufficient cooling can be produced to cool another gas below its critical temperature so that it liquefies under the application of pressure. Thus the production of lower and lower temperatures is linked with the liquefaction of gases; the lower the temperatures which can be produced, the more liquefied gases are available to produce yet lower temperatures and thereby cool other gases so that they are below their critical temperatures.

In the early stage of the liquefaction of gases Faraday used simple freezing mixtures to cool chlorine, hydrogen sulphide and a number of other gases so that they could be readily liquefied. However, since the critical temperature of oxygen is 155 K and that of nitrogen is 127 K, they could not be liquefied in this manner.

Fig. 8.3 shows the principle of the *cascade* process which was first used

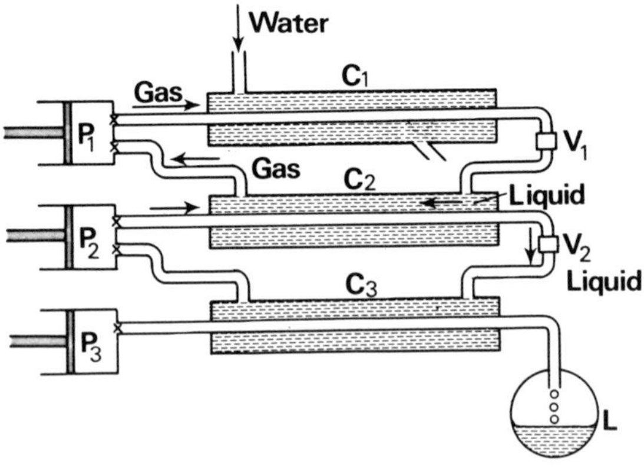

Fig. 8.3

to liquefy air in 1877 by Pictet. The pump P_1 compresses a gas which is below its critical temperature so that it liquefies in the condenser C_1 and the latent heat evolved is removed by a flow of water through the condenser; the condensed liquid flows through a valve to a second condenser C_2. The pump P_1 maintains a low pressure above the liquid so that rapid evaporation occurs, drawing the necessary latent heat from a gas circulating in a pipe in good thermal contact with the liquid in C_2. Consequently this gas is cooled so that it is well below its critical temperature and can be liquefied by the application of pressure from pump P_2. This is repeated with another gas which is passed through C_3 under pressure, and liquefies in the vessel L.

Various gases can be used in sequence to produce lower temperatures in this manner, but a convenient combination employs for the first stage methyl chloride which has a critical temperature of 416 K – well above room temperature. Rapid evaporation of liquid methyl chloride can produce a temperature of 180 K; if ethylene whose critical temperature is 283 K is used as the second gas in the cascade it is readily liquefied after having been cooled by the methyl chloride. By the evaporation of ethylene a temperature of 90 K is easily obtained and thereby air can be cooled sufficiently for both oxygen and nitrogen to liquefy under pressure.

In his original arrangement Pictet used sulphur dioxide and carbon dioxide in succession but this needed pressures of several hundred atmospheres to liquefy the air since the temperature reached was not far below the critical. Another triple cascade that has been used is ammonia, ethylene and methane.

3 THE LINDE PROCESS

The Joule-Kelvin effect was considered in Section 8 of Chapter 6; when a gas expands from a higher to a lower pressure, work is done against the inter-molecular forces even if no external work is performed; above the inversion temperature this effect is masked by other effects of the deviations from Boyle's law, but the magnitude of the cooling increases as the original temperature falls further below the inversion temperature.

The fall in temperature for air at room temperature is of the order of 0.2 K per atmosphere; so even for large pressure changes the cooling is not great and it is obviously advantageous to cool the gas below room temperature before allowing the expansion to take place. This pre-cooling also has the advantage of removing readily solidified impurities such as water and carbon dioxide which would otherwise clog the circulation. After the gas has been compressed into a spiral S immersed in a cooling bath of brine or ammonia which removes the heat of compression it passes through a second spiral C to a nozzle V where it expands to atmospheric pressure; the arrangement is indicated schematically in Fig. 8.4.

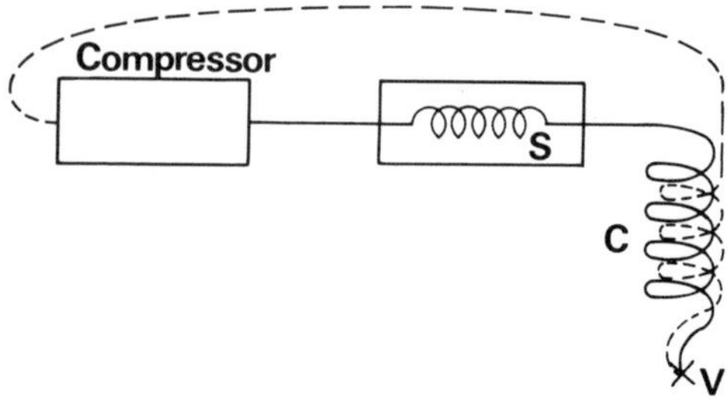

Fig. 8.4

The cooled expanded gas from V passes back through a second spiral which is wound around C; this arrangement of two spirals known as a *heat exchanger* causes a considerable fall in temperature of the gas before it expands, and so the gas subsequently emerging from V is further cooled, It is this process of *regenerative cooling* which enables liquid to be produced eventually on emergence from the expansion nozzle.

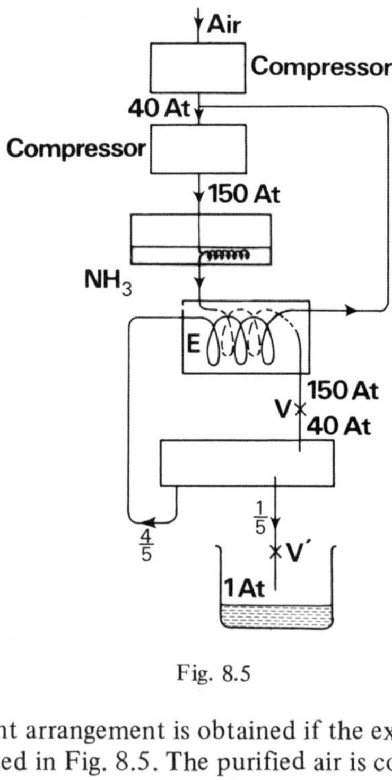

Fig. 8.5

A more efficient arrangement is obtained if the expansion is in two stages as is indicated in Fig. 8.5. The purified air is compressed to 150 atmospheres pressure in two stages and then passes through a bath of ammonia evaporating under reduced pressure. After passing through the heat exchanger E, the cool gas expands to a pressure of 40 atmospheres through the valve V; the major part of this gas then travels back through the heat exchanger to the second compressor, and is again compressed to 150 atmospheres before passing round the closed circuit once again. About 1/5 of the expanded gas at 40 atmospheres passes on to a second valve V′, so that its pressure falls to 1 atmosphere, and eventually liquefies.

In this arrangement the work done in compression is reduced, as only part of the gas has to be compressed from 1 to 150 atmospheres in order to maintain the operation.

4 THE CLAUDE AND HEYLANDT PROCESS

In the original Cailletet method of liquefying air, the cooling resulted from the work done by the gas against an external pressure in an adiabatic expansion. A modification of this arrangement is indicated schematically in Fig. 8.6; after being compressed to 40 atmospheres the gas passes through a heat exchanger E, and then part of it enters the cylinder C of an expansion

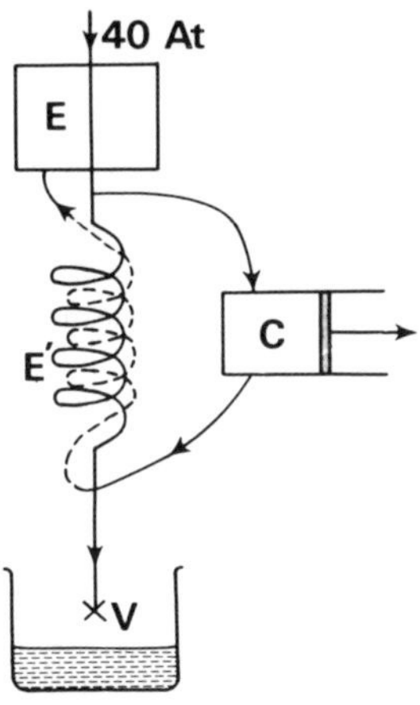

Fig. 8.6

engine. As it expands, pushing the piston back, it performs external work, cools itself and then passes back through the heat exchanger E′. In its passage through E′ it cools that part of the gas which did not enter the expansion chamber, and then it passes through the first exchanger E where it cools the gas which has been compressed.

Thus a stream of cooled gas emerges from the second heat exchanger E′ at a pressure of 40 atmospheres; it expands through a nozzle V, doing work against the inter-molecular forces as in the Linde expansion method, and eventually liquefies: Considerable difficulty is experienced in the expansion engine since the piston has to be gas tight and also well lubricated.

It has also proved possible to liquefy air in a most efficient manner using a small rapidly-rotating expansion turbine; a large mass of air is used, but the expansion is relatively small since the air is only compressed to about six atmospheres.

5 LIQUEFACTION OF HYDROGEN

The critical temperature of hydrogen is 32 K, and it is not possible to attain this temperatures by any liquid boiling under reduced pressure. Consequently the cascade process cannot be used to liquefy hydrogen. Since, however, the inversion temperature of hydrogen is approximately 193 K only a relatively small amount of pre-cooling is required in order to make use of the Linde method for its liquefaction.

After compression the hydrogen is cooled by passing it through a liquid air bath; in this way hydrogen at about 70 K is easily obtained, and as this is considerably below the inversion temperature, a correspondingly large temperature drop due to the Joule-Kelvin effect is obtained. The removal of impurities is a major problem, as the solidication of minute quantities of air remaining mixed with the hydrogen would be sufficient to stop free circulation.

The difficulty of obtaining pure hydrogen can be avoided by using a closed circuit in which a small amount of specially purified hydrogen flows continuously; after a Linde expansion the liquid produced is lead back through an efficient heat exchanging system where it cools ordinary commercial hydrogen under a pressure of a few atmospheres. This impure hydrogen has already been pre-cooled to some extent and is now sufficiently cooled by the liquid hydrogen so that it liquefies.

6 LIQUEFACTION OF HELIUM

Hydrogen boiling under reduced pressure solidifies at temperatures in the region of 14 K, and since the critical temperature of helium is 5 K, there is no liquid available to cool helium below its critical temperature. The inversion temperature of helium is 33 K, and thus Kammerlingh Onnes was able to apply the Linde process to liquefy this last remaining gas. The compressed gas was first cooled in a bath of hydrogen boiling under reduced pressure so that it emerged at a temperature of 15 K; it then carried out an expansion through a nozzle, cooled because of the work done against intermolecular forces, and so liquefied.

It might be thought that it should be easier to employ the Claude method involving the performance of external work in an adiabatic expansion to produce liquefaction, but there were a number of problems involved in the application of this technique. Firstly, as the initial temperature decreases, so does the temperature drop which results. At the same time, once one reaches liquid hydrogen temperatures all normal lubricants have solidified and thus become unusable. However, by leaving a gap of the order of 0.05 mm between the leather packing on the piston and the cylinder wall and at the same time greatly increasing the speed of the piston it was possible to use the compressed gas as a lubricant and avoid losing much gas through the gap between piston and cylinder. A further difficulty arises from the need to provide good thermal insulation to the expansion cylinder. As a result of overcoming these problems Kapitza, a Russian physicist working at Cambridge, built a helium liquefier in 1934 which used an expansion engine which operated only 10 K above absolute zero.

These techniques were further developed in the Collins Liquefier produced by Professor Collins at the Massachusetts Institute of Technology in 1946. This instrument is now in use in all low-temperature laboratories and is the main source of liquid helium.

Liquid helium is frequently used as a low temperature bath in order to cool a substance or piece of apparatus to a temperature of a few degrees above absolute zero as a preliminary to carrying out an experiment. It is therefore often convenient to use the small-scale helium liquefier developed by Simon which is shown schematically in Fig. 8.7.

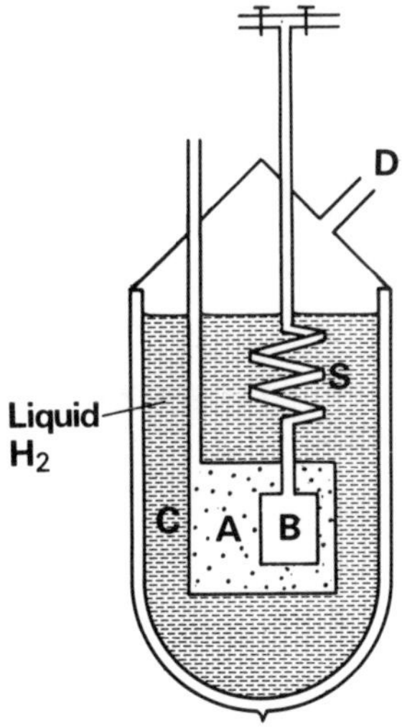

Fig. 8.7

Helium is compressed in the container B at a pressure of about 150 atmospheres; the heat generated in this compression is conducted away through the helium gas in A to the liquid hydrogen which is boiling under reduced pressure in C. The helium in A is at a pressure of a few millimetres of mercury and simply serves as a heat-exchange gas. A vacuum pump is connected to D and maintains a low pressure above the hydrogen in C. Once B and its contents have reached the temperature of the hydrogen bath, the exchange gas is removed by a pump so that B is now completely thermally isolated, and the gas in B is allowed to expand through the spiral shown at S into the open air under conditions that are an excellent approximation to adiabatic; the resulting cooling can be sufficient under favourable conditions to produce enough liquid helium in B to occupy 4/5 of its total volume; this high yield is obtained partly because the density of the highly compressed gas is appreciably greater than that of the liquid, but another important factor is the very small heat capacity of the metal container at these very low temperatures. This is so low that the heat capacity of the gas is very much greater than that of the container; consequently little heat is obtained from the cooling of the container itself.

With this arrangement the apparatus or substance to be used in the low temperature investigation can be placed inside B before the apparatus is assembled.

Fig. 8.8 shows another small-scale arrangement for producing liquid helium; this process depends on the ability of charcoal at these very low temperatures to adsorb immense quantities of gaseous helium and the fact that this adsorption is accompanied by the evolution of a large amount of heat. Thus if the absorbed gas is subsequently removed, the gas and the adsorber are both considerably cooled.

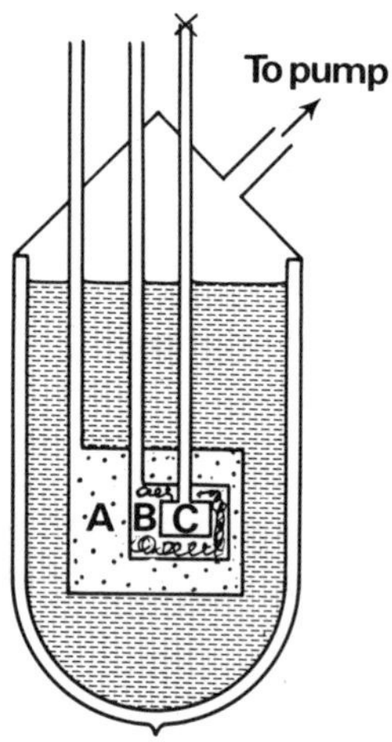

Fig. 8.8

The gas is pumped into the container B and adsorbed by the charcoal, the heat being conducted away by the low pressure helium A in exactly the same manner as in the adiabatic expansion liquefier just described; once again the whole of this part of the apparatus is immersed in a bath of hydrogen boiling under reduced pressure, and after sufficient adsorption has taken place and the charcoal is at the temperature of the liquid hydrogen bath the exchange gas is removed, thus thermally isolating the inner part of the apparatus. A vacuum pump is now applied in order to extract the helium from the charcoal, and the consequent cooling is sufficient to produce liquefaction of the helium under pressure in the closed vessel C.

7 ADIABATIC DEMAGNETIZATION

Rotary pumps are able to produce pressures of a fraction of a mm of mercury above the surface of a bath of liquid helium, and thus maintain the bath boiling under reduced pressure at a temperature of the order 1 K; by the use of special diffusion pumps lower pressures can be maintained, so that temperatures as low as 0.75 K are obtainable with ordinary helium and as low as 0.25 K using the rarer isotope He^3, but a closer approach to the absolute zero is only possible with entirely different techniques.

When a substance is magnetized, heat is evolved and its temperature rises; on demagnetization there is a corresponding fall in temperature if the substance is isolated from its surroundings. The magnitude of this thermal effect is dependent on the rate at which the magnetic susceptibility varies with temperature, and for paramagnetic substances at very low temperatures the effect is large enough to be of considerable use for the production of a significant fall in temperature. The magnetic susceptibility ϵ, obeys Curie's law, $\epsilon = C/T$, where T is the absolute temperature and C is a constant. The form of this relation shows that at small temperatures both the susceptibility and its rate of change with temperature will be large; furthermore, both increase rapidly as the temperature approaches zero.

In just the same way that vaporization represents a change to a more random state and involves therefore an increase in entropy, so dies the demagnetization process. Magnetizing a substance involves an alignment of the elementary magnetic dipoles, which arise from either the orbital or spinning motion of the electrons; this alignment implies a more ordered state, i.e. a decrease in entropy. The subsequent demagnetization involves a corresponding entropy increase, and thus requires an absorption of energy in the same way as energy is needed to convert the relatively ordered liquid into the more random gas.

The essential features of the arrangement used in the adiabatic demagnetization method is shown in Fig. 8.9. The sample of paramagnetic sub-

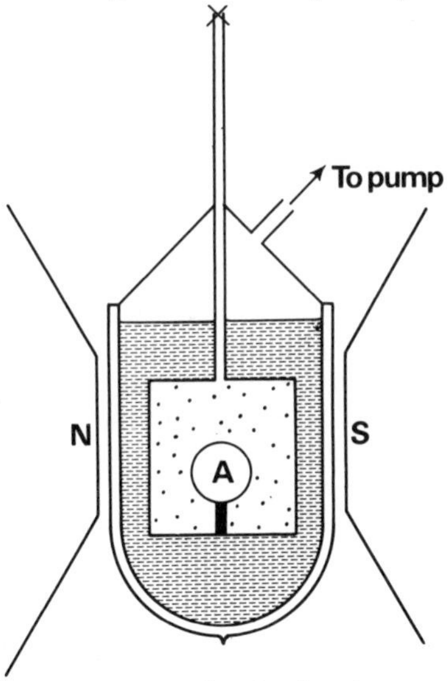

Fig. 8.9

stance A is supported on a poor conducting bar in a container of helium gas under a low pressure and this is in a bath of liquid helium boiling under reduced pressure. The bath is in turn surrounded by similar baths containing liquid hydrogen and liquid air. In this manner the initial temperature of the paramagnetic sample will normally be of the order of 1 K. The whole apparatus is placed between the poles of a powerful electromagnet. When the field is switched on the sample is magnetized and the heat produced is conducted away by the helium exchange gas, which is subsequently pumped away before the magnetic field is removed.

Early experiments using fields of the order of 20 000 gauss and samples of gadolinium sulphate reached temperatures of the order of 0.003 K. If the temperature is required for some particular investigation, the material or apparatus is attached to the paramagnetic sample and is thereby cooled itself. Since most paramagnetic materials have high specific heat capacities, once they are at low temperatures they take a considerable time to warm up through the arrival of heat from outside.

The atomic nuclei possess magnetic moments, and although the associated magnetic moments are more than a thousand times smaller than those arising from the electrons in the atom, these elementary magnets may be oriented in sufficiently strong magnetic fields. Such methods cannot be applied to produce cooling unless a temperature of the order of 0.01 K has already been obtained. If, however, such a temperature is obtained by the methods already considered, application of fields of the order 50 to 100 kilogauss aligns the nuclear magnets; the sample, which could well consist of thin copper wires, is then isolated from its surroundings and demagnetized. Temperatures less than 10^{-6} K have been obtained by this method and it has been estimated that it should be possible to reach very much lower temperatures.

Another technique which has been used to produce temperatures of the order of 10^{-3} K employs the peculiar differences in the properties of the He^3 and He^4 isotopes at these very low temperatures. Below 0.8 K the liquid separates into two constituent phases, one of which is much richer than the other in the He^3 isotope; below 0.05 K the upper phase which is enriched with He^3 on account of its lower density is almost entirely devoid of atoms of the other isotope; the lower phase consists of a constant proportion mixture of the two isotopes. Whereas He^3 has an appreciable heat capacity, that of the normal isotope is almost zero; as a consequence the motion of an atom from the upper phase to the lower one produces cooling. It has proved possible to maintain such motion and thus develop a continuously operating cooling apparatus which gives a temperature of a few millidegrees.

QUESTIONS

1. Explain why a gas isolated from its surroundings cools when it evaporates, and give an account of the application of this phenomenon in a simple refrigerator.

2. Explain why a gas such as air cannot be liquefied by the application of pressure at room temperature, and describe the liquefaction of air by the Cascade process.

3. Explain why the Cascade process cannot be used to liquefy hydrogen, and give an account of one method of liquefying hydrogen.

4. Describe the Joule-Kelvin effect, and give an account of its application in the Linde method of liquefying gases.

5. Discuss the difficulties which arise in liquefying helium, and give an account of one method by which the gas may be liquefied.

6. Give an account of the methods by which temperatures below 2 K may be obtained.

Further Properties of Gases

9

Molecules are continually passing through any particular area in a gas in all directions. If we consider the area as separating two regions of the gas, there is a rate of flow of molecules from one side of the area to the other and also in the reverse direction. If the gas in both regions is identical in all respects, these two rates of flow are equal in magnitude and consequently no macroscopic effect is observed. But as soon as there are differences in density or temperature of the gas on the two sides of the area, the effect of the two flows become noticeable and gives rise to certain effects which will now be considered in detail.

1 DIFFUSION

We saw in Section 10 of Chapter 2 that the number of molecules passing through unit area in unit time was $n\bar{c}/4$. However, these molecules are travelling at varying angles, and a simplification is achieved by considering that there are $n\bar{c}/6$ passing through unit area per second, all of which are travelling normally to the area. It is readily verified that this classification of the molecules, first used by Joule, leads to the same value for the impulse exerted by the molecules, and hence the pressure, as does the more rigorous approach which takes into account the various directions in which the molecules travel. (See Chapter 2, Section 6, page 32.)

The characteristics of the molecules in a stream are governed by the place where they last collided. The molecules passing down through the area ΔS were, on average, last involved in a collision a distance λ above the area, where λ is the mean free path.

In order that diffusion produces a change in a gas there must be a density gradient, i.e. a variation in the concentration of the molecules. In Fig. 9.1, we assume a concentration gradient dn/dy along the y axis, where

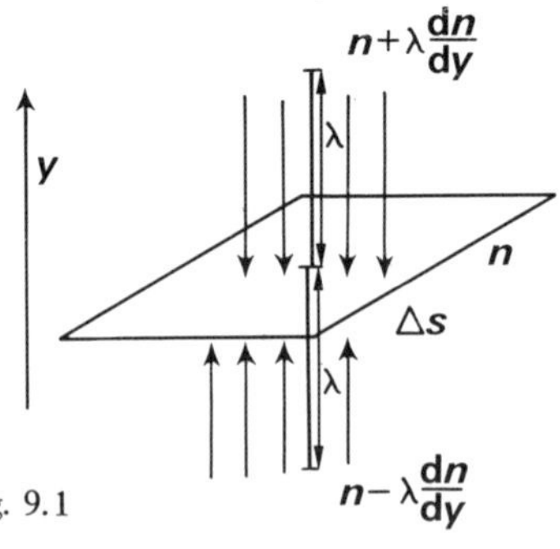

Fig. 9.1

n is the number of molecules per unit volume at any point.

Thus the molecular concentration at a distance λ above the area ΔS is

$$n + \lambda \frac{dn}{dy}$$

so that the number of molecules passing from above to below through this area in unit time is

$$\frac{\bar{c}}{6}\left(n + \lambda \frac{dn}{dy}\right)\Delta S.$$

Similarly, the rate at which molecules pass through the area in the reverse direction is

$$\frac{\bar{c}}{6}\left(n - \lambda \frac{dn}{dy}\right)\Delta S.$$

It follows that the net rate of transfer from above to below is

$$\frac{\bar{c}}{3}\lambda \ \Delta S \ \frac{dn}{dy}. \qquad (9.1)$$

The coefficient of self-diffusion of a gas (D) is defined as the number diffusing through unit area per second per unit concentration gradient, and it follows from eqn. (9.1) that

$$D = \frac{1}{3}\lambda\bar{c}. \qquad (9.2)$$

Various methods have been used for measuring the coefficient of self-diffusion, but all involve determining the change in composition which results from diffusion; this can be done by chemical analysis, but changes in thermal conductivity and optical refractive index have also been used.

Referring back to eqn. (2.16) for λ,

$$\lambda = \frac{1}{\pi n \sigma^2}.$$

Thus, the mean free path is inversely proportional to the molecular concentration, which in turn is proportional to the pressure, if the temperature is constant. It follows that the diffusion coefficient should be inversely proportional to pressure, and this fact is verified by experiment.

2 CONDUCTION OF HEAT

When a region of gas is heated the kinetic energy of the molecules within it is increased; as a result of their random motion these more energetic molecules carry this energy to other parts of the gas. On arrival in cooler parts they collide with other less energetic molecules and share their extra energy with these molecules. In this way there is a steady transfer of energy from the hotter to the cooler regions.

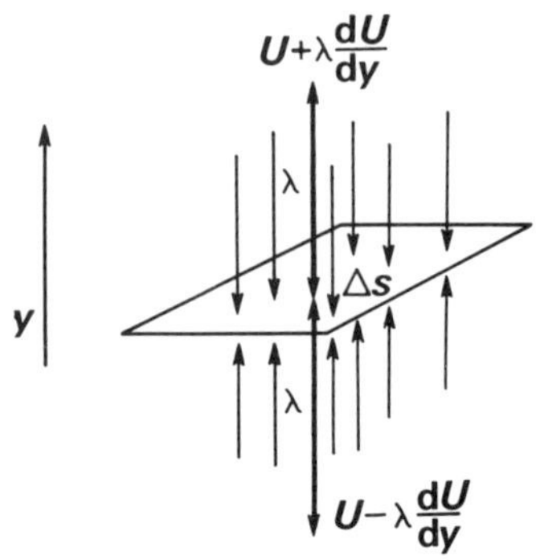

Fig. 9.2

Fig. 9.2 shows a region of a gas where there is a temperature gradient $\mathrm{d}T/\mathrm{d}y$ along the y-axis. Although approximately equal numbers of molecules pass per second from above ΔS to below as pass in the reverse direction, those moving downwards possess more energy than those travelling upwards. If U represents the internal energy of the gas molecules, those travelling through the area from above have, on the average, an energy

$$U + \lambda \frac{\mathrm{d}U}{\mathrm{d}y}$$

and the net rate of transfer of energy is

$$\frac{1}{6} n\bar{c}\, \Delta S \left(U + \lambda \frac{\mathrm{d}U}{\mathrm{d}y} - U + \lambda \frac{\mathrm{d}U}{\mathrm{d}y} \right)$$

$$= \frac{1}{3} n\bar{c}\, \Delta S\, \lambda \frac{\mathrm{d}U}{\mathrm{d}y}.$$

From the definition of the specific heat capacity at constant volume, it follows that

$$\Delta U = m\, c_\mathrm{v} \Delta T$$

where m is the mass of a molecule. Thus,

$$\frac{\mathrm{d}U}{\mathrm{d}y} = m\, c_\mathrm{v} \frac{\mathrm{d}T}{\mathrm{d}y}$$

so that the mean rate of transfer of energy Q can be written

$$Q = \frac{1}{3} n\bar{c} m c_\mathrm{v}\, \Delta S\, \lambda \frac{\mathrm{d}T}{\mathrm{d}y}. \qquad (9.3)$$

The coefficient of thermal conduction, k, is defined as the energy transfer per unit area per second per unit temperature gradient, i.e.

$$Q = k\,\Delta S\,\frac{\mathrm{d}T}{\mathrm{d}y}.$$

$$\therefore\quad k = \frac{1}{3}nm\bar{c}\,\lambda c_{\mathrm{v}} \tag{9.4}$$

and since $nm = \rho$, where ρ is the density of the gas, eqn. (9.4) can be written

$$k = \frac{1}{3}\rho\bar{c}\lambda c_{\mathrm{v}}. \tag{9.5}$$

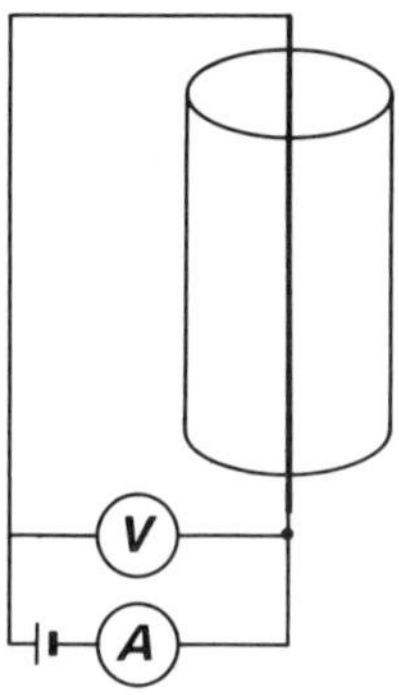

Fig. 9.3

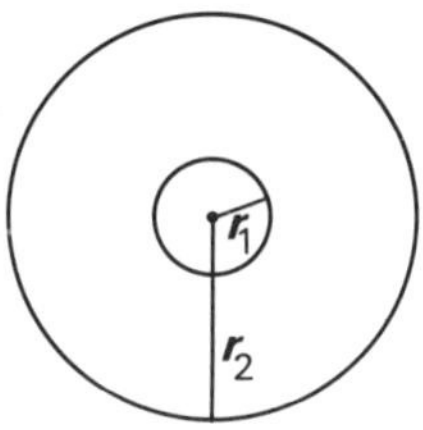

Fig. 9.4

The arrangement of a heated wire which lies along the axis of a surrounding metal cylinder (shown in Fig. 9.3) may be used to measure the thermal conductivity of a gas. When a steady temperature state has been reached, the rate of heat flow, Q, over any cross-section is constant and equal to the input of electrical power to the wire, and this may be calculated from the current and potential difference.

If the temperature is T at a distance r from the axis,

$$Q = -\,2\pi rL\,k\,\frac{\mathrm{d}T}{\mathrm{d}r} \tag{9.6}$$

where L is the length of the wire.

In order that the heat flows outwards, the temperature gradient is necessarily negative and thus the negative sign in eqn. (9.6) is required in order that Q be positive.

Integration of eqn. (9.6) gives

$$\int_{r_1}^{r_2}\frac{\mathrm{d}r}{r} = -\frac{2\pi Lk}{Q}\int_{T_1}^{T_2}\mathrm{d}T$$

or
$$\log_e (r_2/r_1) = \frac{2\pi rLk}{Q} (T_1 - T_2) \tag{9.7}$$

where T_1 and T_2 are respectively the temperatures of the wire and the surrounding cylinder. The temperature of the wire is deduced from its resistance, and that of the outer cylinder is measured using a thermocouple.

From eqn. (2.15), the mean free path is inversely proportional to n, and since ρ is directly proportional to n, eqn. (9.5) suggests that k should be independent of n and hence of the pressure, provided the temperature remains constant. Over a considerable range of pressures this is borne out by experiment, but is also true that although eqn. (9.5) gives the correct order of magnitude for k in the case of most gases, the agreement between theoretical and experimental values is far from exact.

3 VISCOSITY

Viscosity is the property of a fluid whereby slower-moving layers retard the adjacent more rapidly-moving layers. It is a form of internal friction within the fluid, and arises whenever there is a velocity gradient present.

Any solid body travelling in a fluid carries a very thin layer of fluid along with it; thus it gives a velocity to this layer of fluid equal to its own. On the other hand, the fluid well removed from the moving body is at rest, so there is a velocity gradient in it. At slow speeds viscous forces set up in this way are almost entirely responsible for the resistance to motion in a fluid. Similarly, if a fluid flows through a tube the fluid in contact with the walls of the tube is at rest and the velocity increases as the axis of the tube is approached; the velocity gradient thus leads to viscous forces which balance the force driving the fluid through the tube.

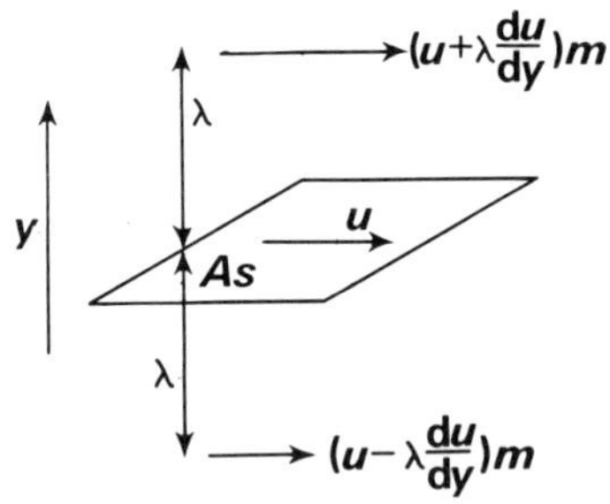

Fig. 9.5

In Fig. 9.5, the gas at the top is moving to the right with a drift velocity u superimposed on the random thermal motions of the molecules. This velocity u decreases as we move downward through the gas, the velocity gradient being du/dy. Each molecule passing through the area ΔS carries with it drift momentum appropriate to the place where it last collided with another molecule; thus there will be a net transfer of such drift momentum from above ΔS to below. The rate of transfer of momentum in this way is the *viscous force* acting on the area ΔS.

On average the $(n\bar{c}/6)\Delta S$ molecules reaching ΔS from above have come from a distance λ above ΔS, and have drift momentum

$$mu + \lambda m\frac{du}{dy}$$

and, similarly, those from below have momentum

$$mu - \lambda m\frac{du}{dy}.$$

Thus the net rate of transfer of momentum is

$$\frac{1}{6}n\bar{c}\,\Delta S\,\left(mu + \lambda m\frac{du}{dy} - mu + \lambda m\frac{du}{dy}\right)$$

$$= \frac{1}{3}n\bar{c}\,\Delta S\,\lambda m\frac{du}{dy}. \tag{9.8}$$

The coefficient of viscosity η is defined by the relation,

$$F = \Delta S\,\eta\frac{du}{dy}$$

where F is the force between the layers, and thus

$$\eta = \frac{1}{3}nm\bar{c}\,\lambda \tag{9.9}$$

$$= \frac{1}{3}\rho\bar{c}\,\lambda. \tag{9.10}$$

We have already seen that the mean free path is inversely proportional to the pressure; since ρ is directly proportional to pressure, eqn. (9.10) predicts that the viscosity should be independent of the pressure. This some somewhat surprising result was demonstrated by Maxwell who measured the viscosity of air at various pressures by the damping effect of the air on an oscillating disc. The agreement in this respect between experiment and theory over a wide range of pressures is a strong piece of evidence in favour of the kinetic theory of gases.

Examination of eqn. (9.10) suggests that the viscosity of gases should increase as the square root of the absolute temperature – a result in sharp contrast to the decrease in viscosity of liquids with temperature. However, although the gaseous viscosities do increase with temperature, no such simple relation as here predicted is obeyed.

The viscosity coefficient of gases is often measured using two discs with their planes parallel and separated by a small distance; one disc is rotated at a high speed and the viscous effect on the other is measured by the couple required in a torsion wire to prevent it rotating (see Question 5). Such a determination of η and a knowledge of $\overline{c}$, provides a means of determining the mean free path using eqn. (9.10).

The results of eqn. (9.2, 9.5 and 9.10) may be combined to give the relations

$$k = \eta c_v \tag{9.11}$$

and

$$D = \eta/\rho. \tag{9.12}$$

Although these equations are not accurately obeyed, the insertion in them of numerical factors of the order of unity does give results which are in accord with experiment, and to this extent the kinetic theory of gases certainly does correlate such diverse gaseous properties as diffusion, thermal conductivity and viscosity.

4 GASEOUS PROPERTIES AT VERY LOW PRESSURES

As the pressure of a gas is reduced, collisions between molecules become very much less frequent; the mean free path increases until it becomes comparable with the dimensions of the apparatus. In the case of air, for example, at a pressure of 10^{-2} mm of mercury it has become 10 cm. Under these circumstances we approach the conditions where in most containers collisions with the walls are more likely to occur than collisions between pairs of gas molecules.

At these pressures the viscosity is found to be no longer independent of pressure, and can be shown to be directly proportional to the pressure; so viscosity measurements can be used as an indirect means of measuring pressure.

It can be established that under these conditions the thermal conductivity is also directly proportional to the pressure. This has lead to the development of the *Pirani* gauge, in which the rate of heat flow and the temperature gradient are measured in a sample of gas between a heated tungsten wire and a cylindrical metal foil. The pressure can then be deduced from the thermal conductivity.

It is the great ease with which diffusion can occur at these very low pressures which is responsible for the effective operation of diffusion pumps.

It is instructive to consider a container which is divided into two compartments by a partition with a small hole, as in Fig. 9.6.

If the temperatures of the two compartments are maintained at T_1 and T_2 respectively, the normal equilibrium condition of equality of pressure in the two compartments no longer applies.

We can only now have equilibrium if the numbers of molecules passing

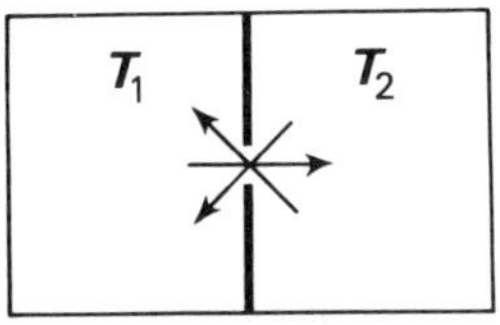

Fig. 9.6

through the hole in any time in either direction are equal.

Thus,

$$\frac{1}{4} n_1 \bar{c}_1 = \frac{1}{4} n_2 \bar{c}_2$$

or

$$\frac{n_1}{n_2} = \frac{\bar{c}_2}{\bar{c}_1} = \frac{\sqrt{\overline{c_2^2}}}{\sqrt{\overline{c_1^2}}} .$$

It follows that

$$\frac{P_1}{P_2} = \frac{n_1 \overline{c_1^2}}{n_2 \overline{c_2^2}} = \sqrt{\frac{\overline{c_1^2}}{\overline{c_2^2}}}$$

$$= \sqrt{\frac{T_1}{T_2}}. \qquad (9.13)$$

Molecular flow of this type is known as *molecular effusion*, and arises because, firstly, there is a negligible chance of any collisions occuring in the region of the aperature; secondly, the small likelihood of collisions with molecules on the other side of the hole means that the two sets of molecules travel through the hole quite independently of each other. Of course, once a molecule is in the other part of the container it eventually changes its energy as a result of collisions with the container walls.

This molecular effusion under a temperature gradient is employed in the *Knudsen absolute manometer*, which measures pressures between 10^{-5} mm and 10^{-8} mm of mercury. Molecules acquire enhanced kinetic energy as a result of collisions with a heated copper block; they then travel towards a vane maintained at a lower temperature and suspended on a delicate torsion wire. The pressure controls the number of such impacts that occur in a given time and thus the force exerted on the vane; this is then measured by the resulting twist in the torsion wire.

QUESTIONS

1. Explain how heat is conducted through a gas in which a temperature gradient is maintained. Discuss whether you would expect the thermal conductivity of a gas to depend on the pressure. To what extent does the mechanism of thermal conduction change when the mean free path becomes very large, i.e. of the order of metres?

2. How does the kinetic theory account for gaseous viscosity? Would you expect the presence of inter-molecular forces to bring about a significant change in the magnitude of gaseous viscosity? Explain why the viscosity coefficient is found to be independent of pressure over a wide range.

3. Discuss the manner in which the properties of gases at very low pressures differ from those at pressures nearer atmospheric, and describe a practical application of the particular properties found at very low pressures.

4. Give an account of the methods available for measuring very low pressures.

5. Two parallel circular discs in air each of diameter 10 cm are separated by a gap of 0.1 cm, and the line joining their centres is perpendicular to the discs. One disc is rotated at 20 000 revolutions per minute, whilst the other is kept stationary by the couple exerted by a torsion wire. If any edge effects can be neglected, calculate the couple exerted by the wire if the coefficient of viscosity of air is 17×10^{-6} N m^{-2} s.

Answers

Chapter 1 (Pages 18–19)

1 8.21 J K^{-1} mol^{-1}
2 2 300 cm^3
3 3.74 atm
4 9 500 mmHg
6 1 160 mmHg
7 801 mmHg
8 1 089 mmHg
9 461 °C
10 839 mmHg
11 1 300 mmHg
12 1/3 molecules dissociated
13 1.49×10^{26}; 0.992 kg
14 Towards hotter vessel

Chapter 2 (Pages 42–3)

1 482 m s^{-1}
2 505 m s^{-1}
3 0.9 per cent
4 1.06×10^7 J
5 91 min
6 414 K
8 Increased by 1/5 per cent
9 9.2 kg m^{-2} s^{-1}
10 3/7 and 4/7 atm
11 202 J K^{-1} kg^{-1}

Chapter 3 (Pages 59–60)

1 $2r$
2 8 300 K; 18.4 atm
3 0.232
4 $r/2$
5 87 per cent
6 12.2 J g^{-1} K^{-1}
7 1.1
8 5.7×10^{-3} m s^{-1}

Chapter 4 (Pages 85–8)

1 9.52 atmospheres; 522 K
2 1 840 cm^3; 172 K
3 $0.341V$; 574 K
4 1.46 atm
5 0.039 8 atm; 1 134 K
6 50 °C
7 2.51×10^6 N m^{-2}; 686 K
8 (a) 5 350 J; (b) 9 030 J
9 302 K; 308 K; 126 J
10 1.46
11 970 m
12 $\left(\frac{C_V + 2R}{R}\right) P_1 \left(\sqrt{V_1 V_2} - V_1\right)$
13 (a) $0.828 P_1 V_1$; (b) $0.5 P_1 V_1$
14 (a) 3.15×10^4 N m^{-2}
(b) 183 K; (c) 238 J
15 8.95
16 566 K
17 187 K
18 (a) 0.509 atm; 232 K
(b) 393 cm^3
19 80 m
20 For a chamber of volume V,

$$l = \frac{V}{a}\left\{(p/p_0)^{1/\gamma} - 1\right\}$$

$$\frac{pv}{\gamma - 1}\left\{1 - (p_0/p)^{\frac{\gamma-1}{\gamma}}\right\} - p_0 al$$

21 (a) 2.5 atm; 300 K
(b) 1.58 atm; 189 K
22 5.1×10^4 N
23 99.7 cmHg, 378 K; 3.59 l, 345 K

Chapter 5 (Pages 108–9)

1 40 mmHg
2 1 706 mmHg
3 111 mmHg
4 141 mmHg
5 (a) 834 mmHg; (b) 1 636 mmHg
6 21.4 cm
7 2×10^3 N m^{-2}; 7.5×10^{-4} g
8 682 mmHg

Chapter 7 (Pages 140–1)

1 2.74×10^{-1} N m^4 mol^{-1}; 3.26×10^{-5} m^3 mol^{-1}
2 9.92×10^3 J; 2.08×10^3 J less.
3 (a) $a(V_2 - V_1)/V_1 V_2$; (b) $2a/Rb$
6 2×10^{-10} m
7 2.1×10^{-21} J
8 7×10^{-22} J

Chapter 9 (Pages 161–2)

5 3.9×10^{-4} N m.

Index